A Student-Centered Language Arts Curriculum, Grades K-6: A Handbook for Teachers

James Moffett HARVARD UNIVERSITY

Houghton Mifflin Company · Boston

NEW YORK   ATLANTA   GENEVA, ILL.   DALLAS   PALO ALTO

The preparation of this book was principally supported by a two-year grant from Carnegie Corporation of New York. The statements made and views expressed are solely the responsibility of the author.

FOR SCHOOLCHILDREN

INCLUDING MY OWN

LISA AND JUDY

Foreword

The last several years have seen vigorous professional attempts to redefine the teaching of English from the preschool through the college, to establish the limits and possibilities of the subject, to assess priorities anew, and to relate to modern programs the findings of scholarship in language and language development which have become recently available. Few trends promise more for teaching than the distinction being drawn today between competence in language and performance in language. Competence is concerned with basic understandings, be they innate or acquired; performance, with the individual's actual use of language as social communication. It is with language *performance* that the model for a new English curriculum presented by James Moffett essentially deals, particularly the productive language of children and adults, their writing and speaking, and the social and psychological forces which affect their growing command of the native tongue. For too long our schools have neglected the importance of oral language and failed to recognize that ability in written language relates in no small measure to facility and command of oral forms. For too long school programs designed to teach our children to read have been separated from those designed to teach them to write and speak. Yet students in child development and psycholinguistics are demonstrating repeatedly the interrelationship of linguistic and cognitive growth, and classroom experimentation is suggesting that for many pupils power in reading is closely associated with power in writing and speech. As Constance M. McCullough asserted at the 1968 national convention of the International Reading Association, "The great dichotomy (between programs in reading and the language arts) must be as one."

In advancing a new model for a K-13 curriculum in English, James Moffett sees oral and written language, indeed all expressive experiences, as central in the educative process. These are the experiences which lead young people to intellectual, emotional, and social engagement. For example, he questions attempts to confine skill development in comprehension to the province of reading alone, feeling that perception, understanding, and evaluation are part of the total language experience. Some readers may question his personal evaluation of different approaches and materials for teaching beginning reading, as they may wonder about the priorities he sets for later educational levels, but they will find the assessment compatible with his view that the crucial element in language learning is the child's active involvement in using his native tongue. It is what the student does with what

vii

he reads that is critical in this curriculum; it is the ways in which he employs and uses language.

Thus, mime, improvisation, drama, and small group discussion take on a new significance. Writing, an active language experience, becomes the key to literary appreciation; discussion in large and small groups, the way to effectiveness in expression. With C.C. Fries, Mr. Moffett would agree that "There is no language apart from the speaker active in expression," and in the classrooms he envisions young people are continuously engaged in expressing their own ideas and feelings.

But more than activity for its own sake is suggested in this curricular model. It is not enough to involve young people in just any experience with language. The experiences themselves must be thoughtfully structured and be cumulative in effect, so that through them children may ultimately be introduced to the entire range of discourse. Behind the specific language experiences advanced in this curricular model, one finds a carefully conceived rationale to guide exploration of an entire range of language experiences appropriate at each instructional level.

Not the least concern of English specialists during recent years has been the lack of clearcut developmental programs for the elementary and secondary years. In advancing his own model for reform of school teaching, James Moffett suggests that sequence may be found not through the allocation of subject matter or through emphasis on discrete skills, but rather through ordering the language experiences in which young people become engaged with reference to both the social and psychological characteristics of the learners and the nature of discourse itself. Both for the potential power of its theoretical basis and for the incisive and practical application presented in this volume, his thesis commends itself to serious professional attention.

James R. Squire

Acknowledgments

In an era when institutions are more apt to deaden than invigorate individual endeavor, it is with particular pleasure that I acknowledge the liberal and sensitive support I have received from three institutions. During the early stages of developing the curriculum ideas presented in this book, the Phillips Exeter Academy provided me a year's sabbatical leave to devote to this study. Later, the administration there released me for further curriculum research by halving my teaching load for the better part of a year, and printed at its expense the experimental book upon which were based the trials reported in this book, even though these ventures went well beyond the needs of the Academy's own English Department, being in fact chiefly concerned with public school education.

At this point Carnegie Corporation of New York awarded a grant, through the Harvard Graduate School of Education, that enabled me to work full time on the project for two years. Besides an office and some services funded by its Center for Research and Development in Educational Differences, the Harvard School of Education provided valuable association with schools and with its own personnel. Since it is not routine for administrators of schools of education and private foundations to risk their resources on the projects of unknown and undoctorated individuals not affiliated with a university, my expression of gratitude to these people is not merely routine either.

The debt I owe the many teachers who tried out assignments for me, and often discussed results after hours without compensation, is too great to discharge here; I will mention them individually in footnotes.

To scores of students I owe nothing less than that portion of this book—rather considerable—which they wrote.

Of the many colleagues whose conversation has helped me to understand my own thoughts about teaching I would like to mention especially Kenneth McElheny, Thomas Hinkle, William Schwarz, the late George Bennett, Joel Weinberg, Davenport Plumer, John Mellon, and Wayne O'Neil. S. I. Hayakawa and his San Francisco associates helped me understand better the processes of symbolization.

Readers who criticized the manuscript prompted me to make important and, in some areas, extensive revisions. They were, for Grades K-6, Jeanne Chall, Blanche Serwer, Bernice Christensen, and William Durr. For the whole manuscript they were John Maxwell, Janet Emig, Robert A. Bennett, William A. Jenkins, and Richard Hodges.

I have already thanked in person my wife Janet for reading and helping prepare the manuscript, not to mention tolerating the author while he wrote it.

James Moffett

Contents

PART ONE   KINDERGARTEN THROUGH THIRD GRADE

PART TWO
GRADES FOUR THROUGH SIX

A Student-Centered
Language Arts Curriculum,
Grades K-6:
A Handbook for Teachers

INTRODUCTION

This book is for teachers on the job, student teachers, and all others concerned with teaching the language arts. I have tried here to describe and illustrate particular language activities that students and teachers would engage in from kindergarten into college. The program thus outlined is meant to be integrated both in the sense that continuity is sustained from one general stage of growth to another and in the sense that reading, speech, literature, drama, composition, and language are learned by means of each other and interrelated to the point of effacing some conventional categories of the field.

I would like to propose a way of teaching the native language that requires almost no textbooks or materials except reading selections and that, indeed, offers an alternative to the installation of a prepackaged curriculum. Featuring the learner's own production of language, and not incarnated in textbooks, this curriculum adjusts automatically to the students at hand. It is therefore meant for use in any kind of school, public or private, and with any kind of student population, advantaged or disadvantaged, of low or high ability. But what I am presenting is not a definitive, thoroughly tried-and-proven course of learning; it is, rather, a chart for further exploration and a kind of rallying call.

Chapter 1

General Orientation

The base of this curriculum is trials, begun a number of years ago in my own classes, picked up and modified by colleagues, proposed as an experiment to a wider and wider circle of teachers, expanded farther and farther into other grades as the need for developmental continuity became critically apparent, and spreading across more and more language activities as the implications of the trials were borne in on me. The ideas in this book have benefited considerably not only from these trials but from reactions by teachers in schools where I have consulted, other teachers who have tried parts of the program on their own, Master of Arts in Teaching candidates I taught in a curriculum and methods course, and my fellow participants at the Anglo-American Conference on the Teaching of English (a one-month convocation at Dartmouth in 1966 of around fifty leaders in English education from the United States and the United Kingdom). So what I have to say is partly a narrative report of trials, partly an extrapolation from experience into possibility, partly a relaying of other people's experience and ideas, and partly a statement of principles.

A K–13 Curriculum in One Presentation

The reason for putting a K–6 or K–13 program in a single book stems from my conviction that, without descending to formulas and mechanical syllabuses, English teaching should build in some sensibly cumulative way. I do not think that important improvements can come about until teachers up and down the line know what their colleagues in other grades are doing and are enabled by their administration to meet and collaborate. The main thing I have learned from experimenting in schools is this: how well a student fares with a certain assignment in, say, tenth or eleventh grade depends enormously on what he was asked to do in the lower grades; sometimes this

3

past education seems even more critical than age and ability. The same assignment can produce extremely different results among students of the same grade and achievement level, these results being relative to what assignments they have or have not done in the past. This relativity partly explains why this book could not have been written merely as a reference book in which the teacher could look up the grade he teaches and not bother with the rest.

For elementary teachers the K–6 sections of this book have been made available in a separate edition. Although it is certainly desirable for these teachers to know how their work is followed up in the later years, it seemed best to acknowledge that many might not want to read more than is actually necessary. To provide some tie, the K–6 edition ends with a summary of what is to come. But every elementary teacher will have to read the whole of the K–6 sequence, not only to find out just where his own classes actually fall on it, but also to know where his work with them fits into the total program. He will have to proceed differently with pupils who have not previously followed the program than with those who have. By understanding how he is carrying forward his pupils' previous experience, and how later teachers will pick up where he left off, he will have more confidence and purpose and gain a greater sense of satisfaction. (By the same token, a teacher working all alone with this program will have a more difficult time.)

Teachers of grades 7–13 will need to read the sections on K–6 for the simple reason that those sections contain indispensible material for *all* years. Not only the second half of the book, but the whole book, is relevant to the secondary and college years, for the presentation is cumulative. Activities and assignments are dealt with in the first half that are only alluded to in the second half but continue in force. Some new assignments grow out of earlier ones that teachers in grades 7–13 must have knowledge of. Also, if students are new to the program, their teachers will often have to dip down into the earlier years to catch them up. In the sections covering 7–13, I have discussed only new work or new developments of old work. Otherwise the book would have become unmanageable. The problem inheres in any effort to present a whole curriculum in a single work.

Present or Future?

In putting this program together I have had constantly to decide whether I was to write it up for the present or the future. In some ways it is directed toward more ideal conditions toward which one would hope some present trends are leading, and yet I have made several concessions to current conditions that are not likely to disappear overnight. Two of the hopeful trends I am banking on are the gradually rising quality of teachers and the increasing local experimentation within school systems. The teaching profession is drawing more intelligent, independent, and dedicated people than it used to. Schools of education may soon begin to give them a better training that includes dramatic work and practical experience with the dynamics of small groups and the realities of writing. School systems are more inclined now to give teachers time off to think about what they are doing, look for ideas, and get in-service training, and many are hiring more specialists, coordinators, and supervisors.

LOCAL CURRICULUM BUILDING

All of this means that more questions are being asked about curriculum than just which publisher's series to order for next year. The dependence of teachers and school systems on prepackaged programs that can be served from books in daily doles may begin to lessen if these trends continue, although some seductive new materials offered by the education industry will perhaps create new temptations. Underlying the teaching of English is this noneducational drama of who is to determine what happens in the classroom from day to day. Will local strength build up fast enough to prevent a very unfortunate meshing of big business interests with the teacher's fears of inadequacy? My point here is that the program described in this book depends on a fair measure of knowledge and self-assurance on the part of the teacher and good collaboration and support within a school system bent on forging its own curriculum. This would, of course, be true of any serious effort at innovation in English teaching. But local educators have a right to expect help from the outside and a mission to look for it. With this book I wish to offer some such help.

HETEROGENEOUS CLASSES

Another prophesy whose fulfillment would ratify this program is that the language classes of the future will be heterogeneously grouped. More learning takes place when students of different ability, achievement, socio-economic class, dialect, sex, and race are mixed together. An English classroom should be as richly varied a speech community as can be mustered. Today opposition to the sorting of students by ability is growing rapidly. The stand taken at the Anglo-American Conference on English was that tracking, streaming, and grouping, within schools and among schools, should be abolished[1]

[1] Recently reported in two books: John Dixon, *Growth Through English*, published in England in 1967 by the Modern Language Association, The National Association of Teachers of English, and The National Council of Teachers of English, and written for the profession; and Herbert J. Muller, *The Uses of English* (New York: Holt, Rinehart, & Winston, 1967), written for the public. This unanimous stand in favor of heterogeneous classes is all the more remarkable if one considers how heterogeneous a group the participants in the conference were themselves, and how little agreement they were able to reach on some other matters.

and a flexible kind of sub-grouping should be instituted within each class. The ideal of the diversified in-class speech community can, of course, no more be attained in an insulated, well-to-do suburban school system than in an urban ghetto. The possibilities of cutting across municipal lines and of eventually redistricting a whole metropolitan area for school purposes are being explored in a number of cities, some of which have experimented with the bussing of students from one part of the city to another. Metropolitan planning may soon make mixed classes a reality. Though the program I am submitting here does not depend on such mixing, it would be most fully realized by it.

Concessions to Current Realities

The concessions I have made to the present facts of school organization concern *the division of the book into blocks of grades,* and *the treatment of English as a separate subject.* To have crept through the grades one at a time would have been absurd. Part of my criticism of some prepackaged curricula is precisely that the work for each grade cannot be specified by someone who knows nothing of the school population and of the past training of each class. Whenever specifying either a grade or a grade-block, I have tried to make it clear that these are relative indications. Pending the supremacy of the un-graded school (and, I hope, also encouraging it) I compromised by emphasizing stages while referring to grades. It is of course, only the stages of development that count.

Sharing the view of some other educators that, ultimately, there should be a total program in discourse running laterally across subject fields as well as longitudinally over the years, I have felt severely constrained at times in trying to keep this program contained within a separate learning area called English. (It is in secondary school, of course, that the problem becomes acute.) The reader will undoubtedly feel this strain at those points where I have advocated writing assignments that might well be done in science and social studies classes. Having to assume a discontinuity between English and other subjects was my most costly compromise, but I have pushed the frontiers as hard as possible, by recommending assignments that place students in the role of natural and social scientists and by recommending some non-literature in the reading program. I hope future reorganization of the total school curriculum will make such pushing unnecessary. If others who try this program feel the same discomfort in this regard that I have felt in assembling it, then perhaps a stronger force will be exerted to break down the compartmentalization of subjects and to ascribe to team-teaching a larger meaning than is generally found in it. (The "Core" program is certainly no answer.)

Material Problems

There are some practical matters to consider in connection with this program. These include the division of classes into smaller groups, arriving at marks, and setting up an experimental program.

GROUP PROCESS

This program calls for the deployment of a class into five or six smaller groups for the purposes of dramatizing, discussing, reading aloud, and commenting on each other's writing. This creates a problem that can be solved in terms of either time or space. That is, either the small groups can operate one at a time while the rest of the class is doing something else, which allows the teacher to lead each group, or else the groups can operate simultaneously in spatially separated areas, which permits the teacher either to pass among the groups or to stay with one group. I am assuming the worst conditions — one teacher, one normal-sized classroom, and 25 to 40 students. Imaginative building, scheduling, and organization of staff could produce better solutions, but I know that teachers have succeeded in running the small-group process even under the least favorable conditions. To picture this process in action, one has to imagine it as a staple school activity in which students would be taught to participate from the earliest years. Serious, effective work in autonomous groups is definitely feasible. The first efforts with uninitiated students give no just indication of this feasibility.

MAKING UP MARKS

Since my focus in this book has been entirely on learning and not on testing — deliberately so, for the two are often in conflict — I suggest a particular way of arriving at marks. A folder of each student's papers is kept and passed on yearly from teacher to teacher. Instead of deciding upon marks by making up tests, putting grades on papers, and doing a lot of bookkeeping, the teacher looks over the folder at the end of the marking period, makes a general assessment of the student's papers, adds in his observations of the student's oral and dramatic work, and either translates this into a letter grade, if the administration insists, or, preferably, writes a two- or three-sentence assessment. Being qualitative, the latter assessment is actually more valuable for most purposes. This procedure, furthermore, has several other advantages: the teacher gets a better picture of trends; the time he spends on marks is less but more meaningful; and the student becomes oriented toward intrinsic learning issues instead of toward grades. Though it is often criticized, the administrative need for tests and marks has tampered with educational processes, especially in English, even more than most of its critics have ever asserted.

SETTING UP AN EXPERIMENT

For school systems wishing to set up a large, longitudinal experiment I suggest the following general plan, assuming some additional funds, perhaps government or foundation support. A wave of students is launched into the program in kindergarten or first grade; at the same time, older students begin it in the later grades in some form that allows for their previous learning background. As the "wave" group rolls through, the teachers who have them for a given year and the teachers who are to take them over the following year are given some time off to meet once a week, review results, make adjustments, and collaborate on the articulation of the two adjacent years. Teachers of all years use this book as a guide and are given some in-service training by specialists in drama, writing, and small-group discussion. A liaison is created with a local school of education, where some faculty member undertakes to give a special course for training student teachers who will enter that system and replace those who leave. An essential part of such a course, which is geared to this program, is to have student teachers themselves do the sorts of assignments recommended in this book, including improvisations and small-group discussion, and to discuss results in workshop fashion. Additional liaisons with psychologists and other researchers would be valuable for both parties: psycholinguists, linguists, and learning psychologists, for example, might find it very useful to follow the wave, and, by some exchange arrangement, might agree to discuss their insights with the teachers.

As for evaluating such an experiment, I will say here only that a learning program should be assessed on its own terms, not shrunk to the narrow limits of conventional, easily quantifiable tests. Fairness would require both long-term evaluation and some way of judging a cross-section of authentic student discourse. I suggested that outside judges be asked to assess samples taken from student writing folders and from tapes of their speech, and perhaps to compare these with samples from a control group. Interpreting of some individual cases should be done, tracing the development of selected students over a span of several years. Broad measures of cumulative effects would be most appropriate, but for the sake of perhaps valuable correlations, I see no reason, secondarily, not to do some standard measuring as well.

Use by the Individual Teacher

I do not mean to imply that only the mounting of a large project would be worthwhile. Many individual teachers have requested copies of the unpublished experimental book from which this book grew, drawn sequences of assignments from it, and used them in their own classes. Often their colleagues became interested in what they were doing, and started an enclave in their department that influenced the curriculum. Many of these individuals were department heads who proposed to their staffs an experiment with some version of the program. In fact, a large amount of unsolicited interest in the program, from individuals who had heard about it, is something that I can offer as some sort of testimonial and is one of the things that encouraged me to write this book. Some of this interest has resulted in the adoption or adaptation of the program by a number of schools and school systems in different localities. But if the book does no more than serve as a practical source of assignments and teaching concepts for the individual teacher, its existence will be justified.

Chapter 2

Principles and Purposes

Summary of Principles

I would like to set down here the main assumptions and beliefs that underlie the program. More of this philosophy will emerge gradually in the course of delineating the program. A fuller argument of rationale can be found in *Teaching the Universe of Discourse*,[1] which is a theoretical companion to this book and may answer many questions unanswered here about the thinking that underlies the curriculum.

1. Most profoundly considered, a course of language learning is a course in thinking. A writing assignment, for example, is a thinking assignment. Conceiving and verbalizing must be taken together.

2. But the stuff to be conceived and verbalized is primarily the raw stuff of life, not language matters themselves. Rendering experience into words is the real business of school, not linguistic analysis, or literary analysis, or rhetorical analysis, which are proper subjects only for college. It takes all of 13 years just to get off to a good start the lifelong learning of how to produce and receive language well. There is no justification for teaching concepts of literary criticism or theories of grammar and rhetoric as an aid to speaking, reading, and writing. And there is neither time nor sufficient reason to teach them for their own sake, except perhaps in separate, elective courses.

3. What a student needs most of all is to perceive how he *is* using language and how he *might* use it. What this requires is awareness, not information. The student will be aided by practical perceptions about what he and others are doing when they speak and write, not generalizations about

[1] James Moffett (Boston: Houghton Mifflin Company, 1968).

what people regularly do with language or formulated advice about what they ought to do with it.

4. The role of teachers is to help students expand their cognitive and verbal repertory as far as possible, starting with their initial limits. The goal is for the student to become capable of producing and receiving an increasingly broad range of kinds of discourse, compositional forms, points of view, ways of thinking, styles, vocabulary, and sentence structures.

5. The sequential pathway to this goal is a growth scale going from the personal to the impersonal, from low to high abstraction, from undifferentiated to finely discriminated modes of discourse.

6. The most effective and best motivated learning process for approaching this goal is trial and error, if the trials are roughly sequenced to provide a cumulative experience, and if, through full feedback, the errors are turned to maximum advantage. This means that, in a general way, the teacher selects the trials — the speaking, reading, and writing assignments — and that he sets in motion classroom processes that allow each student (1) to act verbally and (2) to receive an enlightening reaction to what he has done. This is an action-response model of learning; the student speaks, writes, or reads and others respond to his statement, composition, or interpretation.

7. The only way, short of tutorial, to provide individual students enough language experience and feedback is to develop small-group interaction into a sensitive learning method. The teacher's role must be to teach students to teach each other. Thus he frequently breaks the class into small groups for conversing, acting, reading, and writing, setting the structure of these groups by training them, consulting with them, and relating their activities to whole-class presentations.

8. Using language is essentially a social action, which, however, becomes internalized as a private behavior. The quality of individual utterance depends much on the kinds of dialogues that have been previously absorbed. Thus a good group process provides the external model for the inner processes it will foster.

9. Producing language is more difficult than receiving it. That is, the *composing* act involved in speaking and writing — choosing and patterning words — poses more intricate learning problems than the act of *following* sequences of words as in listening and reading. A student can read some kinds of discourse before he can write them. Also, the problems of writing different kinds of discourse vary much more from one kind to another than do the problems of reading different kinds of discourse. The difference warrants greater attention to the learning problems of producing than to those of receiving, though not necessarily a disproportion in the amount of student time spent on each.

In summary, the approach of this program could be called "naturalistic," and the curriculum, "student-centered." Emphasis is on active output by the learners, on their speech production and their response to others' productions. The goals here are not substantially different from conventional ones; the main departure is in the means. My conviction is that reading comprehension, literary appreciation, compositional skill, and understanding of language all come about most effectively and humanely when these principles are followed.

The main thesis of this book, then, is that learners should *use* language far more than they customarily do in most schools today. Two main misconceptions of the language arts keep the student in a receiving posture and prevent him from practicing language in authentic ways. In discussing these misconceptions I can elaborate some of the principles above.

The First Misconception

The first is that the learner must be given facts about our language system, concepts of literature, and advice about composition. For the sake of this knowledge he must study some textbooks that present him, through exposition and exercises, the history and science of language or the history and science of literature, and that undoubtedly would, if they could, present the history and science of composition. Since rote learning is considered in poor taste today, these presentations fly the banner of "discovery" or "self-instruction." What the student is learning, of course, is still history and science, on the false analogy that one's native language is an informational subject with a content of its own, like empirical subjects. But he is neither using language nor experiencing literature nearly as much as he might.

Historical Determinants of Curriculum

There is no evidence to support the belief that presenting generalizations about language, literature, and composition — by whatever *method* — will influence favorably the development of thinking, speaking, listening, reading, and writing, which are presumably the goals of a language arts curriculum. It is certainly not the *success* of such an approach that warrants it, for it has been tried for generations and found severely wanting. That is one reason why English teaching is ripe for reform today. But reform too often consists of replacing old content with new. What a shame, we feel, to waste the brilliant new theories of modern linguistics and of literary criticisms. Let's turn right around and teach them in the schools! But it is precisely my point that curriculum has been determined far too much by university disciplines and not nearly enough by perceptions about language learning.

The awful truth is that English teaching in America is what it is today mainly because of local historical accidents. The first is that a chronological-critical teaching of literature happens to be the tradition of university English departments and has produced English majors who know virtually nothing about the vast field of language and discourse besides literary periods and influences or how So-and-So achieves his effects.

The second accident is that just as educational research was discrediting grammar teaching there came along some stunning achievements in linguistics that English educators felt must somehow be the godsend they needed to launch a New English like the New Math or New Physics, and to placate the critics who were claiming that after 12 years of studying English students had precious little to show for it.

The False Rationale for Teaching the Science of Language

Linguistics filled the bill to dispel the last wisps of progressivism and to establish the post-Sputnik age of "intellectual rigor." By a deft switch of rationale we could now go on teaching grammar, not as an aid to speaking and writing — for massive evidence forbade that — but as a "humanity" for its own sake, or as an intellectual discipline (like Latin) to develop the mind. A student who is told to learn the different kinds of "determiners" or to transform one arbitrary sentence into another arbitrary sentence might well ask, "If it's a humanity, why is it so inhumane?" It can only be a symptom of hysteria in the profession to swallow the argument that any modern grammar is a humanity or that the study of it has some special virtue for developing thinking. A study of the uniquely human ability to produce language and organize life symbolically is indeed a humanity, but that study is conducted by paying attention to everyday verbal behavior, and, in later years, by becoming acquainted with psychology, sociology, and anthropology, subjects which are hardly even touched on in the overall pre-college curriculum. Yes, language is central to human life, but grammar is a drastically small and specialized subject, limited essentially to nothing broader than syntax, that is, the relations and patterns of words in a sentence.

As for developing thought and intellectual rigor, that comes about in a host of ways as the learner actually tries to symbolize his experience and to understand the symbolizations of other people. Indeed, verbal thinking is the main concern of the program offered in this book. But it does not follow that the student who learns the terms, concepts, and formulations of a rigorous discipline like linguistics is himself learning to think; or if he is, that linguistics is the cause. Study of *any* subject will develop thinking. The only advantage I see in studying the rule-governed system of a grammar is the same advantage one finds in mathematics and symbolic logic, which offer better opportunities for the development of deduction because they are purer logical systems having none of the aberrations of everyday language. Transformational grammar, in fact, represents an attempt to bring order out of everyday language by applying mathematical and symbolic logic to it. Whatever deductive learning would take place in grammar would take place better in a course of mathematics, especially as it is taught today.

This is not a criticism of linguistics itself but a criticism of its inclusion in the language arts curriculum. I return to the point that in our uncertainties about how to teach our extremely difficult subject we too readily drag down university disciplines into elementary and secondary school. (In the case of grammar, this tendency is reinforced by the irrational hold that grammar has on the curriculum because of a long-standing tradition revered by the public perhaps more than by the profession. In the mystique it is equated with "a good basic education," and educators are often exposed to heavy criticism if they drop it.) Besides Noam Chomsky's transformational grammar, we want to teach Francis Christensen's rhetorical analysis of the sentence and the paragraph, or Northrop Frye's mythic theory of literature. For the teacher these are all important things to learn about. They may increase enormously his understanding of what he is trying to teach and help him see how best to go about teaching it. But to teach them directly to his students, or to base exercises on them in the "discovery" manner, is misguided, for this effort to transmit, in one way or another, the generalities of scholarship almost always ends by forcing on students an arbitrary and therefore unwelcome knowledge, and by forcing out of the curriculum much more powerful learning activities such as this book attempts to present. Thus we have students learning what morphemes are, for no reason they can discern, but speaking little and writing less; or answering questions designed to get them to see how "The Millionairess" is an example of satire ("Satire must be something I don't know anything about yet or they wouldn't be defining it for me.") instead of relating the play to their own satiric impulses by acting out scenes from it.[2]

THE BRITISH VIEW

British educators do not at all share our American penchant for scientizing the teaching of English. They are appalled by the mechanized materials that pour forth from curriculum centers and educational publishers here — the programming in minute steps re-enforced by right answers, the highly structured literature presentations, the technical grammar programs for all ages, the inhibited composition assignments loaded fore and aft with solemn rhetorical analyses. In British schools today the strongest trend is away from teaching grammar, marking papers, and using textbooks, and toward creative writing, dramatics (even in secondary school), and a generally more spontaneous curriculum. There is, of course, no reason to think that the British are more right than we are, and this revulsion to our materials is no doubt a reaction against the tyranny of their own external examination and certain rigidities of their recent past. But the point is that until teachers can perceive

---

[2] A fuller discussion, "The Case Against Teaching Grammar," occurs in Chapter Five of *Teaching the Universe of Discourse*.

the ways in which their teaching methods are merely drifting with historical currents it is impossible to think through learning problems and put methods on a relevant footing.

The Second Misconception

The second major misconception of the language arts concerns reading. Or, rather, it does not especially concern reading but — precisely — appears to. A long list of mental activities that any psychologist would consider general properties of thinking that occur in many different areas of human experience have somehow or other all been tucked under the skirts of reading. "Recalling," "comprehending," "relating facts," "making inferences," "drawing conclusions," "interpreting," and "predicting outcomes" are all mental operations that go on in the head of a non-literate aborigine navigating his outrigger according to cues from weather, sea life, currents, and the positions of heavenly bodies. Not only do these kinds of thinking have no necessary connection with reading, but they have no necessary connection with language whatever.

THE FALLACY OF "READING SKILLS"

It is understandable, in a way, that these skills have wound up as "reading skills," because in reading, as in anything else, one is confronted with a set or string of phenomena that one has to make sense of, put together, comprehend. And it is true too that a reader has two simultaneous levels of phenomena to cope with — the letter symbols and the things or concepts referred to. But if he has learned to decode letters into voice, then he has no more to cope with than if someone were speaking to him. A child who fails to understand a text either cannot decode letters, or else cannot understand the text for reasons having nothing to do with printed words; he would not understand even if the text were read aloud to him. In other words, reading comprehension is merely comprehension.

The prevailing assumption in education, however, is that failing to comprehend a text is something more than just a literacy problem and yet still a *reading* problem. This is impossible. If a reader can translate print into speech — read it aloud as sentences with normal intonation patterns — and still fails to grasp the idea or relate facts or infer or draw conclusions, then he has no *reading* problem; he has a *thinking* problem, traceable to many possible sources, none of them concerning printed words. A reading specialist would probably reply that of course these mental operations occur elsewhere than in reading but that he is concerned with them only as they crop up in his specialty; when they operate in reading they are called reading skills. But this has caused enormous confusion in the field and had negative effects throughout the curriculum.

My heart goes out to the reading specialist. Reading has been so broadly construed that his job is in some ways an impossible one. He is made responsible for general mental activities like recalling, inferring, and concluding that belong no more to reading than to any other intellectual activity. Vocabulary building and concept formation are placed in his domain, even though neither of these has any necessary connection with reading. Subject-matter reading, as in science and social studies, is supposed to require additional "skills" that also fall under his charge, when in fact what is difficult for the young reader are the vocabulary, the concepts, and the knowledge context, all of which can be learned without ever opening a book. There are educators who would have us recognize dozens of different reading skills; some even count a couple of hundred.

NEGATIVE EFFECTS

Mis-diagnosis. First, many so-called "comprehension problems" are literacy problems incorrectly diagnosed. Many children have in fact not learned very early to decode letters into voice, and have limped along in reading, understanding some things but missing the individual meanings of some words and the total meaning of some word sequences because they were still having to devote too much attention to unlocking the letters. It is easy to confuse this case with the case of a child who decodes perfectly well but does not have some of the words in his vocabulary or has not grasped certain concepts yet, however they are worded, or has a general cognitive problem in putting facts together, or simply is not motivated to stick with the text. The first child has a problem for which the only *good* solution is the efficient literacy instruction that he failed to receive before. For the other child, the solutions lie in many activities besides reading — conversing, playing games of logic, doing dramatic work, writing, and simply getting more life experience. In brief, I question the whole concept of "reading skills," beyond the level of word recognition.

Misguided assignments. Another result of this misconception is that many children spend a large amount of school time plowing through "reading labs," "skill builders," "power builders," or "practice readers" — that is, reading snippets of this and that and answering comprehension questions afterwards. Then, finally, a considerable amount — in most schools, the majority — of the writing that the students are asked to do is really a check on the reading: it is assigned either to make sure that the reading was done or to monitor the comprehension of it or to "get students to think about it more." (I want to know why students would *not* read the text, or comprehend it, or think about it more. Isn't all this just a poor substitute for other things like motivation before and group discussion afterwards?) This practice drives students away from both reading and writing, because each comes into negative association with the other. An integrated program does not consist of writing about reading — or of reading about writing.

Curriculum imbalance. It is understandable that reading should have become the main preoccupation of a language arts curriculum. It is the pathway to most other school learning and the main measure of successful teaching. But in some ways it has swelled out of reasonable proportion, to its own detriment as well as to the detriment of other activities. Too much is included in it that can be learned better elsewhere. It crowds out those very activities that it desperately needs. It dominates the curriculum at the expense of itself and of speech, drama, and writing — the expressive language arts — which are shunted aside as peripheral "enrichment" because the main business of the day, reading, is not coming along well enough to permit such extravagances. And that is why reading is not coming along well enough.

Let me make it clear that I would not for one moment deemphasize reading, if by that one means reducing the amount of reading or neglecting comprehension. On the contrary, if we dispense with the notion of reading skills and with the practices based on it, it will be possible to let children do more reading of an authentic sort and at the same time to help them develop the faculties necessary to read for meaning.

Causes of Reading Incomprehension

It must also be clear that decoding skills are real indeed. Unlike problems of comprehension, the problems of recognizing vocal speech in print do not involve only universal mental operations but also involve the specific learning of spelling and punctuation conventions, which involves auditory discrimination among speech sounds and intonations, visual discrimination among printed symbols, and the associative pairing of one set with the other so that correspondence is achieved between sights and sounds. When incomprehension results from decoding problems, the case is truly remedial, for inadequate learning of the speech-print correspondences must be remedied by returning to them. The test of literacy is to be able to read a text aloud with normal intonation. This does not mean that the reader understands the text. All literate adults frequently read texts they do not comprehend — even when they know all the words — because of inadequate knowledge of the subject matter, failure to grasp certain concepts, cognitive difficulty in relating statements, or failure of the *writer* to make himself clear. (Writers for children have to take some responsibility for incomprehension). The best way to head off reading inefficiency at the literacy level is an early, intensive, and direct teaching of sound-spelling relations, which is indicated by research and provided for in all the new, and some old, beginning reading materials. (In the chapter, "Becoming Literate," certain materials are recommended.)

Poor motivation. Given a sound literacy instruction, what causes reading problems? A major cause may simply be lack of motive. Some children have not yet become interested in language generally and in books in particular and do not see what they have to gain personally from either. This problem is clearly not going to be solved by practice reading and comprehension questions, but rather by receiving and producing language in social activities — being read to, singing, discussing with peers, expressing oneself in writing, playing word games, and doing dramatic play. Only widespread involvement in language can solve the problem of poor motivation, and that involvement, as most teachers realize, must occur first outside the realm of silent reading; later, self-chosen books, as in individual reading programs, insure against loss of interest.

Environmental deprivation. Another major cause is experiential and, by definition, cannot be removed except in other activities. A book may refer to things with which the reader has no acquaintance. These things may be physical objects, concepts, ideas, or a whole knowledge framework. Because the problem never ceases to exist, it goes far beyond "reading readiness." A layman reading about quasars in a journal of astronomy will probably have trouble comprehending. I once heard Aldous Huxley say that our education is far too verbal, and that much of the literature presented to young people is meaningless to them because they have not yet had the emotional experiences that are prerequisite for understanding it. (Huxley was advocating more nonverbal education to the Friends of the San Francisco Public Library!)

Films and television can help enlarge experience and supply vocabulary. Playing games with picture cards, as described on page 157, will also extend visual acquaintance with objects and living creatures. The practice of taking classes on field trips is well justified in this respect. Emotional experience and point of view can be enlarged somewhat by playing roles in dramatic work. The small-group process advocated in this book provides considerable social experience. Thus schools can, to some extent, acquaint children with the things that words and sentences refer to, but reading comprehension will always stand in some ratio to what an individual has done, heard, seen, and felt in his personal life.

Egocentricity. Suppose a student is missing the point of the text because of subjectivity. Certain words or phrases have special power or private meaning for him; they trigger strong feelings or irrelevant associations that act as static to interfere with clear reception. These words or phrases arrest too much of his attention, causing him to ignore or slight other portions of the text, so that he gives a distorted reading, misconstruing statements or the relationships among statements. Once beyond the early stages, any reader tends to fill in words and phrases subjectively, according to expectancy cues provided by salient letters, syntax, and the drift of the sense. But the problem reader may fail to see how his filling in does not square with meaning cues elsewhere in the text. Or he may be too undeveloped intellectually to infer unstated connections the author is implying. Comprehension questions reveal such failures to understand, but do nothing to help the reader know why he misinterpreted; they test but do not teach. The learner is wrong but does not know why, and will continue to misread. Since egocentricity consists of being unaware that any other interpretation is possible, the learner needs other points of view on the text, which is exactly what he will get in a small-group discussion with peers. When he finds out that others his age read the same text differently, his egocentricity is broken, and he may even be helped to perceive just how his subjective responses derailed him or made him obscure the significant with the insignificant. Such learning is much more powerful than being told by the teacher or the answer sheet that one was wrong, for in the latter case children tend to care only about being right, squaring with the authority, and often take a luck-of-the-draw attitude — "Oh well, next time I'll guess better." In drama work, on the other hand, students enacting a story or poem have to deal specifically with problems of egocentricity because differences in understanding crop up in the enactment and have to be straightened out.

How the Program Develops Reading Faculties

I would not expect teachers and other educators who believe in reading skills to embrace very eagerly the idea that speaking, acting, writing, and playing card games can develop reading for meaning (what other kind is there?) better than "practice reading" itself as found in the skill-building programs. So let me try to illustrate this claim.

It would be hard to find an activity recommended in this book that does not rather directly help to develop the faculties necessary for reading comprehension, for though the program features the language output of the learner, the combining of that emphasis with small-group process actually places the individual constantly in the position of receiver as well. Let's take some of these faculties one by one.

Attention. The ability to attend closely the words of others and to follow their meaning sequences is developed through concentrated, interactive discussions among five or six peers and through dramatic enactments and improvisations. The point here is that what each participant says himself depends on what his partners have just said. Unless he learns to attend he has no basis for his own actions. This habit of interacting makes for active, responsive receivers and generates that attention to the words of others that is the indispensable basis of reading.

Recollection. Recalling depends on attention in the moment and on later efforts to retrieve the information acquired by attending. The writing process set forth in this book frequently consists of taking notes on ongoing events and basing later composition on these notes. The notes may be on the speech of others, when taking a turn as discussion scribe or when recording overheard conversation, or they may even be on reading text themselves, as entailed in some advanced composition assignments. But most often, the notes are on other sounds and sights that the learner is registering. The general habit of deliberately storing and retrieving information — selectively noted — is thus established early and made integral to whatever experience is being registered.

As for recalling texts themselves, this occurs when enacting a piece of literature or when discussing, say, an expository selection. *In order to* act out a story or converse about a topic drawn from the reading, the groups have to recall together the actions or facts. And, of course, performing short scripts requires actually memorizing the text (in which case the actor must try to comprehend it *in order to* perform it). Finally, a regular feature of topic-centered discussion is recalling what the group has said. Since recall is almost always selective, it inevitably leads to the additional skill of summarizing.

Conception. Concept formation is directly fostered, outside the area of reading, by card playing and topic-centered small-group discussion, but the very important impact of those two activities is hard to convey in a book. The card decks remain to be created; and only experience with small-group discussion is really convincing. Whereas card games with special decks present the learner with standard concepts, which he learns by classifying instances of the concept, the framing and pursuing of topics in discussion crystallizes, through group definition, some of the more slippery and ambiguous concepts that underlie words and that cause ambiguity in reading. Since, incidentally, the card games are based on super-classes and sub-classes, they also help the learner to recognize *subordination,* which is also a constant issue in composition and comprehension.

Inference. Let's turn now to the general and major faculty of putting two and two together, reading between the lines — otherwise known as *drawing inferences and conclusions.* From what an author says is true one is supposed to assume that certain other things not said are also true. Inference supplies everything from implied conjunctions of time and causality to the syllogistic reasoning that if statements A and B are true, then a reasonable conclusion would be C. In other words, anything that teaches relating and reasoning will foster this aspect of comprehension. There are many children who do not *expect* things to be related because they are not used to connectedness in their personal or family life and seldom try to tie the facts of real-life experience together, much less statements in a text. They are not *looking* for relations. Until they begin generally to relate facts, they are not going to do so in reading.

Many aspects of the program offered in this book will develop inference. Dramatization is helpful because it elaborates the text and thus brings out what is merely implied. Anything serving as a script — a story or poem or play — is bound to be incomplete. Even stage directions themselves do not by any means spell out everything. The actors must infer many of their positions, movements, expressions, and lines of dialogue, not to mention personality, feelings, and character relationships. Consider also the value of witnessing charades, pantomimes, and performed dramas, all of which require that the spectator put two and two together for himself. An important trait of drama, in fact, is that no guiding narrator or informant takes the spectator by the hand. And for the actor, the enacting of the text is one way of making explicit many of its implications.

A major purpose of small-group discussion of the reading is to allow students to compare the inferences that they have drawn from the text and cite evidence that would justify some inferences and not others. In a more explicitly logical way, students learn to make deductions in earlier years by playing checkers and special card games and in the later years by working directly with verbal syllogisms. But any good discussion, regardless of topic, furthers inference. Since a listener has to infer the implications of what any oral speaker says as much as he does those of what a writer puts in a book — perhaps even more because speech statements are less carefully worded and organized — all discussion teaches this aspect of comprehension. The effect of discussion on reading has never been measured, however, because continuous, regular, and well trained discussion by peers in small groups has seldom if ever played a large role in the language arts curriculum. My claim is that reading comprehension will benefit far more from discussion than from a program of practice reading with comprehension questions. This is so because discussion must deal continually with the speakers' understanding of each other's utterances. The *reasons* for misunderstanding come out. Comprehension can be explored at its very roots. In the case of inference, for example, no matter what the subject is, the *process* of building and cancelling statements inevitably calls attention to the implications in statements and the relationships among them. In fact, a large part of discussion consists, in effect, of testing the implications of statements. If the discussion, furthermore, is about a text the group has read, any disagreement not resolvable by pointing to a certain sentence is almost certainly to be about inference. As the group collectively makes clear the implications, each member not only can see what he missed but also can perhaps see exactly what he failed to relate. Generally, by participating in the group action of putting two and two together, the individual learns how to do it by himself.

The small-group cross-commentary in the writing workshop permits writer and reader to approach inference-making from both points of view at once and thus to see how it is a factor of rhetoric — that is, of compositional decisions that determine what the reader deduces and to which the reader must become attuned. Thus the student-reader says what he understood the student-writer to mean so that when one makes the wrong inferences they can pinpoint together exactly what makes and breaks reading comprehension.

It is interesting that when textbook writers want to make sure that students understand what they are saying they add connectives and state their points explicitly, employing bold type, color, and italics if necessary, leaving nothing to chance, but when they want to test students, they understate. The central issue of all writing concerns how explicitly the writer should convey his ideas and how much he can assume that the reader will fill in. Judging this is no easy matter, for the writer has his own problems of egocentricity. My point is that the learner should, from the outset, be let in on this issue as both receiver and producer. How much the writer has to lead his reader by relating and drawing inferences and how much the reader should be expected to do these things on his own are central to an English curriculum. Comprehension must be approached simultaneously from both reader's and writer's viewpoints, in order to understand how misreading occurs and to realize that reader and writer share responsibility for preventing it. Thus writing is one of the main keys to reading comprehension, especially if it includes commentary by the learners on each other's papers.

A pupil undergoing a reading skills program would be justified in feeling that the writer is always right, for whenever the pupil misunderstands, it is always *his* fault. By implication, when it is the pupil's turn to be writer, the reader can jolly well watch out for himself; any failure of communication is due to poor reading comprehension. The right-or-wrong multiple choice answers unintentionally teach the pupil that only a certain predictable set of implications and conclusions can be drawn from a reading text. Throwing in what-do-*you*-think questions at the end of the exercise does not offset this. (Notoriously, on standardized comprehension tests, brighter students often make mistakes because they see inferences other than the conventional ones the egocentric test-maker had in mind.)

If the learner is given plenty of opportunity, very early, to render his ideas on paper and to have them reacted to by his fellows, he can exercise his ability to relate things in words (composition) and at the same time have the experience of being both understood and misunderstood in print. What did *he* leave out? What made *his* reader take a different direction from the one he was supposed to? The principle I am getting at here is that when *reader and writer can talk together* they can reach a much profounder understanding, than when dealing with printed texts, of what both composition and comprehension hinge on — the incompleteness of a text and how the writer must set cues and the reader look for them. When you become aware yourself of what you are putting in and leaving out, playing up and playing down, you understand that you must, when reading, fill out the text by relating items in it according to cues, the same cues that your own readers indicate you should put in your writing — such as main statements, paragraphing, transitions, emphasis, and subordination.

Interpretation. Here we are into the complex mental operation of putting together inferences and structural cues, and of noting tone, focus, and emphasis. It involves sensitivity to word choice, patterns, symmetry, and form. In dramatic activities, students become attuned to tone and style by imitating characters and playing roles. The structural cues and patterns of word sequences encountered in silent reading can often be translated into visual, auditory and spatial equivalents. An enormous amount of what students miss or misinterpret when reading can be attributed to a kind of childish passivity whereby printed words impose themselves with an authority that makes them seem either inevitable or arbitrary; the learner has no sense of the choices that have been made, whether these concern diction or sentence structure or overall organization. Through writing and discussion of writing he can become aware of how texts are created and therefore of the choices that have been made. In order to interpret well, he must confront choice himself. The inadequacy of trying to teach interpretation through practice reading lies in the fact that a finished text provides no sense of alternatives. Without a background of alternatives there is no way to discriminate what the author did from what he might have done. This is why texts remain featureless to some students and hence difficult to interpret. The writing program presented here is based on compositional choices that range from selection and shaping of the raw subject matter to alternative ways of phrasing part of a sentence. As the learner works constantly on focus and emphasis in his own composing process, he becomes an alert and perceptive interpreter of others' compositions.

Critical assessment. As regards literary form and whole modes of discourse such as poetry, fiction, drama, essay, autobiography, reportage, research, and argumentation, this principle of learning to read by writing is pursued right to the very foundations of this program. Students produce all the modes of discourse that they receive. By learning these modes from the inside, so to speak, as practitioners, they know how to read them. The writing assignments make possible a truly informed evaluation of reading texts, because particular composition-comprehension issues peculiar to each kind of discourse are examined closely under the dual writer-reader aspect of the writing workshop, where criteria for judging are generated.

Organization and Proportions of this Curriculum

This discussion of misconceptions in the language arts has been necessary to make clear what this book is about and what needs it is intended to fulfill. Because the presentation omits some things that readers may be looking for, and reclassifies certain other things, the opportunities for misinterpreting are rife. The emphasis on student language production would seem to cover only half of a total English curriculum, or — which is a more likely misinterpretation — to cover only some secondary activities that can be indulged in if there is time left over from building reading skills, doing analyses of grammar, rhetoric, and literature, and writing artificial papers about the reading. I have been arguing, of course, that the goals underlying these conventional activities can be more effectively and humanely furthered if some aspects of the total curriculum are reconceived and some proportions altered. In short, I know perfectly well that the recommendations in this book about speech, drama, writing, and some other activities will not be taken seriously so long as the misconceptions remain, for there will simply not be sufficient room for them in the total program. One purpose of this book, then, is to right an imbalance. But it is better to think of the curriculum unfolded herein as *replacing* than as *fitting into* the conventional curriculum.

What Is Excluded

While some omissions are founded on educational principles, others are founded on personal limitations. These need to be distinguished. That is, grammar study, pre-arranged literary analysis, rhetorical analysis of models, composition precepts, and reading comprehension exercises are omitted as either inappropriate for the basic, required English course or as misguided methods for arriving at worthwhile goals. During the K–6 years, attempts to "structure" the reading of literature by anything more than general growth seem pointless. The main thing is to give children a rich mixture of whatever literature they are able and eager to read, without schematizing it or thematizing it. A design for sequencing literature in the elementary years is therefore omitted on principle.

The omission, however, of reading lists for all years stems from my own lack of knowledge. I do not feel that I know enough about what reading materials are available and appropriate for different ages to delineate a continuous reading program as specifically as I have detailed other activities. As regards developmental reading suggestions, then, this book needs to be supplemented.

Because the interplay of reading and writing is very important, it is with regret, and not on principle, that I have dealt less with the content of reading, and offered titles only in a suggestive and illustrative way. I would certainly not have students read less than they customarily do; in fact, if relieved of the activities I have deliberately omitted, and if allowed to produce more language themselves, I feel sure that they will have more time and motivation to read. For the sake of righting a balance, I have stressed learning to read by talking and writing, but it is equally true that one learns to talk and write by reading. Without rich input, good production of language is impossible. Similarly, far from being underplayed, literature holds a central place in this program, though teachers should not expect to find the forms of it classified in familiar ways, or to encounter a "literature program" separate from other discourse and from the writing program. (My own background is chiefly in literature.)

What is Included in the Bias Toward Production

Given these reservations and the principles mentioned before, this book is intended to offer a far more nearly complete curriculum than the emphasis on language production might initially suggest. First, its bias is deemed proper because production is more difficult than reception. Second, when students act as audience for each other, they are receiving while they are producing. Third, examining their own productions and their responses to the reading will help them to understand language, rhetoric, semantics, and literary technique more effectively than will programmed presentations of these matters, the critical difference being in whether the matters come up in timely psychological connections or merely under prearranged logical headings. Fourth, many problems that *reveal themselves* in reading are less treatable there than in other activities, mainly of the productive sort. Fifth, the readings in both literature and nonliterature are distributed under categories that make it possible to integrate reading and writing but that also may give to teachers expecting these to be presented as separate programs a false impression that they are being slighted.

The Chapter Divisions of the Book

The last point concerning the organization of this book requires more explanation. The chapters in the Kindergarten to grade six portion are named for *activities,* which are established in elementary school and continue for the most part into secondary school. These activities are acting, conversing, playing language games, reading, and writing. The chapters are about procedures for teaching each activity. The order of chapters is not a learning order, since the activities are concurrent, but an order of exposition. The chapters on writing predominate, but *every writing assignment is a reading assignment,* because children read each other's writing. Laid over against the program of reading in published works, then, is a very full program of reading in pupil productions.

In the second half of the curriculum the reading of published works and the reading of student productions coincide more in time, because published selections are assigned when students are doing a corresponding kind of writing. The chapters covering grades seven to thirteen, consequently, are mostly named for the various sorts of dramatic, narrative, poetic, and expository discourse, to be both read and written. This manner of organizing was essential for showing the integration of activities and the interrelations of the accumulating orders of discourse, in accordance with the theories in *Teaching the Universe of Discourse.* But in cutting across some conventional categories of both teaching and literature, these units based on types of discourse may mislead some readers, especially since the illustrations of the types of discourse are all drawn from student writing.

Purposes of Sample Student Writing

These numerous student papers fulfill several functions at once. First, since student productions are the textbooks in this course, it seemed wise to give a generous sampling of what one is to teach from. I have exploited this sampling for occasions to talk to the teacher about an assortment of things, from spelling to poetic technique, that come up for learning in student productions. This is to demonstrate suggestively an important part of a student-centered approach to teaching aspects of English usually arranged and presented topically.

Second, at the same time that the student papers illustrate the writing assignments, they illustrate the kinds of discourse students will also be reading, because the writing assignments all correspond to authentic discourses produced outside of school. Had I chosen to exemplify kinds of discourse by drawing selections from professional writers, some readers might then even regard this curriculum as literature-centered, and its equal orientation toward reading would have been more evident. But the multiple purpose of the samples would then be lost. Instead, I have referred the reader to titles of works that are professional equivalents and can be assigned for reading. These works can be looked up elsewhere; student papers cannot be.

Again, I have not attempted to supply reading lists for all grades or to structure a strict sequence of reading. *But each kind of discourse is a reading unit despite the fact that it is illustrated with student writing.* A lot of the commentary with which I have surrounded the samples can illuminate, I hope, student problems of comprehension as well as composition, if the teacher will maintain a dual orientation toward reading and writing. This manner of integrating the two activities, however, is *not* to be confused with model writing, whereby a text is subjected to rhetorical analysis and students are then told to compose the way the old pro did. The approach in this program is indeed the opposite of model writing; though reading is meant to influence writing, students are never asked to follow precepts and prescriptions when comparing. Analyzing finished texts is generally unprofitable.

Third, the writing samples also show that young people can create, at their own level of maturity, the same sorts of discourse that they are asked to read, both literary and non-literary. My hope is to interest teachers in what students produce and to make a case that their own working life will be more interesting when they base their teaching on these productions. They will stay in close touch with the minds of learners and discover more clearly what teaching is really about than they ever can when textbooks come between them and their students. Perhaps these samples will give teachers a feeling of familiarity with the kinds of responses they will get from these assignments. My own commentaries about the samples by no means exhaust what is to be said about them. The reader's own responses may often be more helpful to him. It is only after he is steeped in his students' speech and writing that the teacher really begins to understand what he can do to facilitate their learning of language.

Fourth, emphasizing student writing more than reading, with each kind of discourse, is based on the conviction, already expressed, that creating these kinds of discourse is much harder than reading them and that, consequently, it raises more problems and more opportunities for learning. The main difference is in the myriad choices one makes in composing. The *process* of reading does not differ greatly from one kind of discourse to another. Shifting, for example, from first to third person discourse, or third to first, affects very little what the reader *does*, though it may affect very much how he feels. But for the writer this shift changes enormously what he does. As students attempt to create each new kind of discourse, they encounter new learning trials. In arraying the varieties of discourse across a curriculum, I have found it necessary to detail much more what is involved in producing these discourses than what is involved in reading them. I think one of the reasons writing is so often neglected or reduced to sterile exercises is that the problems of teaching the authentic forms of it as actually practiced in the world beyond the school have intimidated teachers. I hope very much that this emphasis on composition will give needed help to the teacher with these problems, and that the small-group cross-commentary recommended here will show teachers that it is possible to handle a very large volume of writing in effective ways.

Fifth, the samples are meant to unfold gradually the panorama of mental growth in language and the building of whole knowledge structures. Writing assignments are thinking tasks, the ones in fiction, poetry, and drama as well as the ones in reportage, research, and generalization. At bottom, both reading and writing are conceptual and cognitive more than they are linguistic, at least when one considers the learning problems they entail. Writing is the embodiment of mind in language. Far too long and far too much, we have thought of reading and writing as technical language matters, when the fact is that composing and comprehending are deep operations of mind and spirit having no necessary connection with the world of letters, or even with oral speech. To solve language learning problems in more than a shallow fashion, the basic approach, paradoxically, has to be extra-linguistic. This program is based on ways in which people process information from the ground up. Though ultimately verbal, the "writing assignments" are really external equivalents for processes of conceptualizing that go on inside us all the time, whether we verbalize or not. Above everything else, a course in one's native language should be about symbolizing experience at various abstraction levels and in various verbal modes. Thus the samples of writing done in response to the assignments of the program depict, however imperfectly, the transformation of sensory data, memories, and vicarious experience into generalizations and fictions, the building of higher abstractions on lower ones, the growth of thought.

Other Aspects of the Presentation

SEQUENCE

This conceptual growth is the developmental basis for sequence in this program. There is much more to say about the abstractive theory of growth underlying this program. Again, I refer the reader to *Teaching the Universe of Discourse*. But as regards the organization of the present book, it is necessary to point out that chapters are not placed in chronological order. Generally, the book traces a progression of activities spanning from kindergarten into college. And I have suggested many sub-sequences along the way. But except where indicated otherwise, the activities described in each chapter run concurrently with those of other chapters in the same grade block. In other words, though framed within a general progression, the chapters themselves are expository and do not follow consecutively as regards learning sequence, but wherever sequences seem indicated by experience or specific trials, I have said so within the chapters. To specify sequences more definitely than is warranted by current knowledge strikes me as poor policy. Thus a fair amount of room is left for local experimentation in the specific timing of recommended activities.

DISCLAIMER OF SCIENTIFIC EVIDENCE

And this is my cue to talk about ignorance, both my ignorance and that of the whole profession. Any book attempting what this book attempts is bound to be incomplete and tentative in some ways. No one knows very much yet about how children can best learn to produce and receive language or what the exact stages of an optimal learning sequence would be. Why, then, attempt to delineate a K–13 program of the language arts, student-centered or not? And what proof backs up the many assumptions and assertions made in this chapter and in those to follow.

The fact is that language instruction goes on and will go on, evidence or no evidence. On what proof rests the teaching that is taking place at this very moment? Precious little. Though many teaching materials claim to be backed by scientific evidence, in actuality there are very few classroom practices that have such backing. Educational research itself is notorious for both inadequate methodology and the verdict of "no significant difference" in its findings. The cry is for better methodology, but truly scientific experiments in a classroom may simply be impossible; controlling variable factors, without converting the school into an unreal laboratory, presents a virtually insoluble problem. And when university research in child development and learning theory is conducted rigorously enough to be reliable, the findings are usually trivial for education; when the findings result in a broad, suggestive and stimulating theory, it seldom gains acceptance beyond one "school of thought" in the discipline. Thus educators can choose B. F. Skinner's "reinforcement" theory of learning as embodied in programmed materials or the very different "discovery" theory as promulgated by Jerome Bruner and others. The theories of the leading figure in child development, Jean Piaget, are disputed; even when scholars and researchers embrace them, they acknowledge that the theories have not been empirically proven in accordance with rigorous research standards and may in fact not be susceptible to scientific verification at all. Though scientific research sometimes helps make decisions when all other things are equal, it has not so far furnished big answers and may never to able to do so.

In any case, of course, education cannot simply wait on research. Pending more knowledge, if it is to come, teachers have to go on making decisions about what to do and not to do, how to do, and when to do. We make the decisions on several bases — practical experience, intuition, definitions of goals, and theories about language, literature, and composition that do not purport to be pedagogical but are attractive for one reason or another. *Very few if any of the practices recommended in this book, or currently reigning in schools, have been scientifically proven superior to others.* By skillfully citing various studies and authorities, one could back up not only the program of this book but virtually any other as well. Research findings and scholarly theories exist to support a host of opposing practices. Therefore I have not attempted to justify the curriculum herein on those grounds. Though these citations might have had scholarly interest for some readers, the effort to document the assertions and practices contained in this book would obstruct considerably its practical purposes and yet prove nothing, though it would give the book a fashionable gloss. Two exceptions are the considerably negative findings about teaching grammar, which all linguists I know of seem to accept, and a general research indication that beginning reading fares best when launched by an early, systematic, and intensive instruction in sound-spelling correspondences, an indication reflected in all new reading programs I have seen that appeared for the first time in the 1960's, as well as in recent revisions of older programs.[3] As I stated earlier, what is determining teaching practices in English is not scientific evidence but historical accident, unproven conventions, abstractly logical conceptions of the field, and intellectually attractive theories about it that were not originally conceived for teaching purposes at all (like Aristotle's categories of language and literature, which were definitions for people who already know, not *pedagogical* concepts). Very little of current teaching is based on research evidence or scientific proof.

---

[3] Useful books for reading about these two research findings are, respectively: H. C. Meckel, "Research on Teaching Composition and Literature," in N. L. Gage (ed.), *Handbook of Research on Teaching* (Chicago: Rand-McNally, 1963), and Jeanne Chall, *Learning to Read: The Great Debate* (New York: McGraw-Hill, 1967).

PERSONAL QUALITY OF THIS BOOK

In line with the disclaimer of scientific evidence is the decision to write this book in the first person. Though I have drawn widely from sources other than my own teaching and experimental trials — from books, meetings, consultations with specialists, countless conversations with teachers, and classroom observation — the main presentation in this book is the work of one person, a fact that I feel the reader should be periodically reminded of, along with whatever hazards and advantages the fact implies. Impersonal, third-person style would undoubtedly have invested the curriculum with a more "professional" and authoritative aura, but would have profited no one. By speaking more personally, I have been able to indicate varying degrees of conjecture and conviction, or at least to help the reader retain a tentative spirit even when I myself may have begun to sound dogmatic. It is difficult to take a flexible stand constantly and at the same time offer definite recommendations. However definite I may sound later, let me say once and for all that *no one* knows the best way to teach English and that my recommendations are made in the belief that this kind of a curriculum offers the most likely way to find out.

I should also head off here the impression possibly created later that I do not realize how much many of the assignments included in this book are in common use today. Just as tedious as repeating "some teachers might like to try . . . ," is the constant sorting of what is standard practice from what is rare or unorthodox. Being more teacher than scholar, I have relied a lot on first-hand trials, in making recommendations, rather than relaying reports of trials third-hand to my readers. To those teachers who have conducted similar trials and who may have employed for some time practices and assignments recommended here, this book may very well be in some way indebted, and to those teachers it is meant in turn to lend support.

If the personal quailty of this book seems arrogant in view of the scope of the subject and the limited knowledge available to us about language learning, I can only repeat that this curriculum is a chart for exploration, not a panacea, and say further that in a time when some educators have declared the teaching of our native language a "national disaster area,"[4] when the drop-out rate is rising and correlates with reading failure, when college students cannot read and write acceptably after 12 or 13 years of language teaching, I would rather risk arrogance than indolence.

Claims for this Curriculum

If this curriculum is no more founded on research evidence than other programs, how does it recommend itself? First, a direct or naturalistic approach, whereby students learn essentially by doing and getting feedback on

[4] Manifesto of the Huntting Conference of Writers and Teachers, June, 1966.

what they have done, embodies the safest assumption about learning. Much general experience supports this assumption in other areas of life. If the goals of the curriculum are to help learners think, speak, listen, read, and write to the limit of their capacities, then the most reasonable premise is that they should do exactly those things. *Whoever assumes anything else bears the burden of proof.* Indirect methods need more justification. To assume that generalities about language aid speaking and writing, that concepts and categories of literature improve literary comprehension and appreciation, that rhetorical analysis and precepts teach composition is to assume also the burden of proof. (Although "practice reading" designed to build "reading skills" seems to fit the principle of learning by doing, this is an illusion caused by a misnomer. As I have tried to show, the skills that need practicing are general thinking skills that have no necessary connection with reading.) Learning by doing is not simple, however; practice of the target activities can be a sterile perseveration in old habits from which little is learned. This is why the small-group process of interacting and feeding back is essential. Also, the teacher must propose a variety of tasks that allow the learner gradually to expand his verbal and cognitive capacities across the whole spectrum of discourse.[5]

Second, since it is student-centered, this curriculum offers the best opportunity for teachers to learn what they need to know to teach well. We would know a lot more than we do now if textbooks had not been allowed to bypass the teacher and present over-structured materials to students. Learners have been transmitted to so much, and attended to so little, that after generations of teaching we are still very ignorant of what makes for good language learning. Fancily rationalized indirect approaches falsely centered on a "subject" have been given a long and humanly expensive trial that is merely perpetuated by most of the new materials for English. Virtually the whole national school system has been the lab for this bit of research. A student-centered curriculum, on the other hand, is a teacher-teaching curriculum.

[5] See also "Learning to Write by Writing," in *Teaching the Universe of Discourse.*

Part One

KINDERGARTEN THROUGH

THIRD GRADE

As stated in the last chapter, the order of the ensuing chapters is not chronological. Each, rather, centers on a language activity that, throughout these years, weaves in and out of other, concurrent activities. Most chapters, however, contain suggestions for sequencing the work they treat. And certainly the introduction of dramatic activity, speech, and literacy instruction before reading and writing makes a certain rough developmental sense, if only as a reminder of what the latter are founded on. I begin with drama, which, taken in an everyday sense, is the wellspring of language activities. It is that preverbal way of understanding, expressing, and representing that underpins not only literacy but oral speech as well.

Chapter 3

Acting Out[1]

"Acting out" is meant to have a double sense — both "expressing oneself" and "filling out" a ready-made story. Thus dramatic activity breaks down into two main kinds — inventing one's own dramas and enacting the stories of others. Both are improvisational; the difference is in whether the pupil makes up the main situations and actions or merely makes up the details of word and movement that flesh out the borrowed story. In both cases there are "givens" — some concrete points of departure or stimulants that both suggest and limit the dramatic idea. Putting on a crown, for example, invests the pupil with kingship and thus provides a source of ideas at the same time it restricts the range of possibilities.

What we will be concerned with here is drama, not theater. Drama is the acting out of feeling and takes the point of view of the participant, for whom it exists; spectatorship is an irrelevance and, until a certain stage of development, a hindrance. Theater concerns performance before an audience, whose point of view is included and for whose benefit effects are calculated. Theater is a secondary effect of drama, an outgrowth appropriate only much later, after elementary school. ("Children's theater" — the performing of plays for children by adults — is a different matter; I am speaking here of what the *child* does.)

The purposes of acting out at this age are: (1) to promote *expression* of all kinds, movement and speech harmonizing and reinforcing each other; (2) to limber body, mind, and tongue; (3) to *begin* to single out the verbal mode from the others and thus to activate speech in particular; (4) to forge drama

[1] The suggestions for dramatic activities in this curriculum have been amalgamated from many sources, including some reading in the area, but mostly from talk with teachers, first-hand trials, observation of special classes, and personal participation in dramatic activities. I am particularly indebted to Douglas Barnes and Anthony Adams of England for discussions that helped sharpen some ideas in this and later chapters on drama.

into a learning instrument for continued use throughout all grades; (5) to make the first school experience with language fun and meaningful in children's terms; (6) to habituate pupils to working autonomously in small groups; (7) to further peer socialization of a learning sort not usually possible outside of school; (8) to gain intuitive understanding of style as voice, role, and stance, and of rhetoric as achieving effects on others; (9) to develop in the more familiar mode of dramatic play those characteristics necessary for the less familiar process of discussing, such as attending, responding, inter-acting, and turn taking; (10) to exercise and channel emotions.

Younger children seem to invent more freely and feel more comfortable when dressed in borrowed robes and otherwise stimulated from outside. Therefore I suggest that dramatic work begin within a framework of conven-tions of the sort children like — familiar props and settings, stock characters, and symbolic pieces of costume. They want to "be" an ogre, or a fox, or a fireman. They seem to have to be themselves by being something else. In primitive fashion, they wish to take on — to invest themselves with — the qualities and powers of some object, animal, or fantasy figure. Or they wish to test out adult roles symbolizing powers they wish to have. They work out realities through fantasies and thus prefer the symbolic and ritualistic to the actual and original. This does not mean, however, that play-acting conven-tional roles in borrowed situations is learning to be unoriginal and stereo-typed. It is simply that small children require masking and stereotyping as conditions for being creative. They are less interested in what they are — weak, fearful, dependent — than in what they want to be — powerful, fear-less, and self-providing. Sometimes they act out both roles at once by assign-ing to a toy or a puppet the weaker role and assuming the more powerful role themselves. Realistic role-playing, imitating various kinds of adults, may be both an assumption of power roles and also an effort to understand adults.

The various activities described in this chapter represent different ways in which children can be stimulated to act out. They take place concurrently in the curriculum but should be introduced, I suggest, in staggered fashion, following the order of their presentation in this section.

Play with Objects

The first dramatic activity is solitary play. At first, toys are the stuff of drama. For the small child, they automatically imply some words and deeds; he has a point of departure. Grasping a stuffed animal, a Dorothy of Oz puppet, a wand, a sword, a stethoscope; donning a feather, a cap, a belt, or a kerchief; standing before a moon or gate or counter — all these tell a child what to do, by evoking a host of associations in which the item is embedded in his mind. (Of course these associations vary somewhat among cultures; a southern Negro or a Harlem Puerto Rican may find meaning in different objects than a middle-class white.) The classroom of the early school years should contain many dolls, puppets, toys, bits of costume, props, and sets, some of which the children themselves could certainly make or bring from home. For all grades, rostrum blocks (small, portable platforms) can be important equipment, since they permit children to work with vertical space. All the teacher need do at first is to provide a time and climate — a period every day — for this activity, and to help the child come together with the right objects. The teacher's only role is to foster and facilitate, to sponsor a play process that takes care of itself if there are plenty of fantasy objects and playmates.

Experience suggests that a natural sequence is from playing alone to playing in pairs to playing in larger groups. Children will vary, of course, in their social growth. An advantage of acting out at school rather than at home is that individual play soon becomes group play as children become interested in and influenced by what others are doing. A child may begin by monologuing his fantasy as he plays, or by making up a conversation between two puppets, and end by playing doctor to several patients. Certain props, such as a pair of telephones or a cash register and money, naturally call for social play and promote interaction. Furthermore, chatting over a phone or buying and selling over a cash register promotes the specific social play of talking.

Movement to Sound

The second point of departure for dramatic activity is sound, including rhythm and music. As a stimulant, sound has some advantages over toys: it leaves more to the imagination, and it prompts the child to use his body more. Since the teacher makes the sounds while the children react, a controlled activity of the whole class becomes possible.

MATERIALS

As for most drama work, a large floor area is needed, preferably a special room set aside and equipped with piano, record player, and other sound instruments, but a classroom will do if the desks can be moved. Cafeterias and gymnasiums will also serve well but may not be available for enough hours of the day. For strong rhythms and tattoos, percussive instruments — drum, tambour, and tambourine — are needed; for arresting interjections, cymbals and gongs and whistles; for tones and note sequences, a pipe, flutaphone, or other simple wind instrument; for rhythm and melody combined, a piano or record player, if not both. Such equipment allows you to create a wide variety of stimuli which the children can translate into a correspondingly wide variety of body movements. Many sound-makers, of course, can be improvised from common materials like cans and sticks.

Providing the Stimuli

Diversifying the sound is important for perceptual discrimination, emotional range, and bodily articulation. Play with all the possibilities: shift the stress in rhythms, speed up and slow down tempo, raise and lower or shorten and lengthen the notes, widen and narrow the intervals between notes, make the sound skip or trip or drag or slide, alternate quiet and turbulence. Isolate one at a time the various dynamics of music — staccato, glissando, crescendo, accelerando, ritardando — then join them later into little sequences that create reaction sequences for the children. The ability to act with the body — to pretend to be a rabbit, or an old man climbing a snowy mountain — depends a lot on the repertory of body movements a child can bring into play. As in all other matters, access to a broad spectrum of possibilities directly increases one's creative invention. Enlarging the repertory, in this case, need not be done through systematic exercises; if frequent enough, diverse stimulation will eventually lead children to discover the repertory. Learning to discriminate various auditory dynamics will sensitize them to pattern and structure in other media, including literature. And running the sound spectrum is running the emotional gamut — exercising feeling in a controlled, communal fashion.

These movement-to-sound sessions, which I recommend two or three times a week for younger children, can progress from movement of the whole class in concert (not in unison) to individualized movement and thence to interaction of individuals. I suggest this because personal invention comes slowly, and because many children are shy of bodily exposure, which is minimized when everyone is doing the same sort of thing together. In so many areas, the individual develops by shedding his dependence on the group. But once he is able to express himself somewhat in his own way, the child can learn to interact with other individuals in a more truly social way than when he was merely a herd member. The following procedural suggestions reflect this progression. The three stages are for convenience, and I will not attempt to say how long a period of time they span.

1. *Herd movement.* Beat a strong, simple rhythm that children will take as a cue to either skip or run or tiptoe or slide-step, directing them only to "move the way the sound tells you to." They almost always fall into a circular movement, often following one or two leaders. Both this ritual and your control of the sound production impose order on this mass energy. Try out many of the variations mentioned above, gradually complicating the sound sequences by producing different dynamics in succession.

2. *Individual invention.* Begin to alternate these locomotions with movements-in-place by directing them sometimes to move each in a small area of his own, and occasionally even telling them not to move their feet. But first make the sound while they are resting and ask for ideas about how to move

to it. Let the class then try out these ideas one at a time in concert. The question would be: What is happening? Who are you? Where are you? This so that they can verbalize or demonstrate the movement idea in dramatic terms. Then dispense with the practice of asking for ideas and just tell the children to move in place as the sound tells them to. Those who still have to imitate will do so, and those who are ready will invent. Occasionally repeat a sound sequence and tell them to do a different movement to it than they did the first time. Continue the sound variations. Encourage the children to imagine a setting, an action there, and a personage. Have them be that person or thing doing that action in that place. Introduce more extended pieces of music, especially music suggestive of mood and action. Let them know that they may speak as they move. Let them move about, each in his own area.

3. *Small-group interaction.* Place the class in pairs, trios, and quartets (gradually increasing the number in each group) and direct them to share space with their partners. The point is not to make children act or dance together but simply to clump them for spontaneous interaction, to let them influence each other in a group-defined space. They may move in place or move about, but in either case they should remain in their areas. Recompose the groups on each occasion. Continue sound variations.

These stages are cumulative; to enter a new stage is not to abandon previous ones but to add to them.

Pantomime

After movement to sound has become a regular activity and has reached the stage of individual invention, those sessions may be combined with pantomime. Instead of toys or sounds, the stimulant now is an *idea* of an action.

EARLY PROCEDURES

Ask the children to pretend to be all sorts of things, at first selecting simple acts: a giant striding, a hobbled prisoner, someone hauling on a rope or pulling a sled, someone opening a door or window or umbrella or difficult bottle, someone drinking something unpleasant or pleasant. Select actions that will continue to enlarge the repertory of movements — bending, twisting, contracting, stretching — with all parts of the body, and in all directions. Tell them, for example, to imagine that they are standing close to a building, facing it, and straining to look up at someone in a very high window; then the person at the window throws something out that curves slowly over their head and falls behind them; they follow it with their eyes, bending back until, as it nears the ground behind them, they finally have to twist around. Or station them all along the walls and tell them to try to push the wall over in as many different ways as they can think of without *striking* the wall.

Once the children are familiar with the game, ask them for suggestions, and from then on merely relay individual ideas to the group, which can try them out one at a time in concert. Continue to select the ideas, however, both for muscular and dramatic variety. Then give them an action made up of a series of acts, such as entering a window, taking something from a chest, hiding it on one's person, and leaving. Narrate or read aloud a story step by step, and expressively, allowing the children time to pantomime each new act and to "be" each new character that comes up. All children play all roles, including objects. Next, help them make up together a verbal story that they can proceed to act out in the same step-by-step manner as you tell it over.

LATER PROCEDURES

As with movement to sound, progression at this point is two-fold — toward individuals doing different things at the same time and toward individuals forming small groups that also do different things at the same time. For the former, direct them each to think out and execute alone an action of his own, and then pass among them and try to guess what some of them are doing. You may provide very helpful feedback just by saying what you think you see. If this is different from what the child has in mind, you can then say also what he did or did not do that gave you your impression. That is enough for the child to learn from; there is no point in either gushing praise or correction of technique. In fact, if commenting seems to spoil the children's involvement or to create self-consciousness, it would be better to defer it to a later age.

As for the small-group work, this can begin after the pupils are well experienced with solo pantomimes and after they have achieved some social maturity. The class is divided into groups of three or four and directed to make up a short scene or to enact one from a story they know. Tell the groups to start thinking of an action that has parts for everyone and say that you will pass among them to help them organize. This planning talk itself is important as task-centered conversation, and, although you should help the groups to settle on an action and on the casting if they cannot resolve these matters, the ideal is self-organization as soon as they are able. (Many later assignments call for small-group projects, and the children should become habituated early to running their own groups.)

Remind the class that the game of pantomime is played without words and without props; their bodies alone tell the story. Objects are suggested by movement in feigned relation to them or can be played by other children (rock, tree, revolving door, etc.). When they have been through their pantomime once, they are directed to discuss making changes, to rotate roles, and to do it again. Both the revisions and the role reversals are important. Doing different versions of the same basic action is a form of composition and also draws some attention to technique (the commentary coming from the participants, not from the teacher or any other audience). Recasting roles establishes early the principle of flexibility and point of view in role playing and breaks the type-casting based on traits of personality and physical build that children by themselves are apt to institute. Again, the main value is in the acting itself and in the pupil discussion entailed by it; the teacher does not even hint that one group should perform while the others watch. When children think of this, it is usually because they got the idea from adults.

Relation of Physical Movement to Language

Though movement to sound and pantomime do not seem at first glance to relate directly to the development of speech, they in fact lay an important base for it. For small children, speech is only one physical activity among others (as indeed it really is), and not a preferred one. As a specialized mode of communication and expression, speech only gradually singles itself out from movement and gesture until, in print, it becomes totally separate. For children generally — and boys especially — speech *accompanies* other action and justifies itself only when it can do what other actions cannot. Movement to sound and pantomime permit the child both to develop his powers of nonverbal modes of expression and to run up against their limitations. Too often schools attempt to make speech abruptly supplant these modes, forcing the child off native ground onto strange territory. The fact is that the two realms blend without a seam, and the nonverbal expression can provide the best pathway to speech development. The sheer socialization of school helps to promote speech — or can, if the activities permit socializing. The teacher can insure that speech grows out of physical play and bodily movement by extending nonverbal expression into the verbal. More concretely, the teacher orchestrates play with objects, movement to sound, and pantomime into full-blown improvisation, which in this curriculum will be a major method of learning to use language.

Combining Movement and Speech

ENACTING READY-MADE STORIES

When a teacher feels that his pupils are ready, he may combine the three foregoing activities by breaking the class into groups and directing the groups to act out a short familiar story with speech and movement. The assignment is broached before the whole class, and the children are asked to nominate stories. They are to understand that they will take the main action of the story and do it in their own way, filling it in, making up the details and dialogue, or using details and dialogue that they remember. It should be clear that they will improvise, not learn their parts. They should feel free to change and add things. The story could be one they have read together, one the teacher has read, one a pupil has written or dictated, or one that all the children know anyway. The teacher moderates the selecting of a story or scene and leads preparatory discussion in which the story is recalled if necessary and decisions are made about: the number of parts, which props if any are needed, whether some inanimate things should be played by people, which roles need to be played by boys and which by girls, whether musical or rhythmic accompaniment is wanted, and whether individual or choral singing seems called for (as in enacting some story songs).

Another possibility is to enact a story just after reading it. This strengthens two of the aims of drama — to tie the printed word to the physical world of behavior, and to sharpen reading comprehension by translating the subject into another medium. For example, during the preparatory discussion, the teacher would have the children refer to the book when making decisions about how to do the story.

The reason for holding all groups at first to the same story is that preparatory discussion is then class-wide and led by the teacher. This discussion can become the model for small-group procedure when several groups are going to act out different stories and hence must organize themselves more on their own. After a certain amount of experience with enacting, the groups might indeed select different stories. If, in the whole-class nominating session, several factions feel strongly about different choices, they can become the nuclei of groups to act out those choices. The class would then break up, and some time would be allowed for small-group planning with the help of the teacher when he comes around. Whether doing the same or different stories, the groups proceed as they did with pantomime: they act out the story with one cast, discuss that version, rotate roles, and do further versions.

Free improvisation

The "minimal situation." A free improvisation is based on a story idea, the least elaborated, most summarized statement of character and event that will give the players the feeling of having enough to go on. This idea may be called the "minimal situation." The difference between enactment and improvisation is necessarily a matter of degree only, since there are always some "givens," suggestive ideas that are the starting point for acting out. In improvising, one makes up more of the story as he goes along; when enacting, one has more details specified in advance. Since small children's inventions are drawn so much from familiar stories anyway, the distinction breaks down even more at this age. Nevertheless, launching the children from a minimal situation rather than from a known story does place them farther along the way toward individual creativity.

Minimal situations might come from a number of sources — the children's own captioned drawings, ideas suggested in class, local events, and common real-life circumstances. In regard to the last, a first-grade teacher[2] and I tried such situations as: two teachers chatting during a coffee break; a parent and teacher having a conference about a pupil; two brothers arguing; and several other family scenes. Despite a number of mistakes I made due to my ignorance at the time, these trials were successful enough to suggest that under the right circumstances children can work well with realistic minimal situations. The procedure would be to select a situation in preliminary class discussion, then to break into groups and improvise it with the usual rotation of roles. The teacher passes among the groups to offer an occasional suggestion when a group seems to need more priming.

Conclusions from some trials. I will pass along a little more of the experience of the trials just referred to, pointing out at the same time that what I learned the hard way is well corroborated in books by drama specialists.[3] I will let my trials stand as typical of what would probably happen to any well intentioned but not well informed teacher who should blunder into improvisations too soon (for himself and for the pupils). (Often in this book, my advice will be not to do what I did.)

When the children were asked who wanted to be so and so, hands waved furiously, but once they were front and center many children became blanks (which never seems to happen when playing unwitnessed). They wanted to "be" but did not know what to do. Masking themselves behind puppets and costumes helped, but even then the boys resorted to an embarrassed kind of physical banging, and both boys and girls uncreatively repeated action or became "silly." If the group was as large as four or five, the participants left the initiative to others, or in effect dropped out and stared or smiled at the audience. Good movements came only when an unusually poised child — almost always a girl — could stay in role and invent ways to stimulate fellow actors. The teacher was held in tension between wanting to maintain a free climate and feeling that the unnatural silliness and physical violence was a perversion of the whole activity. The children asked for time to work out the main story idea or situation before improvising, but such planning did not usually reassure them or help them to maintain involvement with the action rather than with the audience.

My conclusion was that the spontaneous play process should not be tampered with by having it witnessed. Most children of this age are not really

[2] My thanks to Miss Mena Topjian of the Franklin Elementary School in Lexington, Massachusetts.

[3] For such a book, by perhaps the most important pioneer in this area, see Peter Slade, *An Introduction to Child Drama* (London: University of London Press) a book I read only in the course of revising this book, but which accords rather well with most recommendations made here. To find more detail on method and rationale, teachers should become familiar with Slade's work.

interested in performing before others, do not do it well, and become considerably inhibited when asked to do so. The name of the game changes. *They transfer their involvement with the original objects or people to the audience, and yet they do not allow for that audience.* That is, they become self-conscious and tongue-tied, and at the same time they speak too low, unwittingly hide some of their action, and do mysterious things that only their partners understand.

If a puppet theater is available, as it should be, one or two pupils may ask for an audience; the teacher could then watch and let other children join her as they want. This is an easy kind of first audience because the puppets are the focus, and the puppeteers, feeling hidden, can act through them. They will use their voices more boldly because they think of them as issuing from the puppets. (The child's feeling of identity with the puppets is especially strong when he has made them himself.) Despite the common belief that small children are born show-offs and have unfettered imaginations, I think the fact is that premature performing can spoil the very important evolution of play into other dramatic activities. Furthermore, first grade is too early for free improvisation, which should be gently and thoroughly led up to. A slow growth through the activities I have described, fostered by a watchful but patient teacher, will promote the most effective learning in drama.

Chapter 4

Speaking Up

Rationale

The Need for School Talk

To develop their language powers the simple fact is that children must talk a lot. They must *use* language and use it an enormous amount. Learning to read and write will depend in large measure on the growth of oral speech. Like dramatic play, conversing is something the child does before he comes to school, a fact that implies two things. First, it is something that the school can build on from the outset, a familiar medium to extend and use as a substratum for reading, writing, and thinking. Second, since children learn to talk out of school, their talk within school should provide additional learning not easily acquired anywhere else.

School should be a place where children talk at least as much as outside, for fostering speech is the business of the language classroom. Too often there is the hidden inscription above the door that says, "Abandon all speech ye who enter here." The kids get the message. "Speech is not wanted (that is for another time and place). Here you sit quietly and don't socialize; paper work is what they care about in school except when they want you to read aloud or answer a question. Talking to other children is bad behavior." So long as talking is excluded from the curriculum and not utilized within it, peer conversation can only appear as a disciplinary problem. As the last section was concerned with harnessing play for learning purposes, this section is concerned with formalizing peer talk sufficiently to provide learning of a sort that seldom occurs in casual out-of-school conversation.

45

"CLASS DISCUSSION" AND SMALL-GROUP DISCUSSION

What I will recommend here has little to do with what is generally called "class discussion," which is rarely a real discussion. Although class-wide talk is often helpful or necessary, it cannot *teach* discussion; it can only *benefit* from discussion's having been learned some other way. So far as I can tell, the only way is pupil-to-pupil talk in small groups of no more than six. The sheer size of "class discussion" precludes a high enough degree of attention, participation, and interaction — essential qualities of discussion. The teacher has to talk too much to maintain continuity, and invariably does talk too much. He resorts to prompting by questions, and except for occasional solos by a loquacious few, the children play the very restricted role of answering these questions. As vocal exchange, such a process is severely limited. The heart of discussing is *expatiation,* picking up ideas and developing them; corroborating, qualifying, and challenging; building on and varying each other's sentences, statements, and images. Questioning is a very important part, but only a part, and should arise out of exchanges among students themselves, so that they learn to pose as well as answer questions. For his part, the teacher should be relieved from the exhausting, semi-hysterical business of emceeing.

Serial exchanges between teacher and pupil A, pupil B, etc. may serve some other purposes such as checking information or soliciting scattered opinions, but children should never be allowed to think that this is discussion. Discussion is a process of amending, appending, diverging, converging, elaborating, summarizing, and many other things. Most of all, it is an external social process that each member gradually internalizes as a personal thought process: he begins to think in the ways his group talks. Not only does he take unto himself the vocabulary, usage, and syntax of others and synthesize new creations out of their various styles, points of view, and attitudes; he also structures his thinking into mental operations resembling the operations of the group interactions. If the group amends, challenges, elaborates, and qualifies together, each member begins to do so alone in his inner speech. This is not a proven point, but I believe that general experience bears it out. The teacher's job is to establish the forms of discussion that, when internalized by individuals, will most enhance the growth of thought and speech.[1]

RELATION OF DRAMA TO DISCUSSION

Dramatic interaction will further the goal of developing thought and speech considerably because it promotes the diverse forms of expatiation. Indeed, therein lies much of the ultimate value of improvisation. Using the words of others as cues for one's own response is the heart of both improvisation and discussion. But discussion differs from drama in valuable ways

[1] The full theory of internalization of speech is set forth in "Drama: What Is Happening," in *Teaching the Universe of Discourse.*

that enable it to carry on where drama leaves off. It is more abstract and more verbal. Relatively, it immobilizes the body and detaches itself from things. The vocal mode is singled out. Emphasis is more on the content of speech than on speech as a behavior. Appeal is more to reason than to emotion. But none of these differences represents a clean break; in fact, discussion retains a dramatic underpinning that provides continuity from one to the other and should never be lost. Any experienced discussant acknowledges the big part that "group dynamics" plays in discussion, however intellectual the subject. What the teacher should keep in mind is this whole relation of drama to discussion and its importance for an articulated curriculum.

STATUS OF DISCUSSION IN THE CURRICULUM

Peer discussions in small groups should be a staple learning activity for all grades, alloted a large amount of time in the curriculum, and conducted with the same regularity and sense of method that, for example, the traditional reading groups are accorded during these early years. I am aware that a number of teachers do from time to time permit children to talk about something in separate groups. But discussions need to be carried out with frequency, regularity, and method. Usually teachers feel that they are indulging the children in a side activity, and do not bring to it nearly the conviction and professional confidence that they do to reading and other activities. The lack of conviction and professional confidence derives directly from lack of experience and method. Too few teachers feel that they know how to manage small-group discussion, and indeed there has not been much precedent or support for it.

What I would like to do here is to make small-group discussion respectable and show that it can have method. This will not be easy because it has been explored very little as a serious, staple activity. And it does not, like writing, break down into a variety of specific assignments; it is a basic process that grows gradually over the years in ways not easy to define, at least not yet. Given these difficulties, I will approach the matter by describing some trials that I know about, and by extrapolating this experience into guidelines for further experimentation.

Unstructured Discussion

ACCOUNT OF SOME TRIALS

I asked the teachers of two classes combining second- and third-graders (called the Beta team)[2] to break their two classes into heterogeneous groups

[2] At the Franklin Elementary School in Lexington, Massachusetts. I am indebted to the teachers, Mayrae Means and Charles Mitsakos, who were assisted by a student teacher, Tina Feldman.

of three and four and direct them to discuss some magazine photographs for five to ten minutes in different parts of the same room at the same time. We provided no adult leadership after the general directions were given to the whole class. No pupil leader was appointed, but one often emerged. After two rounds of small-group discussions of the photographs, which were deemed provocative for children, the teachers felt that the subject was too open and the children did not have enough to go on. So they directed them first to jot down notes about the photographs first, as demonstrated on the chalkboard, and then to use these as a basis for talk. Still there was too little interaction. Often the children made a few remarks on the photo, then talked of other things or gazed away. Some children would not talk to certain others, presumably for personal reasons. Next, the groups were asked to make up a story about the picture. One teacher described the results as "awful," another as "the best yet" (contradictions spice life for the researcher), but the one had hoped for single, unified narrative and the other had settled for description. Results were indeed mixed: often the stories were good, often they were flatly descriptive of the photo; some children inferred motives and circumstances, some elaborated a single idea, some gave several interpretations.

We considered what might precede and follow the group discussion. Whereas our question initially was, "What do children really want to talk about?" it later became, "Why do they talk when they do? In what circumstances?" For children to discuss photographs and live animals (another subject we used) seemed somehow arbitrary and unmotivated, even though we knew they were in some sense interested by these subjects. The assignment came from nowhere and went nowhere. We began to feel that the children needed the talk to produce something, to be a means toward some other end. Thus we considered talk centered on a task, like making a magnet — planning talk, problem-solving talk. The idea was for some of their action to engender the task and for the talk, in turn, to make possible other action. We replaced isolated talk for its own sake with purposeful talk continuous with other tasks.

This change led to two major procedures — setting a larger goal that would *require* talk along with a series of other activities, and having a scribe take notes of the talk to use in panel discussions. The following example will illustrate both procedures. The process evolved in a groping fashion from the imaginative efforts of the participating teachers to solve the problems raised above. I offer the process here as a teaching method that can be used many times with the same children but with different subjects. I would, however, expect other teachers to want to ring variations on it.

The participating teachers first learned from the children what would be for them a "burning issue" to deal with practically. The petty stealing of pencils, rulers, and erasers turned out to be such an issue. Feelings ran very high — higher than most adults would ever have foreseen — about this ubiquitous daily problem that involved every child in the classes. The children were told that they could try to solve the problem of stealing and each class was broken into eight or nine groups of three members each (four being considered a bad number because of the tendency to pair off). The function of the talk was to produce some ideas about how stealing occurs and what might be done about it that could then be relayed to the whole class. The groups were given five to ten minutes. In each group a scribe was appointed to record whatever ideas occurred. The groups were told in advance that the scribes would later form a panel so that ideas from all the groups could be pooled. Armed with their notes (brief, to be sure) the eight or nine scribes met as panelists before the rest of the class. Actually, these meetings were not so much true panels as series of reports, but the remarks of the scribes could be compared for similarities and differences, and some interaction did take place among panelists. Afterwards, the teacher asked the rest of the class to comment on the panel. Some disagreement came out as well as an occasional new idea.

At this point each of the two classes decided on a second phase of action: one was to make posters about stealing, and the other to prepare a publication about it. The class doing the publication brainstormed in the small groups for five minutes about items that might go in it, then looked these ideas over. After scribes reported these ideas at the panel, the whole class refined and pared them down to eight items: a report of a survey about sentiments on stealing, ads, lost-and-founds, tall-tales about what happens to stealers, "wanted" pictures of those who steal, what-to-do-when-you-find-something, what-to-do-if-you-don't-want-something-stolen, and an invitation to form a club. Some children were to explain the campaign to other classes to whom the publication was to be distributed. Two children wrote the survey questionnaire and two others compiled it with the teacher. Participation in the brainstorming was total, and every child wrote an article, even those who were hitherto "non-writers." The articles were read in the small groups, the good but not necessarily best ideas were singled out in discussion, and the papers were revised. Thus, through rewriting and proofreading in the groups, final copy was produced. Then each group discussed these and selected one for the publication, which was called *Beta-Gram* and is reproduced on page 142. After distributing the posters and *Beta-Grams* to other classrooms, the participating children went in pairs to garner reactions to their ways of dealing with stealing. The small groups discussed these reactions, and their scribes compared notes at a panel that stimulated a final class discussion about actually implementing a campaign in the school.

Probably no adult of sound mind would have thought up in advance such an intricate rigamarole. Being of sound mind myself, I certainly did not offer it as an experimental idea to the participating teachers. They had the courage to pursue my bare notion of small-group discussion wherever it needed to go, the wit to improvise and orchestrate activities, and the sensitivity to play by ear with the children. The process just described, which spread over two or three weeks, did not go off without a hitch, but the problems were those of a first trial, when teachers did not know what the next phase was to be. Certainly this air of adventure and freedom accounted for a lot of excitement and involvement, but, as the teachers felt, some things such as the assemblage of *Beta-Gram* and the visiting of other classes was hasty and sloppy. One visiting educator was concerned about how a scribe should be chosen and his role explained, and also whether he imposes a list format on his group discussion. To answer the last question first, I think he does impose a list format in some measure, but enumeration is a primary form taken by any young children's discussion anyway, one which they need in the earliest stages of learning to converse. Other forms of discussion, of course, should grow from it, as I shall try to sketch later. In the experiments the scribe was chosen first by the teacher but later ones were volunteers. The first time the process is run through, the teacher should probably choose a more verbally able child, but on other occasions the role should be rotated automatically.

Conclusions from the Trials

As one of the teachers said, the project may not prevent stealing, but it works well for language development. For motivating pupils to speak and write, and to do so in real and meaningful ways, it seems indeed very successful. The teachers felt that the pupils came alive and became involved in language as they never had before. Four features of the process account for this, I believe, and would be desirable traits of other speaking and writing assignments for this age. (1) Though paramount to the teachers, speech was, in the pupils' eyes, incidental to the goal of social action; it was a means to a real-life end, solving the problem of stealing. (2) The various speaking and writing tasks formed a long-range continuity that imparted practical sense to each task and accumulated momentum as one led into the next. (3) Pupils were allowed to socialize, make decisions with peers, and exercise some independence as groups. (4) The high motivation cut out distraction and impelled the children to interact within their groups. Obviously, other teachers using the process should keep the spirit of it and never formularize it. For the hardships of playing somewhat by ear they will be rewarded by keen response and a sense of progress.

These trials, especially the picture discussions, undoubtedly resemble some that other teachers have conducted. They may stand as generally representative of what happens when second- and third-graders are asked to talk in small groups about a preselected topic without adult leadership and without special training in the art of discussing. Assuming a goal of autonomous peer discussion, my approach was to start with the most open situation and then to note where structure was needed. I drew these conclusions: (1) Unstructured, leaderless discussion needs to be embedded within a larger project that entails the discussion, thereby giving it a practical function and an end beyond itself; (2) even such task-oriented discussion would benefit considerably from prior training under adult leadership. In other words, the key issues are the motive to talk and the learning of good talking habits. These habits concern qualities mentioned earlier — participation, attention, and interaction — none of which are very easy for children who are still learning to socialize and to focus. To some extent, high motivation itself reduces these problems, but the natural egocentricity of their age may still cause children to listen only to themselves and to make irrelevantly subjective remarks. Although the stealing project showed that children can talk effectively on their own, and want to, I felt convinced that specific training in small-group discussion should provide a model and basic experience that pupils could transfer to other discussions and that would enable them to participate most advantageously in groups not led by the teacher.

Drawing on the experience of these trials, of leading small-group discussions in my own secondary classes, and of participating in adult "awareness" groups, I settled on a notion of training whereby the teacher would lead one group at a time — directing the group process, not joining in the discussion of the subject — and would establish at the outset a few common-sense principles about listening, responding, and sticking to the subject.

Structured Discussion — "Grouptalk"

At this point I came upon the work of Dr. Babette Whipple, who had been doing research among fifth-graders with just such a training, which she called, as a kind of trademark, Grouptalk. This research, more extensive and systematic than my own, was first conducted under the auspices of the Elementary Social Studies Project of Educational Services Inc., at a Newton (Massachusetts) public school, and is being continued at the same school under the Newton school system. She reports a very enthusiastic response from children and a high degree of success. She and teachers under her guidance are currently trying Grouptalk with children of lower grades, including second, the method being adaptable to all ages. Since her Grouptalk illustrates essentially the kind of training method I have in mind, and has undergone a substantial trial, I will give an account of it here.

DEFINITION AND PROCEDURE

In a monograph entitled *The Grouptalk,* Dr. Whipple has defined Grouptalk as

A formal discussion of a question by a small group and a leader following the specific rules that all members of the group contribute relevantly to the discussion and that all help in the effort to summarize it.[3]

[3] Occasional Paper Number Ten, Educational Development Center, Cambridge, Mass., 1967, obtainable by writing to EDC, 44a Brattle St., Cambridge, Mass. Undoubtedly, she will produce further reports as she continues to explore Grouptalk.

"Formal" refers to the governing influence of the rules, not to the atmosphere, which is relaxed and lively. "Small" means three to six. The group is heterogenously composed. "Implicit in the definition are three primary functions of a leader: (1) to direct strategy, (2) to keep the group relevant, (3) to see that summary is achieved." The group shares with the leader the responsibility for calling attention to departures from the rules, and, by this means, "the teacher prepares for a gradual transfer of leadership to a student." Dr. Whipple stresses the point that the teacher concerns himself with group process, not with content or information. He is teaching children "*how* to think, not *what* to think."[4] The topic, always worded as a question, may be chosen by the teacher or suggested by the children. It is written on a chalkboard so that it can be read aloud and referred to. Ideally, the group meets in a separate room, for 30 to 45 minutes, and has the use of a tape recorder.

The rules are printed on cards, and are read and paraphrased by individuals during the first few sessions. As most recently formulated by Dr. Whipple, they are:

Rule 1: Understand. Everyone thinks about the meaning of the question before the group tries to answer it.

Rule 2: Contribute. Everyone tries to answer the question.

Rule 3: Listen. Everyone tries to understand what is said so that he can respond.

Rule 4: Be Relevant. Everyone keeps to the point.

Rule 5: Sum up. Everyone tries to state the main point of the discussion.[5]

As I see it, Rules 2, 3, and 4 merely crystalize, as concepts for the child, certain common-sense principles. Perhaps the same is true for Rules 1 and 5, but Rule 1 is also a more specific bit of method for getting children to define key words and for insuring that discussants are assuming the same meanings in common. (Do they agree to include birds and fish in the meaning of "animals"?) And the summary (Rule 5), which is usually initiated by the teacher after a certain time has elapsed, is also designed to elicit a special activity, selective recall.

CONDITIONS FOR SIMILAR SMALL-GROUP DISCUSSION

Dr. Whipple has developed Grouptalk under research conditions that do not characterize the normal teaching situation. The group has been taken

[4] These quotations are from pages 8 and 9 of *The Grouptalk.*

[5] I am indebted to Dr. Whipple for this provisional reformulation and for criticizing this portion of the manuscript dealing with small-group discussion.

aside to a separate room while the regular teacher remains in charge of the rest of the class. Regular teachers who have led Grouptalk have been trained to do so by participating themselves in Grouptalk led by Dr. Whipple. And the children's sessions have been taped and played back to them immediately afterwards so that they can become more aware of the way they interact. Children love to hear themselves, and through playback they become aware of how they converse and of how to improve. Experimenting teachers, moreover, can gain skills by analyzing the tapes later. In short, the rather ideal conditions included a separate room facilitating concentration and recording, a separate teacher, in-service training, and a generous time allowance of 30 to 45 minutes per group. Can the school approximate these conditions?

First of all, the essentials of Grouptalk or of any other small-group discussion do not require all of these conditions. Though valuable, playback is not necessary.[6] Eliminating it would cut the duration of sessions in half and reduce the importance of a separate room and separate teacher. A teacher can take one group at a time into the corner of the classroom while the rest of the pupils are doing something else, as is the practice now for reading groups. The presence of a student aide or a student teacher would of course solve the problem more gracefully. As for in-service training, virtually any important innovation in the curriculum calls for some new knowledge or skill on the part of the teacher, as was certainly the case in revisions of the teaching of mathematics and the physical sciences. Until schools of education provide direct experience with small-group process, the experience will have to be gained in-service. Two able teachers who, at my suggestion, tried Grouptalk without special training[7] certainly achieved worthwhile results from the beginning and quickly learned a lot about the technique from criticizing the first few sessions, which were taped, but I am sure that Dr. Whipple is right to insist on special teacher training for the best results.

And this is my second point about achieving ideal conditions: the effort should be made. Makeshift is always possible but not always efficient. Dispensing with playback, for example, may save time but may equally well protract the learning period by rendering the whole process less effective, so that the moment when pupils can take over leadership of the group is deferred longer then if playback were allowed. The problems of small-group discussion can be solved in better ways than by making shift — by reconceiving uses of time, space, and staff. When educators become convinced that a certain kind of instruction is vital, they find the means. The power of verbal interaction to develop thought and speech is so important that I would go so far as to say that it obliges every school to make room for it, whatever the effort requires. Educational needs should dictate routines and facilities, not merely conform to them.

[6] In recent correspondence, she has informed me that "the current definition of Grouptalk incorporates the tape recorder, which is no longer considered optional." Thus discussion of playback becomes a key feature.

[7] Frank Lyman and Kayda Cushman.

Grouptalk is only illustrative. For developing verbal interaction in a way not necessarily practiced by children outside of school, it offers the best method I have heard of to date, but it may not be the only method or the best. I endorse it heartily, but I have given an account of it here mainly because it helps to fasten down my main concept of training in small-group discussion and exemplifies the problems entailed. Henceforth "small-group discussion" will refer broadly to any peer discussion with six members or less, whether led by the teacher or not. The following pages represent my own thinking on the matter, but I gratefully acknowledge the influence of Dr. Whipple's research.

Small-Group Discussion Led by a Teacher

Since not enough experimentation has been done to differentiate methods for K–3 from methods for 4–6, these recommendations will stand generally for all of elementary school, and even for later years, although I will try to sketch, roughly, some lines of sequence. The more detailed the suggestions, the more tentative they must be. But I can advance the general idea rather confidently.

Two kinds of small-group discussion are set in motion. One is of the problem-centered or task-oriented sort, embedded in a project, not led by the teacher. Probably, but not necessarily, these groups discuss at the same time in different parts of the room, and their membership will vary with the occasion. The other kind of discussion, led by the teacher for the purpose of teaching discussion itself, often has a nonfunctional topic but one that is of great interest to the children. Of necessity, only one group discusses at a time, and membership will remain constant over long periods of time. The two sorts of discussion take place concurrently, the first being employed on many occasions in connection with acting, writing, and reading, and the second being scheduled regularly, at least once a week for each group. The assumption is that what is learned in discussions structured by the teacher will transfer to the autonomous, temporary groups. Since the operation of these self-governing groups depends on what pupils bring to them, and since a lot of what they bring will depend in turn on the operation of teacher-led groups, I will concentrate on the latter. Because of its spontaneous nature, the talk of working parties cannot be separately dealt with here. What happens in these groups will be determined by the kind of task, as well as by the habits acquired from training.

CONDITIONS FOR CONCENTRATION

For children of the K–3 age the two new and difficult things to learn will be: concentrating on a single subject, which is a matter of focal attention, and adapting their talk to interlocutors, which means abandoning egocentric chatter and allowing for a listener. Attunement to the group is, in short, the main quality. And the main problem is distraction, whether it comes from outside the group, from private associations of ideas, or from entanglements of personalities. So at first, the teacher exerts an influence against distraction and for concentration.

This need not and should not be done in a disciplinary way. Physical distraction from outside the group should be minimized by taking the group aside to a quiet corner of the room (carpets help), preferably partitioned off, or ideally, to another room, while the rest of the class is doing something else. Like the reading group, the talking group is seated in a circle, perhaps around a table. A specific visual focus may help: write the subject on a placard or chalkboard close by, or place the picture or object within easy view. I have noticed, however, that first-graders cannot look at an object and talk about it at the same time; they seem to need to alternate. This needs more experimentation. I am not sure at just what stage of maturation children can do both at once and when they may have to look first and talk later, away from the object. In any case, placing the written topic before them does help them to focus and to stay on the subject. But, most of all, it is motivation that overcomes distraction. Interacting and sticking to the subject depend enormously on the interest of the topic.

SIZE AND MEMBERSHIP OF GROUPS

The size of the group should probably not exceed six, simply because participation and interaction drop below a desirable level in groups of larger numbers. Research in group process, mostly with adult subjects indicates that five is an ideal number. If the group is smaller, the cross-stimulation is likely to be insufficient for nonfunctional discussion. Small, even-numbered groups tend to split in two, and trios tend to produce a situation of two against one. The number may quite possibly need to change with maturation, discussion experience, and the degree of teacher direction or non-direction. The children should stay in the same groups for weeks or months so that trust, understanding, and a sense of group identity can build up. Shifting individuals from group to group sets off a lot of emotional static, and the new group regards the individual as an intruder. If changes are to be made, it is better to recompose all the groups completely. For the sake of an enriching variety and the development of communication skill, groups should comprise *differences* — of dialect, sex, socioeconomic status, verbal ability, intelligence, and so on. Speech develops best when one has to talk to people *unlike* oneself, because overcoming differences requires more clarifying and explaining. This principle is important enough to warrant heterogeneous composition of classes themselves (from which homogeneous sub-groupings can be formed for other purposes). I think that the teacher should compose the groups, but an argument can be made for sometimes letting pupils choose whom they are to be with. This matter needs trial and would depend perhaps on age and the makeup of the whole class.

Ground Rules

I do not think that discussion rules are the same for all ages or that they are always necessary. Their purpose is to induce certain speaking habits, such as listening and responding, and certain conceptual habits, such as defining and summarizing. Once the habits have been formed, the rules can be dropped. Rules about participating, listening, and sticking to the subject are appropriate for beginners only and would be discontinued once children learned to do these things (well before fifth grade if they began in first). On the other hand, a rule about summarizing may not have much interest or meaning for children before third grade. Small children like rules and rituals, but I think this aspect should be emphasized no more than is necessary to induce the habits.

The initial presentation of rules on cards is probably a good idea; Dr. Whipple may well be right in maintaining that reading aloud and talking about rules help children to *conceptualize* the behavior expected of them, which in turn helps them to achieve the behavior. But I think the main thing that shapes small-group process is adult direction and the children's imitation of it. Children's departures from the rules will have more to do with distraction, impulsivity, poor motivation, and egocentricity than with ignorance of common-sense discussion principles, and the teacher would do better to gain insight into these causes, as he will through experience, than to harp on the rules.

One rule that I suggest for beginners concerns taking turns. The understanding should be that a discussant who wants to talk does not raise his hand; his cue to speak is someone else's stopping. One of the main problems of teacher-led discussion is that children tend to talk to the teacher instead of to each other. If the teacher calls on children who raise their hands, he inevitably becomes the focus of the group, which is difficult to avoid in any case, since he is being directive in other ways. A rule about hearing out the last speaker and then starting to speak without signalling will help children to focus on each other and reinforce the rule about listening.

Finally, it may well be true that a very experienced teacher need not set up rules at all but can let the children generate their own as they criticize the playback of their discussions during early sessions.

General Role of the Teacher

The most basic thing is to create the proper climate for talk — relaxed but concentrated. The tone is warm and friendly but not saccarine. The teacher does not have to revere children's words; but everything he does should show that he truly values what they say. The art of conversing is a profound cognitive activity, not an application of etiquette like practicing table manners. It must be understood that this is the time for children to talk, and to talk to each other; the teacher is there to facilitate this by setting up and maintaining certain conditions. He does not participate as a discussant of the subject matter; his participation is at the level of process and not of content. The measure of his success is how well the discussion goes without him, how soon the children can take over his role and function autonomously. If he enables them to exchange with their peers in learning ways he has given them a great educational gift for the rest of their lives. After all, the ultimate goal of a teacher is to eliminate himself. But a teacher who needs too much to feel needed unconsciously keeps the students dependent on him.

Establishing the meaning of the topic. Specifically, the teacher does several things, *all of which should eventually be done by the pupils themselves.* First, make sure that they all understand the topic in the same way, by asking someone to say what it means to him and asking the others if they agree. It may be necessary to ask how they define certain key words. If they define "animals" so as to exclude birds and fish, that definition stands, though it is incorrect. Correction can take place at other times. Actually, as Dr. Whipple points out, these sessions give the teacher insight into children's concepts and knowledge so that he can better fit his other teaching to their needs. Discussing key words is also a way for children to acquire vocabulary and sharpen concepts. This agreement on the meaning of the topic is the touchstone for relevance throughout the discussion when teacher or pupil remarks that some utterance is off the subject. After settling on the sense of the topic, the children start where they will.

Encouraging participation. If someone does not participate for a long time, say, "Bobby, we haven't heard from you yet," or "What comes to your mind about this, Bobby?" Sometimes just looking at a child will draw him out. Children who habitually withdraw may need a skillful alternation of encouraging and letting alone.

Keeping the focus. Usually all that an off-subject utterance requires is a neutral reminder. But try to be aware of why children digress. If too many children wander frequently from the topic, you had better ask if the topic really interests them, or determine what else the matter might be. They might discuss what would be a better topic. Digressing is, after all, mostly a matter of involvement. Think of how difficult it is to divert a child from something he wants to do very badly. But digression may also arise because of involvement. Something just said may remind a child that "Daddy locked himself out of the house yesterday" or set him to wondering "What would happen if a locomotive got too hot and started to turn red all over."

Though irrelevant to the group's present focus, these are legitimate private associations and should not appear as enemies to the teacher or as mistakes to the child. The teacher simply says, "That might be a good incident to act out next time" or "You can suggest that for a later topic." No remark is ultimately inappropriate, only immediately inappropriate. All ideas will get their time; another idea has the floor now.

Focusing attention. If a child is not listening well, this will probably show up in a high percentage of non sequiturs and repetitions. In the latter case, simply say, "Joan has already mentioned that," or "Did you hear Joan say that before?" This lets the repeater know that he may have missed something, and also shows that you are setting an example of listening.

A major reason children do not listen to each other is that they do not value what peers have to say. Their first inclination is, in school at any rate, to assume that they can learn only from adults, who are all-powerful and all-knowing, not from other small critters like themselves. If the teacher attends and values their peer talk, they will also. As in many other matters, real attention establishes value. If you praise and blame, or otherwise make yourself the motive center of the group, children will talk to and for you, not to and for peers, and consequently will listen only to you and use the time while another child is talking to prepare their next bright remark for you to praise. Listening to peers, then, is directly related to honoring peer ideas, and the problem of inattention decreases as the peer-to-peer nature of the group becomes real to children (they may not believe it at first).

Some non sequiturs, however, are not born of inattention; a child may be breaking new ground in another aspect of the topic. When you feel that the abrupt switch shows that the speaker did not hear his predecessor, you might ask him if he heard, then ask that previous speaker to repeat what he said, then let the present speaker continue. Occasionally, when you feel that a certain remark is especially fruitful or difficult or deserving of thought, ask someone to paraphrase what was said. Such feeding back can help the speaker to know how well he was understood as well as sharpen listening among peers. Part of the teacher's role is to influence pace so that ideas are given their due and the discussion thickens and thins at appropriate places.

Handling the impulsive interrupter. If someone seriously interrupts another's sentence, say, "Ellen hasn't finished yet," in a factual rather than accusing tone of voice, or "Remember about waiting your turn," or make a simple gesture that says, "Hold off a moment." In extreme cases, when a chronically impulsive child habitually interrupts, you may as well focus the group momentarily on this problem and discuss it before proceeding, if the group seems mature enough. Ask what they all might do to help Plunger listen more and wait for his turn. The lesson is that when an individual problem impairs group functioning it is then a group problem also, and time should be taken to restore functioning. Turning in annoyance on the individual as culprit makes him defensive and makes matters worse; he needs rational help. If the group can think of no solution, ask Plunger to act as recorder for several minutes, listening only, and perhaps taking notes, and then, when the time is up, to tell in his own words the gist of what the group said, and to voice what he thinks of what they said. If this is done to help the individual and not to punish him, I think it will bring him around. At the same time, as it causes him to delay his responses and to become involved in listening during this delay, it also assures him that he in turn will have a definite and full hearing. Plunger's difficulty in waiting usually stems from one or more of these three things — impulsive inability to delay responses, egocentric disregard for what others say, or overanxiety about having a chance to get attention.

Leading the summary. Since the teacher controls the duration of sessions, it is up to him at first to initiate summary, but pupils should take over this function too as soon as they are able to follow time and to sense when discussion is ready for a summary. Ask the group to try to recall the main ideas that have occurred to them. Summarizing is important for developing thought because it is abstracting. Younger children will content themselves with selective recollection, but as they grow, their manner of summarizing will also grow; it will approach the drawing of conclusions. Sometimes new ideas occur as previous ideas are reassembled, thrown in a different order, paraphrased, and checked for omissions. Once all the returns are in, perspective is sometimes different. At this point the teacher can call for suggestions about the next topic, or air his own suggestions. Tying the summary of one session to the choosing of a topic for the next increases the likelihood of good continuity and momentum.

Helping with hang-ups. Besides insuring adherance to ground rules, the teacher looks for blockages and hang-ups. His job is not just to get the children over a difficulty but to help them understand what the difficulty was and how it can be overcome. He makes them aware of what makes and breaks communication so that they can eventually solve these problems themselves. Disagreement is not in itself necessarily a blockage, but it *may* be. Dr. Whipple has neatly classified disagreement into three categories —disagreements of definition, information, and value. Certainly the teacher needs to be adept at spotting mere definitional hang-ups, where different children are attaching different meanings to the same word or concept. The initial agreement about what the topic means should head off some definitional misunderstandings, but of course as new words and concepts are introduced into discussion the problem may crop up again. Say, "Mary, I think when you say 'transportation' you are including a lot of things Stephen isn't thinking about." Or ask another member if he thinks those two children mean the same thing by the word. Either another pupil or the teacher should try to say what Mary means and what Stephen means. Stephen and Mary can be asked if that is in fact what they mean. In other words, hang-ups should come under discussion until, again, the group process continues unimpaired.

Definitional disagreements should make way for more important ones. If the teacher believes a disagreement stems from different information — Alice has seen so and so and Elmer has heard or read something different — he may ask, "How do you know?" or "Where did you learn that?" or "What do you think proves what you say?" Partly, this questioning is intended to establish the habit of asking for, and giving, evidence. Identifying and documenting *factual* statements is something that small-group discussion should pursue later in many ways. Mainly, for now, the teacher helps them to see how some disputes may be resolved by getting more or better information, or at least to see that different information is the source of dispute. This could lead to research that could be brought into the next session. For disagreements founded on different values, you can only remark that "Beauregard and Abigail seem to be arguing over a difference in what they like. He considers machines very important and she doesn't because she cares a lot more about live things." This does not, of course, resolve the disagreement — which is not the point — but it serves to clarify the basis of the disagreement.

Often blockages reflect personal relations among the children. If doing so does not embarrass them too much, the teacher may remark that "Ed and Rick always seem to disagree, no matter what the subject is," or ask, "Do you always agree with Julia?" Another child may say, "Sure, they like each other" (giggles). "Do you think you can like each other and still disagree sometimes?" It is true that an adult cannot meddle much with children's interrelationships without creating fear of exposure. He can say, however, that when feelings they have about each other interfere with the activities of the group, the group may need to talk about them. Ganging up, jeering, or chronic arguing for the sheer sake of contest certainly play havoc with discussion. Since the whole purpose of the group is to learn how best to talk together, no malfunction can be ignored, whatever the reason for it. If members do not seem aware that discussion is being determined by personal feelings, the teacher should at least say that he thinks that it is. How far he should go beyond that is too difficult to say here; playing by ear is wisest in such sensitive matters.

QUESTIONING

The teacher's role in discussion will shift as the children become adept and begin to follow the rules for themselves. He does not need to try to do all things all the time. The less he has to concern himself with the fundamentals of the process, the more he can concentrate on making discussion more sophisticated.

The first way the teacher makes discussion more sophisticated is by sparely interjecting questions calling for elaboration, clarification, or qualification. These questions are not mere conversation prompters; they should express the teacher's real feeling that what a child has said is incomplete, unclear, exaggerated, or overgeneralized. Whereas a declarative statement to that effect sounds critical and omniscient, a question or request makes the speaker think a little more and sets an example of questioning for the listeners, who may well have found the statement incomplete or unclear too but were not aware that they did, or, with childish acceptance, did not realize that questioning might relieve their uncertainty. The teacher might say: "Will you explain that a little more?" (clarification); "*All* animals?" or "Is there a time when that is *not* true?" (qualification); "Tell us some more about what they do because I'm not sure yet how that fits in" (elaboration). Since the teacher is in the same role of listener as the other children, each question suggests what they too might have asked, or could ask in the future. At the same time the speaker is given feedback to help him come more on his true course by adding to or adjusting his first statement. This elaborating and adjusting under the influence of feedback will become an increasingly important learning process in later years. Though children are less interactive in these early years, if the teacher sets the example of questioning, small-group discussion can begin to become already a model of good thinking for the child to internalize.

FRAMING TOPICS

Topics may be of all sorts, but in the early grades they should be specifically stated in some predicated form, not just named with a noun or phrase. This would usually mean a question like "What are the different ways animals get food?" not "Animals" or "How Animals Get Food." The topics should be of the greatest possible interest to children, whether they come from the children or from the teacher. This means *emotional involvement.* For very young children, try topics into which a lot of feeling can be projected: "What would you do if the animals got loose in the zoo?"

Common information will provide a good basis for discussion among second- and third-graders, though teachers have to remember that it is not the purpose of these discussions to *convey* information; that should be done elsewhere. Films might serve well, but other experiences can furnish common information to all children — trips, reading, classroom pets, and, of course, universal life experiences outside school. To choose topics for their moralistic value to the teacher would be to pervert the whole intent. Subjects such as safety rules, good and bad manners, or the behavior in the auditorium yesterday would be dead give-aways that the teacher is merely converting small-group discussion into an agency of indoctrination and law enforcement.

Interest is considerably increased if subjects can in some way be carried over from one session to the next. Continuity and momentum are created by dove-tailing related topics and by framing a series of sessions within an overall goal or project.

One means of increasing the sophistication of discussion is to frame the topics in ways that progressively call for more difficult thinking tasks. *Why* questions, for example, are relatively difficult, entailing as they do not only a grasp of continuity of events and a concept of cause and effect but also a certain analytic ability to distinguish and classify events. Causation in familiar physical phenomena is easier, moreover, than causation in abstracter realms.

Topics inviting enumeration. The kind of topic most appropriate for beginning conversationalists calls for listing or enumeration: "How many different ways does an animal get food?" First, listing is a simple kind of thinking but an important one, and we know that small children can do it and learn from it. Cognitively, the process is one of furnishing positive instances of a category, Animal Ways of Food-Getting or Uses of the Magnet. This relates to concept formation. Disagreement occurs when an instance is offered — say, birds flying south to get food — and another child objects, in effect, that the instance is negative, not positive. (Birds fly south, he says, for reasons other than to get food.) If the category is "vehicles," "sled" may be disputed as an example. These disputes lead to precision of concepts and finer discrimination, to more analytic thinking.

Second, listing requires the least interaction among pupils. Essentially it is a piling of ideas, or "brainstorming." One pupil influences another mainly by thought association: a suggestion by one makes another think of something along the same line. Disagreement over instances, however, does represent greater interaction and a step upward from mere influence by association.

Enumerative topics may be of different sorts that can be roughly scaled to form a progression. One scale can run according to the abstractness, complexity or novelty of the category — its difficulty: "How many things can be done with a bottle?" "How do people get other people to do what they want?" "How can you tell what things will cost a dollar and what things a dime?" (Isolated, such topics are arbitrary, but they could be very pertinent in a context.)

Topics inviting comparison. Enumeration can lead to comparison topics by making the category one of similarities or differences, but taking only one or the other at a time. "In what ways are cars and airplanes alike?" "What are the differences between dogs and cats?" Dealing simultaneously with both similarities and differences — full comparison — is rather advanced and should probably be deferred to grades four through six. Researchers in the development of children's thought disagree about whether the perception of similarity or of difference comes first. This indicates, perhaps, that the order does not make much difference and that both kinds of topics could be dealt with alternately.

Topics inviting chronology. Another kind of topic for beginners calls for chronological ordering — making up a group story, planning an action, or telling how something is made. Such topics could be interspersed with the enumerative kinds. Most often they will relate to other activities such as drama, writing, and making things. The purpose of discussion is to work out an order of events that is going to be carried out in some way. The process is one of building, act by act or step by step, which is relatively simple in itself but usually entails reasons for choosing one suggestion over another. Thus, the main form is easy but invites some more complex kinds of thinking. Undoubtedly children will leap ahead and then later think of things that should have gone before. This backtracking and readjusting is something a summary could help put to rights.

The fixed groups led by the teacher should be used sometimes for planning, so that when children are placed in temporary groups for certain projects, they can exploit the experience. The topic might be a story problem to be enacted afterwards: "How does John get his bicycle back?" or a planning problem such as working out the stages of a campaign: "What steps should we take to prevent stealing?" or a planning problem about how to make something: "How should we go about making a bird feeder?" The enumerative and chronological may dovetail. For example, a listing of things that birds will be attracted to and will peck at might have to precede a session on construction , in order to settle on the type of feeder. The groups that selected the kinds of writing to be included in the *Beta-Gram* on stealing resorted to enumerating (ads, lost-and-founds, etc.) in the midst of carrying out one of the chronologically planned phases of the campaign.

SCRIBES

One of the many aspects of discussion that needs much more exploration is the use of a scribe, some pupil designated to take notes during a session and, after the group has summarized at the end, to read his notes as a summary to be compared with theirs. This would provide individual as well as group practice in summarizing, and would also act as a check on memory and perspective. Another procedure is for the scribe to participate in discussion until the summary and then take notes on the summary alone. Either way, children have opportunities for well motivated writing and the group has a record of their talk for the next session or for carrying out a plan. (The record may be helpful to the teacher also, in lieu of or in addition to a tape recording.) Of course many children are not able to write well enough or fast enough to act as scribe before the second grade, but even a few key words would be a good beginning.

PANELS

A further use for notes, as in the *Beta* experiment, is to form a panel when the class wants to pool ideas or to know what other groups have thought on the same subject. The scribes meet in a semicircle in front of the class, and each reports what his group has said. These panelists are invited to comment on each other's reports, and then the class is invited to comment.

Many of these recommendations not only apply to grades four through six but would be inappropriate before then. But not enough is known about small-group discussion among children, and especially its evolution over the years, for me to be able to distinguish two main stages of it, as I have for most other activities in elementary school. The ways in which topics, rules, grouping, and the role of the teacher should shift as pupils mature are critical matters for experimentation. Especially moot issues are: (1) the point at which groups can become self-governing for discussion of designated topics (so that, for one thing, simultaneous discussions can take place); (2) the uses of pupil leaders; (3) the likelihood that the teacher should periodically resume leadership of the groups to train pupils in new skills of thinking and discussing made possible by their increasing experience and maturity. These new skills might entail some changes in procedure and in the leader role (examples being a more abstract way of summarizing, or the citing of evidence to support statements). With a sense of method, such as these recommendations are intended to instill, the teacher should be able to cope with the problems of further experimentation and to enjoy the excitement of it.

Holding Forth

Solo talk, monologuing, is a special case of "speaking up" that I shall call "holding forth." The utterances of children in the lower grades tend to be short. The purpose of encouraging monologues is to let children practice extending their utterances. Whereas the continuity of dialogue is provided by the give and take of social exchange, the continuity of a monologue must come from within the speaker, from his perception of how to string his utterances together to develop a subject. He does this spontaneously, of course, without thinking ahead, but practice in holding forth can improve what he does spontaneously. Since developing a subject is what composition is generally about, holding forth is, in a real sense, learning to write without paper. After all, writing is a more sophisticated form of monologue.

Although I do not believe that monologuing can be carried very far in the K–3 years, because extended utterances must wait on several kinds of maturation, a definite beginning is possible. Monologue is born of dialogue, when a single voice takes over momentarily, like an aria in an opera. Holding forth means elaborating, which is not a small child's first tendency. He is at home with the reciprocal prompting of dialogue, where his thought can develop in bits and pieces under the influence of others, and where the problem of linking sentence to sentence, idea to idea, does not come up in a serious way. He should not be pushed to monologue, but he can be helped at this age to start stringing his bits and pieces into some kind of continuity.

SHOW-AND-TELL

The basic idea of talking while showing is very sound because it is transitional between play prattle and addressing an audience, between talking to toys and talking about them. Though monologue in the sense of sustaining a subject to a group comes slowly, nothing comes easier to a child than prattle, talking to himself and to his toys as he manipulates the toys. This kind of soliloquizing is fluent and may make for some very long continuities indeed. What provides continuity is the ongoing play to which the prattle is an accompaniment. What he does with the toys supplies a steady stream of cues for speech.

The value. Show-and-tell allows the child to take off from prattle but requires him to modify his speech for the sake of an audience. His subject is a familiar or loved object that he knows a lot about, but he must allow for outsiders who do not share his familiarity with the object. As he talks he can look at the object and do things with it, which will suggest things to say, but his speech continuity can no longer merely follow the blow-by blow continuity of his play. What he does is tell stories about how he got the object or what he has done with it, or give information about what it is and how it works. The difference is essentially that speech diverges somewhat from the ongoing action, becomes more independent, and necessarily becomes more abstract. While pointing, he inevitably talks of some things that cannot be pointed to — the past, feelings, purpose and function, and certain general information. But to be an important kind of learning, show-and-tell must be taken seriously and shaped into a distinct process.

Procedures. First, since nearly all small children are shyer in large groups, they are likely to talk more freely in a small group. Thus, holding forth could occur in the same teacher-led groups used for discussion, either before discussion begins or, if that makes too long a session, on another occasion. Once experienced, children can be placed in groups around the room and directed to take turns.

Second, the other children should question. Let the shower-teller begin as he will. When he has said all that initially occurs to him, encourage the audience by solicitation and example to ask natural questions. "When did they give it to you?" "What happened to the wing there?" "What's the red button for?" "What do you do if you want to get the money out again?" "Where do you keep it?" "Do you let your brother use it?" These are model questions calling for anecdote, explanation, and information. They are asked at first by the teacher and then by the children as they grasp the possibilities. Questions act as cues or prompts that replace play as a source of ideas. They cause the speaker to sustain his subject, to elaborate — fitfully, it is true; but I assume that, with experience, the speaker will anticipate questions and supply more information and background without waiting for questions to prompt him. Thus the monologue element will grow. A lot of practice in oral explaining can even influence the *order* of information — the mentioning of certain items first so that later items will be clearer. Questioning, then, is fixed as a part of the procedure.

Third, specialize the talk by asking the children to bring, on different occasions, something that (1) has a good story behind it, (2) they made or grew, (3) especially means a lot to them, or (4) moves or works in a funny or interesting way. This is how show-and-tell can become somewhat like a composition assignment. Narrative, exposition, and explanation are emphasized in turn by calling for objects associated with memories or having certain characteristics. Some objects were acquired in an interesting way or have had curious things happen to them; thereby hangs a tale (narrative). Drawings and paintings that the child has done also contain stories — fantasies or real events — that the artist can relate as he explains his picture. If the object was made or grown, the child tells how he made or grew it (description of a process). If it has special meaning for him, he tells how he feels about it (personal essay). Gadgets, machines, and other apparatus elicit explanation of purpose and operation.

Show-and-tell will grow as children grow, for their meaningful objects will reflect their maturing amusements, crafts, thoughts, and feelings. It is another staple activity that will continue beyond elementary school, and it is an important element in the later development of composition.

Chapter 5

Becoming Literate

Two main ideas underlie the following remarks and recommendations. The first is that *literacy is a two-way street.* When we go from speech to print, we call that writing; when we go from print to speech, we call that reading. The teaching of literacy must do equal justice to both, whatever that may require. It is necessary to say this because literacy instruction is traditionally biased toward reading, to which writing is attached as an adjunct.

The second idea is that *reading is mere decoding of print into speech, and writing is mere transcription of speech into print.* Speech is the given, the base, which children acquire before school and out of school. With speech goes a stock of meanings that has no necessary connection with reading and writing, that is independent of both, as indeed it must be for illiterate people. At the outset, then, I would distinguish, in reading, between decoding and comprehension, and, in writing, between transcription and composition. This distinction between literal and conceptual levels is obvious but easy to lose sight of.

The real issue of learning to read is not "getting meaning from the page"; we get meaning from the speech sounds that the letters represent. The real issue of learning to read is decoding the letters into words we already know and to which meanings are already attached. Reading comprehension is merely comprehension. Difficulties in comprehending are difficulties with concepts, ideas, and their relationships, not with printed words. A text that presents a problem of understanding to a child when he reads it will present the same problem of understanding when he hears it. Does he hear a voice behind the words when he reads them? *That* is the real problem of learning to read — decoding letters and punctuation into speech.

The same argument holds for writing. Just as comprehension is independent of reading, composition is independent of writing. We acknowledge this when we speak of oral composition and oral literature. The problems of composition are problems of selecting and ordering speech units — words, phrases, sentences, and whole monologues — and are essentially the same for the speaker as for the writer. Rendering a meaningful sequence of images and ideas into graphic symbols, on the other hand, is mere transcription, taking dictation from oneself. Spelling and punctuation belong to transcription, not to composition. It is understandable that transcribing and composing should become confused, since a person writing does both at once. And, of course, the fact of writing does influence composition and cause written speech to differ from vocal speech: writing down thoughts permits revision and relieves the memory load. (In an oral culture, one revises by memorizing and retelling.) But transcribing and composing are quite distinct activities and entail very different learning problems.

In this view, then, reading and writing are matters of getting between one symbol system and another, between some sounds and some sights that one learns to pair off — letters with vocal sounds, and punctuation and other typographical signals with intonation. Comprehension and composition, on the other hand, are deep operations of mind and spirit, concerning the relations between symbols and those complexes of perception and conception that we call meanings. There is no way simply to pair off meanings with symbols by rules of regularity. So the two-way street between speech and print is a symbol-symbol relation involving an essentially perceptual learning that for most children seems no longer developmental beyond the age of about first grade. I cannot imagine what the future maturation of a student can contribute to the problems of decoding and transcribing if he has not already learned by then to do those things. The rest is remedial.

This is not to minimize, however, the obvious difficulties that many children have learning to decode and transcribe. My point is that these difficulties can be greatly reduced by treating the two activities as nothing more than what they are — the matching of an auditory symbol system with a visual symbol system — and by treating meaning as nothing less than what it is — the matching of thought with speech. In short, literacy, I am convinced, can be better learned if it is not confused with the much broader issue of meaning. But this separation does not argue for a split in the learner's experience, only for a conception of literacy that helps to bring out which problems of reading and writing are *unique* to reading and writing and which are general problems of thought and language encountered in oral speech as well.

Since some recommendations in this chapter will consist of referrals to particular published materials for literacy instruction, I would like to propose criteria for choosing some materials over others. These criteria are based on the indications of research and on certain principles. Let me take the research first.

Research Indications

In a recent book, *Learning to Read: The Great Debate*,[1] Jeanne Chall presents an interpretive synopsis of what is known so far about beginning reading. This three-year study for Carnegie Corporation consisted of reviewing the old and new research on reading, analyzing textbooks, interviewing proponents of different methods, and observing literacy teaching in classrooms. It is because Dr. Chall has tried to characterize the present state of our knowledge about the subject, rather than merely to report certain research, that I would like to relay some of her points. She calls the central controversy one of *emphasis* as between a decoding approach and a meaning approach. The decoding approach would teach the phonographemic relations sooner and more systematically, as the key to unlocking new words, whereas the meaning approach would preteach whole words before they are read and feed in phonics gradually over several years as a supplementary way to recognize words. For new teachers especially, a somewhat fuller definition of these approaches may be helpful.

Two Basic Approaches to Reading

The *meaning approach,* incarnated in the conventional basal reader series[2] and enjoying almost unquestioned supremacy until recently, is based on these tenets, according to Dr. Chall:

1. Comprehension and interpretation should be a part of reading instruction right from the start.

2. Early reading should consist of recognizing words already pretaught by the look-say method.

3. Children should begin with whole words and sentences.

4. Silent reading should be stressed to avoid oral difficulties and "word calling."

5. After sight recognition of 50 words, instruction should begin in sound-letter relations.

6. The attack on new words should be through picture cues and contextual clues and through visual analysis and substitution.

7. Phonics and word analysis should be spread over six years of school, phonics gaining momentum in grades two and three.

8. Separate, systematic teaching of phonics is bad because it is boring and difficult; separate sounds should not be blended into words, but rather words broken down by phonic analysis.

[1] New York: McGraw-Hill Book Co., Inc., 1967.
[2] Typified by the Scott, Foresman and Co. Series of 1956 (now revised) and the Ginn and Company Series of 1961, which Dr. Chall analyzed in detail.

9. In grades one to three, the words in readers should be repeated often on a meaning frequency principle, the number of new words being very low in ratio to old words (necessarily, since new words are pretaught by sight).

10. Beginners should move slowly after a readiness or prereading period.

The *decoding approach* has been variously represented in the past and is even more variously represented in the present, now that the swing is back toward phonics. The only thing that all the different decoding methods have in common is an early and systematic teaching of sound-letter relations as an analytical tool to enable children to attack new words. Some people are opposed to certain tenets of the meaning approach, some to others. The variations among them concern principally whether phonic regularities are to be taught explicitly or inferred from controlled spelling of the reading matter, whether components are to be synthesized into words or words analyzed into components, whether words are to be spelled out or sounded out, whether devices such as machines and artificial alphabets are to be used, whether the alphabet is to be learned first by naming letters, whether pictures are to accompany stories, whether the method is to be used independently or in conjunction with conventional basals, and whether oral speech, writing, dictation, and activities other than reading are to be a part of the method.

What verdict does research evidence render on these two general approaches? In interpreting the evidence, Dr. Chall insists on one point that has often been a source of conflict in the past: one approach or method seems more effective at the end of the first grade but not at the end of second or third grades. (In any case, the evidence at present does not go beyond the beginning of fourth grade.) Given this, her general conclusion is that after two or three years, children read with better understanding, and recognize and spell words better, when they have learned by a decoding-emphasis method.

> Most schoolchildren in the United States are taught to read by what I have termed a meaning-emphasis method. Yet the research from 1912 to 1925 indicates that a code-emphasis method — i.e., one that views beginning reading as essentially different from mature reading and emphasizes learning of the printed code for the spoken language — produces better results, at least up to the point where sufficient evidence seems to be available, the end of the third grade.

Here are other conclusions from the findings:

1. Early decoding may result in lower comprehension and rate at the end of grade one but surpasses whole-word learning by the end of grade two. Decoding may achieve an early superiority in word recognition that does not show up on standardized silent reading tests (comprehension and vocabulary) in first grade, but by second and third grades the greater facility in word

[3] Chall, p. 307.

attack increases the ability to read for meaning, as measured by these same tests.

2. Children of lower intelligence and background seem to do better with an early code emphasis. (Children of higher intelligence and better background also gain from it, but the effect is not so great.)

3. Correlational studies support the experimental findings that an initial code emphasis produces better readers and spellers.

4. Learning the names of letters and their sound values before beginning to read helps early reading. In primary grades, a knowledge of letters and sound values appears to have a greater relation to reading achievement than intelligence.

5. There is some evidence that inferring phonic relations from texts that are controlled for spelling regularities is insufficient, that explicitly taught sound-letter knowledge is required in addition. The best results will probably come from controlling vocabulary for spelling *and* from direct teaching of phonic relations.

6. Clinical evidence shows failures in both camps, but the meaning approach seems to produce more serious failures than the decoding approach.

7. Children with a specific language disability all share a great difficulty with decoding, not with comprehension, and can be helped by phonic instruction combined with special kinesthetic and perceptual experience.

Although the findings clearly call for a reversal of the conventional emphasis — already apparent, as we shall see, in all the new materials — they do not give the nod to any one method of teaching the sound-letter relations, unless one is to give weight to the indications about teaching the names and sound values of letters before introducing reading texts, and about teaching the sound-letter relations explicitly rather than by inference or "discovery." These indications would distinguish some materials from others, since some withold the alphabet and some refuse to single out sounds and letters from whole words. The indication about explicit instruction, for example, would presumably give an edge to sounding-and-blending methods (synthesis), since they do present phonemes and graphemes in isolation from words, whereas the "linguistic" methods present them only in whole words grouped for minimal difference (analysis). But both aim for a phonic understanding that will enable children to decode new words for themselves.

Since Dr. Chall's synoptic research was conducted, a fresh set of research projects have been undertaken, under the auspices of the U.S. Office of Education, that constitute an essentially separate source of information from those that she synthesized. (In *Learning to Read: The Great Debate* she was able only to mention briefly the first reports.) The Cooperative Research Program in First Grade Instruction comprised 27 reading studies whose results were correlated at the University of Minnesota Coordinating Center. These studies compared several different beginning reading methods with "the" conventional Basal method. Ten of the studies have been continued through second grade.[4] Those methods for which results are available through second grade were designated Linguistic, I/T/A, Language Experience, and Phonic/Linguistic (the Lippincott *Basic Reading Series*). The 27 research projects compared one or more of these four methods with the Basal method *but not with each other*. There were other very important goals besides these comparisons, however, as the following findings indicate.

At the end of first grade it was found that whatever the method used, phonics-supplemented programs produced greater reading achievement. At the end of both grades, little significant difference was found between Basal and Language Experience or between Basal and Linguistic, though the latter tended to show a slight edge in word recognition and spelling. I/T/A did not differ significantly from Basal in reading comprehension but was superior in word recognition and spelling. The transition from I/T/A to traditional orthography appears to be a relatively simple task. Phonic/Linguistic (Lippincott) produced superior achievement over Basal in reading, spelling, and general language ability (but only two projects comparing these two, and hence much fewer subjects, remained at the end of grade two).

Several general results of these coordinated studies corroborate Dr. Chall's findings: (1) An early code emphasis appears to be highly related to word recognition and spelling achievement at the end of second grade (certainly as compared with basals). (2) Phonetic control of vocabulary helps the child recognize more words at an earlier stage. (3) Writing symbols in connection with phonic instruction aids the learning of both sound-symbol correspondences and irregular words; writing is an effective component of beginning reading. (4) Children can learn new words at a faster rate than has been commonly assumed in reading programs; expectations of pupil reading achievement can be raised.

The Cooperative Research report differs with Dr. Chall's in at least one important respect. Whereas Dr. Chall asserts that a decoding emphasis produces not only superior word recognition but also superior comprehension, thereby suggesting a strong relation between the two, the authors of the coordinated studies say:

> The superiority in word recognition of pupils in various phonics emphasis programs is not, as a general rule, demonstrated in the area of reading comprehension. . . . This finding does not support the contention that the pupils' only task in learning to read is to develop the ability to translate graphemic symbols into sounds on the assumption that once he has decoded the words he will understand their meaning. Direct instruction in comprehension is apparently essential.[5]

[4] The results for first grade alone are reported in *Reading Research Quarterly*, Vol. II, No. 4 (Summer, 1967) (Newark, Delaware: International Reading Association). The results for both grades are reported in *Continuation of the Coordinating Center for First-Grade Reading Instruction Program*, by Robert Dykstra, September 1967, Final Report of Project Number 6–1651, Minneapolis, Minnesota: Bureau of Research, U.S. Office of Education, University of Minnesota.

[5] *Ibid.*, p. 162.

First of all, Dr. Chall's evidence runs to the end of *third* grade. One of her points about such comparative research is that comprehension gains of the decoding approach show up late rather than early. Second, it is obvious that whether decoding will lead to comprehension or not depends on factors of attention, cognition, experience, motivation, environment, and so on that were not dealt with in these studies. It is indeed true that word recognition does not guarantee comprehension. A main contention of this book, in fact, is that comprehension involves so much more than letters that it should not be classified as a "reading problem." Finally, even if "direct instruction in comprehension" were possible, which I doubt, the purely logical assumption the authors make about its being essential should be regarded as a dangerous inference in a comparative study not purporting to analyze the learning process itself.

Fortunately, the coordinators of the USOE project have themselves stressed very hard the limitations of these studies. Thus, what may well be the most significant evidence they offer concerns the validity of most reading research itself. A striking finding was that reading achievement varied more within one method than it did between one method and another. And some differences in achievement seemed unrelated not only to method but even to pupil readiness or teacher qualifications, or to the particular class, school, and community the pupil was in. Variation, then, must be ascribed to factors not measured, about which one can only speculate.

> In general, projects appeared to have a greater influence on the reading ability of pupils than did the particular instructional method or materials utilized. Specific programs were relatively effective in one project, relatively ineffective in other projects. On the other hand, all programs used in the same project were found to be quite similar in effectiveness. This would indicate that the entire instructional setting is involved in the effectiveness of an instructional program in reading. Differences in method or materials alone do not alter, to any great extent, the reading growth of pupils. The section of the analysis again points out the importance in future research of focusing on teacher and learning situation characteristics rather than methodology and materials.[6]

Although in our ignorance we have no choice but to give some credence to reading research, the fact is that it is tremendously inadequate and should play only a limited role in determining curriculum. What it has produced so far simply must not be taken too seriously, for several critical reasons. Many severe limitations that are scrupulously acknowledged in these USOE studies characterize in fact practically all other classroom research as well, when it has not been downright amateurish and biased. Sophisticated computering and modern methodology are still not equal to the task of controlling all the variables that are operating in a classroom situation.

But to the sheer difficulty of establishing convincing controls, one must add the staggering problem of properly conceptualizing beforehand the nature

[6] *Ibid.,* p. 164.

of reading and the nature of learning to read. The USOE studies have performed the great service of showing that *we don't know what some of the more significant variables are.* The net catches a few fish, but suppose the secret is in the makeup of the sea itself? The power of research can be no greater than the power of the concepts by which it is designed. It is this poverty of conception, perhaps more than anything else, that accounts for the inconclusiveness, contradiction, and irrelevance of most reading research. Caleb Gattegno has put his finger on one telling weakness of this research:

> Reading research to date has "measured" not absolute learning, but the relative advantages of one method of teaching reading over another method. However, research in reading has not attempted to discover under what conditions a learner can acquire the skills of reading and writing as readily as he acquires the skill of speaking.[7]

For a good initial effort in the direction of better conceptualization I refer the reader to "Reading and Reading Difficulty," by Morton Wiener and Ward Cromer.[8]

"Action research" in classrooms has a practical look about it but has not in fact got us very far and may have done as much harm as good. Patient observation of particular children, as exemplified by John Holt[9] and by some clinical workers, plus basic investigation into the reading process of proficient readers, may help us much more to understand how children can best acquire literacy. The recommendations made farther on in this chapter attempt to allow for both the few safe generalizations and the many limitations of research as it stands today.

How New Materials Meet Objections to Decoding

The Objections

The materials now available for direct and early teaching of phonographemic relations show a very strong awareness of the long-standing objections to the decoding emphasis. Besides the general objection that phonics is dull and difficult, the principal ones mounted in the past and frequently still reiterated today are:

1. The building up of words from letters causes *confusion,* since alphabetic names usually differ from the pronunciation of the letters in a word, and *distortion,* since the combination of separately sounded phonemes results, for example, in *kuh-a-tuh* instead of *cat.*

2. Analytical word attack produces mere "word-calling," instead of mean-

---

[7] *Words in Color, Teacher's Guide* (Chicago: Encyclopedia Britannica Press), p. 3.
[8] *Harvard Educational Review,* Vol. XXXVII, No. 4 (Fall, 1967).
[9] *How Children Fail,* 1963, and *How Children Learn,* 1967 (New York: Pitman Publishing Corp.).

ingful reading. The term is a pejorative one denoting a mechanical sounding of one word after another as if words were not related in sequences of sense.

3. In basing word recognition on phonic clues, the approach deprives children of a very important reading aid, the meaning cues of context.

4. Many words in English — some of the most common, in fact — are irregular and hence not learnable through phonic instruction.

5. Memorization of whole words is a natural, humane, and meaningful way to become literate that the decoding approach discourages as being a bad habit.

Avoiding Confusion and Distortion of Letter-Sounds

Those of my readers who nodded in agreement with the criticisms above should look closely, if they have not already, at how current materials meet these objections. They do so in several ways. Some programs do not teach the alphabetic names of letters at all, or do not ask children to spell words aloud in connection with reading. If naming of letters and spelling are advocated (as in the linguistics-based programs), sounding and blending are dispensed with, the sounds being presented not in isolation but in whole words grouped for spelling regularity. When names of letters are taught in a sounding-and-blending program, care is taken to divorce the learning of one from that of the other. Some programs simply avoid sounding and blending phonemes, and among those programs that advocate it only one that I have looked at allows consonants to be pronounced artificially as in *kuh-a-tuh*. This is usually avoided by presenting them only in combination with vowels, frequently in whole words. On this matter one feels, in virtually all of these programs, the strong and beneficial influence of modern linguistics, which will not tolerate phonetic distortion and which, moreover, through its emphasis on structural patterns, has facilitated the use of whole words grouped for spelling regularities, whether these regularities are to be "discovered" or taught directly.

Avoiding Word-Calling

Likewise, "word-calling" does not inhere in a decoding approach. The authors of one supplementary phonics method declare, "No mechanical word-calling in Phonovisual; we must have comprehension."[10] But how is word-calling to be avoided if, one way or another, sounds are isolated as phonetic components and words have to be "figured out" accordingly? A child who reads smoothly and meaningfully because he has memorized all words in advance is not confronting the issue. The test of "word-calling" is whether he can read *new* words in such a way that the sentences containing them come out as meaningful wholes uttered with a natural intonational

[10] A picture caption in the *Phonovisual Method* of Lucille Schoolfield and Josephine Timberlake. Washington, D.C.: Phonovisual Products Inc., revised edition, 1961.

contour. A child who has to puzzle out each word so laboriously that he loses the continuity of sense and intonation simply has not learned to decode well enough. As all proponents of a phonic approach emphasize, the point of the teaching is to make decoding second-nature, fast and automatic. It is the child who lacks inadequate tools for decoding who must drop sense and intonation to devote all his attention to puzzling out new words. Today's materials for early, intensive phonics are speech-based, having as their chief goal the unlocking of spellings into familiar vocal sounds to which meaning is already attached. In the *Lippincott Basic Reading Series,* the authors say frankly that reading *is* word-calling, giving the term a positive sense, because a child who has learned to decode efficiently is thereby permitted to call out words in the continuous and comprehending manner with which he would *speak* the word sequences.

The influence of modern linguistics is again felt in its reinforcement of the oral approach to reading and in its insistence on the importance of the *patterning* of words into syntactic and intonational sequences. In short, the assumption that focusing on components of words will exclude meaning and vocal continuity is unfounded. More likely, what produces word-calling, in the bad sense of haltering gibberish, is the child's having to focus on individual words because he does not know how to translate them into sounds and sense.

Contextual Clues and Whole-Word Learning

What I have said so far implies how the remaining three objections are met. "The whole phonic pattern and the whole meaning-pattern are joined in a single unit of perception.[11] As regards both contextual clues and whole-word learning, all of the current decoding programs that I have looked at recognize, as indeed they must, that these are natural and valuable aids in reading so long as they do not prevent the child from learning to crack the code itself. Although some new programs eschew *picture* cues, they do assume that children in their later reading will always use the verbal context of a word as an aid in recognizing it, their point being simply that children should not depend on context as the main means of word attack, for it is inadequate by itself. And every program includes some whole-word learning of frequently occurring words like *come* and *as* that need to be presented early to initiate reading but that are phonetically irregular.

Irregularity of English Spelling

Finally, to deal a bit more with the objection about irregularities, critics of phonics sometimes forget that even when part of a word is irregular the

[11] Glenn McCracken and Charles C. Walcutt, *Basic Reading Series* (Lippincott), p. vii, teacher's edition of all readers.

rest is often perfectly phonetic. Furthermore, far more English words are phonetic than not (about 80%). In reading, this means that knowledge of sound-letter correspondances provides powerful cues for beginnings, middles, and endings of irregular words so that contextual and other cues can operate more effectively in recognizing the whole word. In writing, it means that even when a child misspells a word, he will misspell within a relatively small range of phonetic possibilities (e.g., *ir, ur, er*) so that his task of memorizing which spelling is actually correct is greatly reduced.

All this is to say that the critics of the approach have been closely listened to, and that the practical experience of the last 30 years or so has been thoroughly incorporated in today's materials. But this is not to say that all of the materials are alike. Far from it, for when one comes to the point of committing himself to choices among them, differences loom large. Some of these differences have little to do with the matters just discussed, which I have turned over mainly in order to assure those of my readers who think of themselves as belonging to the meaning camp that the recommendations to follow will not be so much at odds with their experience and beliefs as they might have thought.

Criteria Other than Research

Since research indicates mainly just a general criterion, without providing *strong* reasons for choosing some decoding-emphasis materials over others, the teacher must invoke other criteria for making decisions — goals, convictions about learning, and other considerations such as how long the materials have been tried and how much of other things besides literacy instruction they include. In addition to what research indicates and what the individual teacher may want to judge by, I propose the following criteria:

1. The presentation of sound-letter correspondences should launch equally well and equally early both reading and writing.

2. This presentation should begin before or at the same time as reading and last only a few months, leaving most reinforcement and rehearsal of phonographemic knowledge to actual reading and writing instead of to continued drills and workbook exercises.

3. When a literacy program includes readers, these readers should comprise, by at least the end of the sound-letter presentation, real children's literature of the highest quality. Material written by the producers of the program should be limited to the earliest texts controlled for spelling regularities and presented only during the period when sound-letter correspondences are being learned.

4. An independent literacy program that limits itself to word attack, handwriting, and basic spelling is preferable to a large package that includes grammar, reading comprehension practice, discussion, or composition and

dramatization, some of which should not be taught and some of which should be taught more extensively, not as an adjunct to reading. Materials should permit flexible combination with other approaches. The integration of the language arts, moreover, takes place in the head of a learner, not in a package.

5. The more a program takes phonics out of a book and puts it on the chalkboard or in the air or in card games the more it is to be preferred, all other things being more or less equal. For general pedagogical reasons, this principle is directed against isolated bookishness in favor of a livelier, social learning medium that will also make use of cross-teaching among pupils.

6. Materials should enable teachers to become sensitive to childrens' learning problems in reading by enhancing, rather than obstructing, opportunities for insight.

7. Given an equal effectiveness for word recognition, synthetic phonics should be preferred over analytic phonics because it offers an extra benefit in the form of creative word building whereby the pupil may combine components into words of his own choice, according to all of the English possibilities, instead of merely breaking down words according to some internal similarity (as with *shall* and *wish*).

The gist of these criteria is that an ideal literacy program gives the key to the code at the outset, fast and intensively, so that children can begin to read and write authentically and independently very early in the game. The teacher is free to make separate decisions about how to teach comprehension and composition, instead of having to "buy one, buy all." He is also free to combine the phonics instruction, for which materials are truly needed, with other methods of teaching literacy, to be mentioned later, for which materials are not always necessary.

Reading Readiness

It is important that the concept of "early" instruction in sound-letter correspondences not be misunderstood. It means that the literacy program begins before or simultaneously with reading and lasts for a relatively short while. It does not mean that children are pushed into the world of books and letters before they are ready. In other words, "early" refers to what comes after, not to what comes before. I fully accept the principle that children's readiness for literacy depends on their attaining a certain development in perceptual and motor skills and a certain amount of emotional and experiential maturity. Most literacy programs include materials and practices intended to enable children to discriminate letter shapes, make the writing movements, and acquire the top-bottom, left-right spatial orientation. But children who have not been talked with, not been read to, never even been shown a book, and seldom been given the opportunity to experience the things books talk about will see no meaning in literacy and have no motive to undertake it. These deprivations simply have to be overcome first, as the Headstart Program acknowledges so well.

It is terribly hard for one teacher alone to give a roomful of deprived children what they need. He can read to them, try to get them to talk, give them objects to play with, let them look through picture books, and take them on visits. But, I would like to submit, he can go much farther if well developed children are mixed with the underdeveloped, so that the one can help the other, and if dramatic play and peer talk are included in the activities. Those children who have not been talked with should talk with children who are used to conversing. They should have a chance to play with more emotionally mature children of their own age, and to pick up from the latter some of their knowledge of the world. The teacher alone cannot possibly provide enough of these experiences for each child. He can, however, set up social games among small groups and lead the class in some activities described in Chapters 3, 4, 7 and 10. What has not been sufficiently exploited in reading readiness is peer interaction, the teaching of some children by others. In a heterogeneous class, advantaged or abler children can begin the literacy program before disadvantaged or slow children and help bring along the latter. Besides talking with them, they can read to them, interest them in books, and even impart some of their knowledge about letter formation and spatial orientation. According to both Dr. Chall and the USOE reports mentioned earlier, the second most effective predictor of reading achievement — outranking intelligence — is auditory discrimination, which can be developed only by hearing many meaningfully discriminated sounds, mainly human speech. In short, since the timing of literacy instruction depends on individual development, and since some children will consequently be starting it before others, an additional and powerful force — pupil cross-teaching — can be brought to bear on the critical problem of reading readiness.

Brief Survey of Literacy Materials

Let me roughly classify for convenience the materials that teachers have to select from. I have examined most current materials, but I am sure I have missed some, and new ones are appearing all the time. The purpose of this survey is to narrow down the field in accordance with the criteria just discussed.

The first group comprises those basal reader series of the conventional sort that stress meaning and comprehension but do not begin with an intensive sound-letter program. I will not name them. Although some have appeared in revised editions that afford a greater decoding emphasis, they are still far inferior to the new materials in this respect. A quick repair job is just not enough. In addition, almost without exception, the basal texts are very poor, being mostly editor-written material based on a small vocabulary and on the

Dick-and-Jane principle that children want to read about familiar family life. Unfortunately, this group includes reader series especially created for racial minorities. In contrast to the saga of the neighborhood, a collection of folk and fairy tales, fables and legends, poems and songs has the advantage that, by not specifying familiar environments, it fits any school population, whatever the race or class. Besides being convinced that any small child would rather read about the remote or fantastic, I think it is impossible to make a reader series truly realistic, especially when children come from a subculture filled with crime, obscenity, and despair. A couple of ashcans do not depict a ghetto. The co-basal, or supplementary, reader series, however, sometimes contain very good children's literature and might be used with a literacy program taken from somewhere else. But both the teaching of sound-letter relations and, to a lesser degree the reading material of the basal programs are faulted by the criteria.

The second group of programs is based on spelling patterns derived from modern linguistics and on the inductive or "discovery" theory of learning. Thus sounds and spellings are focused on by presenting groups of words that are alike in spelling pattern but differ minimally with respect to one sound or letter (*mat, map*), with the intention that children should infer the patterns (consonant-short vowel-consonant) and discriminate the contrasts (*t* and *p*) themselves. This is a structural kind of whole-word learning that teaches phonographemic regularities without isolating phonemes and without sounding and blending. The early reading has a phonetically controlled vocabulary plus some irregular sight words of high frequency. All have some readers but vary in the number of them. Since all were put out for the first time in the 1960's, none has had a long trial in its present form. This group comprises *The Merrill Linguistic Readers,* by Fries, Wilson, and Rudolph (Columbus, Ohio: Charles E. Merrill Books, Inc.); *Let's Read,* by Bloomfield and Barnhart (Bronxville, N.Y.: Clarence L. Barnhart, Inc.); *The Linguistic Science Reader,* by Stratemeyer and Smith (New York: Harper & Row, Publishers); *The Basic Reading Series,* by Rasmussen and Goldberg (Chicago: Science Research Associates, Inc.); and *Sounds and Letters,* by Hall (Ithaca, N.Y.: Linguistics).

One effect of the inductive, word-grouping approach is to lengthen the time it takes to teach literacy. The presentation of the phonographemic relations in these materials takes a year or more. It seems to me that both the effort to cover all or most of the spelling patterns and the effort to do so by means of copious word groups make these programs unnecessarily heavy and academic. Another effect is to provide a perhaps less "direct" decoding approach than the research in reading seems to indicate is needed. As I said in discussing Dr. Chall's work, there is some evidence that many children need more explicit learning of sound-letter relations than inference affords, though the explicitness need not necessarily include statements of phonic rules. In fairness, this evidence may not be strong enough to warrant great consideration, and most of these linguistics-based programs have not had enough trial to be given a good chance to prove themselves or to be included in research.

The content of the readers is not the best obtainable for first grade. Though some delaying of literature may be caused by the slow presentation of the sound-spelling system and the prolongation of phonetically controlled vocabulary, the problem is partly that the reading material is often editor-written even when it might be drawn from children's literature. In general, the content of the readers in these programs is disappointing, not only for first grade but often for later grades as well.

In addition to the general objections to these programs, there are others applying to them individually that prevent me from recommending them. Some do not lead well into writing, either because they explicitly exclude it or because they provide insufficient writing of sounds and words, and little or no dictation. Some include comprehension practice, or otherwise overburden and overstructure the package.

The materials of the third group could actually be classed as linguistics-based programs but differ in that they are programmed for self-instruction. The first two try to cover considerably more than literacy. They are *Reading in High Gear,* The Accelerated Progressive Choice Program, by Woolman (Chicago: Science Research Associates) and *Programmed Reading,* by Buchanan and Sullivan (New York: McGraw-Hill Book Co., Inc.). Both teach whole words grouped according to spelling patterns. Both teach spelling and writing. The programs consist entirely of booklets that pupils fill in by themselves under some monitoring by the teacher. The booklets contain blanks to fill, questions to answer, reading passages, and (very poor) composition assignments. Though self-pacing may be an advantage, these programs suffer the same drawbacks as the linguistic programs and are even longer and heavier. Paperwork is the order of the day; speech and social interaction are virtually lost. And not only is the package far too big, with great emphasis on comprehension practice, but the whole idea of embodying self-instruction in a long series of workbooks based essentially on the reinforcement of right answers seems very dull and uncreative to me. Except for the far overstructured composition assignments, the whole learning sequence is specifically predictable.

In contrast to these two programs, and to American self-instruction in general, is *The Programmed Reading Kit,* by Stott (Glasgow, Scotland: W. & R. Holmes, Ltd.), which consists of nothing but a teacher's manual and 30 teaching aids — all sorts of matching and interlocking cards for playing a wide variety of games, frequently in pairs and groups. These materials do not attempt — mercifully — to cover nearly as much as the preceding ones, but word grouping is used and the children progress at different rates, playing each game as long as they need to. What the children do is predictable only within the broad limits of the game rules; they create and transform words and sentences. Writing is not included, but the program is easy to supplement because it is open. *The Programmed Reading Kit* has been tried a number of years. *Reading in High Gear* and *Programmed Reading* are in the development stage.

The fourth group comprises some admittedly rather varied materials that do have in common, however, the presentation of sound-letter relations through whole words grouped in patterns, some of these patterns deriving from linguistics and some not. In all but one, sounding and blending is avoided, as in all the other programs mentioned so far. Three of these, all of which appeared in the 1950's, are *Phonetic Keys to Reading*, by Sloop, Garrison and Creekmore (Oklahoma City: Economy Co.), *The Royal Road Readers*, by Daniels and Diack (London, England: Chatto and Windus); and *The Structural Reading Series*, by Stern (Syracuse: The L. W. Singer Company, Inc.). All three programs spend a year presenting the phonographemic relations and include reviews that go beyond the first year. All avoid isolating sounds from whole words. The reading material is almost entirely editor-written. In *Phonetic Keys to Reading*, which contains readers for grades 1–3 but no workbooks, the material is thin Dot-and-Jim stuff. This program seems to do little with spelling and writing. *The Royal Road Readers*, a full softcover and hardcover series for the elementary years, with accompanying workbooks, has more interesting texts but is still not an anthology of children's literature, as I think such a series should be. Children write words and letters in the workbooks but apparently do not take dictation. *The Structural Reading Series* runs from grades K–2, consisting of workbooks, reading booklets, and cards. Word grouping is employed in a particular way — to teach sound-letter correspondences principally through initial and final sounds. Spelling and writing are given their due. Professing to be half allied to the meaning approach, this program does stretch out phonic instruction and would presumably be used as a supplement to a basal series.

From Sounds to Words, the Silver Burdett Spelling Readiness Program (Morristown, N.J.: Silver Burdett Company, 1966), a single workbook for pupils with a teacher's edition, focuses on hearing and saying speech sounds, on seeing and writing the letters that spell these sounds, and on the building of words. Letters are learned from initial and final positions, and the presentation of sound-spelling relations is based on patterns from linguistics. The program is to begin at the time when pupils are reading at "the first-reader level," can already write the letters of the alphabet, and have a desire to write. I wonder, however, if it could begin sooner, its utility being to supplement a reading-biased literacy program such as *The Programmed Reading Kit*, with which it might be combined.

Read Along with Me, by Allen and Allen (New York: Bureau of Publications, Teachers College, Columbia University) also has a very special limitation: since the learner reads part of the text along with the teacher, only one to four pupils are accommodated. It is essentially a tutorial method for parents or for teachers who can work with very small numbers. It is partly based on spelling patterns from linguistics, but also presents phonenes in isolation. The sounding-and-blending does produce artificial syllables (*kuh* and *tuh*). This program contains a picture alphabet chart, a book of "rhyming words" and simple sentences, a manual, and a book of stories with the sentences to be read by the teacher in small print and those to be read by the child in large print.

The fifth group consists of three older supplementary phonic programs, employing sounding-and-blending, that have been tried for 20 or 25 years and revised somewhat in recent years. They all present the sounds and spellings of English in isolation from whole words, or single them out from whole words, but the sounding-and-blending process avoids distortion by sounding consonants in combination with vowels, and word grouping is used to bring out sound-spelling regularities. In fact, hardly any program available today does *not* exploit word grouping in teaching children to grasp spelling patterns and discriminate component sounds and letters. But some programs, like this group and a few in the preceding group, may base the groups and the sequence of groups on practical teaching experience rather than on the descriptions drawn from structural linguistics. Often linguistic grouping and pedagogical grouping coincide, and there is certainly reciprocal influence, but grouping is central to Group One and Two programs and only secondary in the third, fourth, and fifth groups and some of the other programs. The chief divergence, however, between the present group and those described up to here is between the whole-word methods of focusing on sound-spelling components, which work by inference and "discovery," and the more "direct" methods of presenting the components separately as well as in words, which work by sounding and blending. As noted before, research so far seems to give an edge to the latter methods, but it is difficult to know how heavily this indication should weigh.

The members of this group are *Reading with Phonics,* by Hay and Wingo (Philadelphia: J. B. Lippincott Co.); *The Phonovisual Method,* by School-field and Timberlake (Washington, D.C.: Phonovisual Products, Inc.); and *The Writing Road to Reading,* by Spalding and Spalding (New York: White-side, Inc.). Appearing first in the 1940's, these three programs were designed to supplement conventional basal reader series emphasizing sight reading. They present the sound-letter correspondences gradually during the first year and review them in the second. They state some phonic rules. They offer readiness instruction that can begin in kindergarten. They can be used remedially for older children who have not had such a program before. All three programs have the children hear, speak, read, and write each phonene as it is presented. Dictation and written spelling get strong attention, though *The Writing Road to Reading* stresses them the most.

The *Phonovisual* materials are slim, relying mainly on charts, cards, games, the chalkboard, and oral work. Emphasis is on recognizing initial and final consonants, then on "tucking in the vowels."[12] There are a consonant work-book and a vowel workbook but no readers. *Reading with Phonics* is a hard-cover textbook containing mostly word groups and accompanied by several softcover reader-workbooks, the texts being phonetically controlled. It is the most detailed and thoroughgoing of the three — too much so, I believe. It covers more of the uncommon spelling patterns, gives many more phonic rules, and takes the strongest bent toward reading. The program includes "Talking and Writing Stories" (in a phonetically controlled vocabulary). *The Writing Road to Reading* centers around 70 "phonogram" charts repre-senting 45 sounds and has no readers or workbooks. It teaches handwriting before reading, and in addition to giving frequent dictation from Ayres lists, lets the children write new words in sentences.

Phonovisual and *The Writing Road* are generally recommendable if modi-fied. Though the latter emphasizes writing more, both lead well into it. In both cases, I would suggest dropping the second year, which in the Spaldings' program includes not only a review but the keeping of a spelling notebook. I would prefer these two over *Reading with Phonics* because the latter is overloaded and also because it prepares less well for writing. The fact that these programs are supposed to spend a year presenting the sound-spellings need not disqualify them, since, so far as I can see, there is no serious reason, except in the case of *Reading with Phonics,* why they could not be worked through in a half year or less. The original pace seems to have been set more by their association with conventional basal readers than by necessity[13]

The sixth category combines a sounding-and-blending method, as in the materials above, with a grades 1–6 series of hardcover readers and contains only one very recent program, *The Open Court Basic Readers,* edited by Arther Tracy (La Salle, Ill.: Open Court Publishing Co.). This program represents the classic package of a literacy course embedded in a reading series. But it differs from conventional basal series, and the revisions of them thus far, in several important respects. The literacy program, called the Foundation Program, is over by the middle of first grade. During this period the children complete two workbooks, which are sensibly limited and full of poems, and read six editor-written stories with a phonetically controlled vocabulary. The

---

[12] In experiments reported by Crovitz and Schiffman in "Visual Field and the Letter Span," *Journal of Experimental Psychology,* Vol. 70, No. 2 (1965), it was established that adults given very brief tachistoscopic glimpses of eight-letter words remembered better the initial and final letters, even though their eyes were fixed on the middle of the words, where vision should be best. The finding presumably reflects reading habits. Common experience also supports the notion that proficient readers identify words first by these salient letters and fill in the interiors of words according to meaning cues, subject to verification. Thus *The Phonovisual Method* and *The Structural Reading Series* may be well founded as regards the scanning-and-processing movements of eye and mind.

[13] *Breaking the Sound Barrier, A Phonics Handbook,* by Sister Mary Caroline (New York: The Macmillan Company) is aimed completely at reading. It is a reference book of practical rules and procedures for attacking new words.

first hardcover reader, for the second half of first grade, is a fine anthology of children's literature. The teacher asks a few comprehension questions, mostly open-ended ones, but the emphasis is on children's responses.

The Foundation Program presents sounds in isolation but also in poems and in word groups. Alternate spellings for the same sound are presented together. Children see, hear, speak, and write the sounds. A readiness program makes use of many sorts of cards, tracing paper, and games. The sounding and blending avoids false syllables. For every reading lesson there is a writing lesson. Though sounds and spellings are presented before the whole class, those children who need more practice are screened down and given additional sessions, so that some individual pacing is possible.

The creators of the series have clearly set out to make the large package still viable by removing or revamping those things for which the old basals have been so heavily criticized. This is especially reflected in the readers, which, with some unfortunate exceptions, continue in the later grades to be anthologies of poems, fables, legends, folk and fairy tales, and myths. (Grades 5 and 6 have not been published yet.) The high literary quality begins in the pre-reading stage, when the teacher reads poems to the pupils from his manual. The exceptions occur in sections of the second- and third-grade readers that are devoted to science and stereotyped social studies content.

Other aspects of the large package are less desirable but could be omitted. In aiming for an "integration of the language arts," the producers have again made composition an adjunct of reading. Though the composition assignments that ask children to write from literature are like those recommended later in this book, others are poor, and in general this "integration" merely gives the illusion that composition is seriously dealt with when actually it is considerably underplayed. In addition, the series has a curious and unnecessary moralistic vein running through it. Finally, the teacher's manuals for each of the readers make rather heavy going, partly because the inevitable review sets in after first grade, but partly also because the reading selections are overworked for word study (including diacritical marks) and suggestions for discussion and composition.

For grade 1 alone — for the Foundation Program and beginning reading — the Open Court materials look very good. For succeeding grades I would suggest that the readers be used only for content as any other anthologies. Except for some suggestions and information about the literature itself, the teacher's manuals could be ignored. Dramatization, discussion, and composition should not be handled in this limited fashion, though of course the selections themselves will often provide good stimuli for these activities. With these reservations I recommend this program as one of the better possibilities available today.

The seventh class of materials features the use of a special alphabet and is represented by the recent Early-to-Read i/t/a Program, *by Mazurkiewicz and Tanyzer (New York: Initial Teaching Alphabet Publications, Inc.)*

The Initial Teaching Alphabet (i/t/a) puts the 44 sounds that it recognizes into one-to-one correspondence with just 44 written symbols, thus reducing drastically the number of spellings the beginner has to deal with. The program is designed to last 15 months, beginning in the sixth month of kindergarten, or one year if begun in first grade. The most rapid learners, we are told, can be introduced to all 44 sounds in three or four weeks, but a slower rate is desirable. The transfer to the regular alphabet is normally accomplished by degrees toward the end of grade 1. Fears that the i/t/a would create learning problems during and after the transfer — that it would have to be unlearned — do not seem to be borne out by several years of trials, for which a high degree of success is reported in comparison with conventional beginning reading. But research does not show that the alphabet itself is responsible for the results; as Dr. Chall suggests, it may be that teachers who use it tend naturally to emphasize decoding. At any rate, though the i/t/a is not itself a method, it has become associated in America, and in these materials, with an early, intensive teaching of word components.

The materials consist of an i/t/a alphabet book, a number book, a readiness workbook, symbols-sound cards, and six serial readers with workbooks. Except for some excerpts, the texts are editor-written up to Books 4–6, and these are made up of selections from *Humpty Dumpty Magazine,* which puts out fairly good reading material but not superior literature. By a joint publishing arrangement, some of the selections of Scholastic Book Services are made available in i/t/a, but in general, teachers do not have a wide choice of reading texts since they are limited to what is printed in the special alphabet. This problem, of course, might be eventually overcome, as it should, because an important claim of the program is that children can read early and are not limited by a highly controlled vocabulary.

Unfortunately, this program attempts to teach Comprehension, Concepts, and How to Think. I doubt that this lingering alliance with the meaning approach constitutes a strong enough reason to reject the i/t/a. There is no program I could recommend that does not contain some things better ignored, though admittedly the conjunction of this defect with the drawback in available reading material does make it harder to weigh the great advantage that i/t/a has in permitting children to read and write sooner and less restrictedly. All the other programs mentioned so far are working under the hardship of teaching the correspondences between 40-odd sounds and some 280 spellings. Any method that can make English phonetic deserves special consideration, because one-to-one matching can shortcut learning problems. Certainly teachers should follow the development of these materials and whatever reports issue from research in which the results of this program are compared with those of other *decoding* approaches. (And one should not forget that i/t/a itself is just an alphabet and may be used independently of any particular materials.)

The eighth class contains again a single member. Caleb Gattegno's Words in Color (*Chicago: Encyclopedia Britannica Press*) *also reduces sound-symbol relations to a one-to-one correspondence but without altering traditional orthography.* That is, each of the forty-seven English sounds he recognizes is represented by a color that stands for it in the spellings. The program is organized around sounds, for the sound-color relations remain constant whereas spellings change color according to their sound in a given word. Children read and write earlier than in any other program except perhaps the *Early-to-Read i/t/a.* From the outset they read and write in black and white. The program has been tried since 1961, and a series of books on classroom experiences with it has been begun,[14] but no research summaries so far include comparison of it with other methods.

The color symbolism is not Gattegno's most important innovation in literacy instruction. A profound part of his method concerns playing with letters and words in ways that strike me as capable not only of teaching very thoroughly the phonetic components of words but also of exploiting this for truly creative intellectual development. In what he calls "games of transformation," for example, children change one word into another word by reversing, substituting, inserting, and adding letters. The same game is played with words in sentences. (These activities are similar to some recommended later in Chapter 10, though the latter were not derived from Gattegno. Indeed, I do not mean to imply that no other materials contain interesting games with letters and words, but his games go farther because they are such a critical part of the method itself. In the beginning, children make up real and nonsense words from the sounds they know, however few. The set of sounds and letters they know at any given moment constitutes a "restricted language" with which they do everything possible. By pointing rapidly from one symbol to another as children sound them, the teacher gives "visual dictation" whereby the combining of sounds and symbols in any order becomes habitual. I should think that children who had run Gattegno's course would know words inside and out, having developed both a very strong attention to sound-letter relations and a playfully intellectual involvement in language. Furthermore, the word building and "visual dictation" should prove very effective for children having a specific language disability, whatever labels (dyslexia, cross-dominance, etc.) or causes are assigned to it.

The quickest way to become acquainted with Gattegno's method is to read the teacher's manual or *Background and Principles.* A demonstration would be better. The materials themselves are: colored chalk, 21 colored charts, a phonic code chart, a pack of word cards, 14 worksheets, three "basic" books that introduce sound-signs, a word building book that unfolds the entire set of sounds, and a book of stories, editor-written and phonetically controlled.

[14] The first book is *Creative Writing,* by Sister Mary Leonore Murphy (Berkshire, England: Educational Explorers Limited, 1966), a log book of a trial in Australia.

These materials may be used in different ways and orders. Gattegno, in fact, shows great respect for the independence and creativity of both teacher and pupils, though he has said that forthcoming revisions of *Words in Color,* by the Zerox Company, New York, will contain more detailed instructions to the teacher. Emphasis is always on the building of words from sounds, the building of words into sentences, and the building of sentences into stories — all of this predictable only within the limits of the "restricted language" of the moment. After Book One a pupil can work through the paper material on his own, but a considerable amount of the work is oral. The program, it is claimed, can be completed in a few weeks or months, depending on age and intensity.

The ninth and final category comprises a single and unusual reader series that flies in the face of research and yet is not of the basal type — The Sounds of Language, edited by Bill Martin (New York: Holt, Rinehart & Winston, Inc., 1967.) The series consists of nothing but five readers for the first three grades — not even manuals or literacy materials of the sort surveyed so far. Though it is possible to look on this series as a pure anthology — and a very good one, the selections being drawn almost entirely from the Little Owl books — such a view would not do justice to the astute and attractive ways in which Martin exploits the "melody of language" and the "sound of sense" to teach beginning reading. ("The sound of the sentence is the fundamental sound in language.")[15]

Each selection is marginally annotated, in the teacher's edition, with imaginative and useful suggestions about how the selection should be orally read and about how to help children relate the sounds of language to the structure of words and sentences. The pupil edition contains nothing but the selections themselves, but varied and arresting typography singles out words and patterns and calls attention to the visual aspects of language. Vocabulary is uncontrolled, and the very first selections are from authentic children's literature. Many suggestions for writing are derived from the selections, which are considered a storehouse of words, sentence structures, and ideas, and the suggestions incorporate Sylvia Ashton-Warner's idea of giving out the children's favorite words on cards to be accumulated and learned through use.

Martin's method partakes of the whole-phrase, whole-sentence approach (not to mention the pure-love approach). Although he rejects any systematic phonics, and emphasizes sight learning, his method is different enough from that of basals or of look-say to justify claiming that it has not been covered by research. Whole words are not pretaught or taught in isolation. Children learn the visual equivalents of speech sounds, initially at least, by hearing the teacher read selections as they follow in the book. They are invited to soak up and savor the sounds of sentences in poems and stories, then they memorize

[15] P. 13 of supplement to teacher's edition of each reader.

the text, say it aloud together, and, as they begin associating strings of sounds with strings of letters, read back to the teacher chorally and in voice parts. Each selection is handled somewhat differently, depending on the accumulating word knowledge of the children and on particular verbal features of each selection that may be exploited to further this knowledge. Similarities, differences, and patterns in the sounds and spellings of words are brought out constantly but informally so that the child's global perception of whole sentences becomes refined into perceptions of component words and word-particles. Essentially, the method relies on the incantative power of literary language and on the child's desire to possess this language by eye as well as by ear and tongue.

The combination of pure love and shrewdness has a lot going for it that experienced teachers will recognize. Many bright, alert, clearheaded children would undoubtedly learn to read well by this method alone. But the general evidence suggests that the risk for many, if not most, other children might be great (though we can hardly claim that the pure-love approach has been satisfactorily researched out!). My thought in including *The Sounds of Language* is that it ought to be seriously considered as a program to use *in conjunction with* one of the independent phonics programs described above. Furthermore, whatever materials teachers select, they should look at this series for its superior presentation of the sight-meaning approach and thus for its value in maintaining an open mind.

Recommendations

Preferred Materials

My first choice among current literacy materials would be a combination of *Words in Color* with *The Sounds of Language,* closely followed in preference by either The Open Court program through first grade, for teachers who want an accompanying reader, or by *The Phonovisual Method* or *The Writing Road to Reading,* the latter two in conjunction also with *The Sounds of Language. Words in Color* probably requires the most learning and effort on the part of the teacher. Teachers who are to use it should see demonstrations of it or, better still, attend a workshop given by one of Gattegno's associates. (Arrangements may be made by writing Dr. Caleb Gattegno, Schools for the Future, P.O. Box 349, Cooper Station, New York, New York.) *Words in Color* seems best to me because it meets the criteria and, all other things being equal in the eyes of research at the moment, has some additional merits as described above. The spirit of Gattegno's materials, moreover, is close to that of the curriculum in this book, and his method, as he says, lends itself well to creative writing and to the "language experience" approach, which is also a part of this curriculum.

VERSATILITY OF APPROACH

This is the place to emphasize that opting for *Words in Color* or any one of the other methods recommended above does not settle the whole problem of beginning reading and writing. For one thing, methods and materials are not everything. As we have seen, they may be less important than the relationship of teacher to pupils, the general learning atmosphere, and many other things as yet unknown. But at least there is no necessity for using inferior materials simply by default, by not knowing what *else* is available and by not assessing their worth in the light of reasoned criteria.

Second, if there is any consensus among researchers and reading specialists it is that no one emphasis is adequate for all learners. However much statistics indicate that *most* children learn better with explicit sound-letter instruction, we know from common experience that many children have learned to read and write very well with absolutely no phonics, and that some children have learned with no instruction at all. A case was reported recently of a five-year-old Negro boy of illiterate parents who learned to read alone at home with no printed matter at all — apparently from watching television, that old archfoe of literacy![16]

The second sort of recommendation, then, concerns versatility. In becoming literate, a child should be able to avail himself of several learning modes, since it is either true that one mode in particular is best for him, in which case he needs to try them all out, or that all modes help him through reciprocal reinforcement. This means in turn that either the teacher can conduct testing and screening to determine which mode fits which child, or he can use multiple approaches on all children on the assumption that even if one is best for a given child any child will benefit enough from all to make them worthwhile. Though it may seem that individual tailoring would be ideal if feasible, there are two arguments against it. First, the amount of perceptual, cognitive, and emotional testing it takes to match child to method is so great that the disruption and loss of time may not be worth it, especially if the tests are fallible. Second, chances are that other modes of learning will be worthwhile for a child, even if one is dominant for him, either because the others indeed reinforce the one or because they further his general growth in other ways. Thus a child who does not "need" *Words in Color* in order to become literate will most likely learn to read and write better and faster if he has it, and will at the same time develop his logical and creative powers (through discriminating, combining, and reversing at will the components of words).

But in a versatile classroom, where children participate in all the literacy practices offered but are free to partake more of some than of others, or to shift emphasis as they feel the need, it may be possible to enjoy the benefits of

[16] Reported in a talk at the Harvard Graduate School of Education on November 14, 1967, by Jane Torrey, Connecticut College.

both individual learning and multiple approaches for all. This versatility seems the most appropriate strategy to recommend.

Language experience. One of the other modes of learning I have in mind is embodied in the so-called language experience approach, whereby children discuss experiences or make up stories, dictate them, see how their own words *look* when transcribed, then read them from memory. This and many related practices are described elsewhere in this book, being distributed over the chapters on speaking and writing. Indeed, it is a major article of this whole curriculum that literacy and later reading should not be conceived as specialties but as aspects of total verbal growth. Certainly, however much a child may need phonics, he also must be able to integrate this small-focus work with the true function and value of written language — to share experience. The language experience approach teaches literacy through the whole word and the whole sentence. Children memorize and look at letter strings that mean something to them because they have uttered them for their own expressive purposes. High motivation brings a powerful psychological force to bear on visual memory.

Listening while reading. Another approach recommended also exploits the perception of the whole word and the whole sentence. It consists of the pupils' listening to a text as they follow the words visually. So far as I know this has been done little, though, as we have seen, *The Sounds of Language* includes it. Apparently it is not considered a method, for the practice is rarely if ever compared, in research, with other approaches. The virtue of this practice is that the child sees and hears words *simultaneously* and has the opportunity also to associate intonational contours with sentence endings. As an extension of merely being read to, the method is simple, and there is no question that it is pleasurable for children. They learn unconsciously as those children do who climb on their parents' laps during story time and follow along in the book.

The obvious drawback is that a child may be looking at one word while the teacher is sounding another. But once they have acquired a certain reading vocabulary, children can follow known words well enough to be sure of encountering the unknown words at the same moment the teacher sounds them. Also, new words that are repeated, as in rhymes and jingles, can be identified by the fact that the new shape recurs at the same time its sound is heard again. The old bouncing ball that was used in community-sing film projections to synchronize the singing of the audience could solve this problem if the text is projected. A flashlight arrow-indicator may be used so that children can chant or sing along following the movements of the indicator. Machines such as the Controlled Reader may also be of help. In any case, by one means or another, perhaps by language laboratory equipment, I am sure that the problem of synchronization can be solved if the listening-while-looking method is taken seriously, as common experience certainly warrants, however inadequate research is on this score.

Some publishers of readers have put out tapes of their texts so that pupils can listen as they read. By using either these or locally recorded tapes of other books, this method may be used with an individual reading program, if enough tape recorders are available.

A number of reading specialists I have talked with agree that reading while listening has great potential, and have difficulty explaining its neglect. Apparently such a homely practice has been deemed too unsophisticated to warrant thoroughgoing experimentation! I see no inherent reason why it should not be placed on a par with other kinds of literacy instruction.[17]

AN OPEN MIND

The last recommendation is to keep an open mind about the various possibilities of teaching literacy. Not only has it been an area of heated controversy in the past, but future developments will undoubtedly generate more dispute. For one thing, I am thinking of electronic machines with which children can interplay, not just O.K. Moore's automated typewriters but other machines only now being pondered. Since literacy learning consists basically of perceptual pairing, electronics may conceivably offer some very real help. "Computer-Assisted Instruction in Initial Reading," by Richard Atkinson and Duncan Hansen, will give some notion of the possibilities in this direction.[18] But aside from electronic machines, other yet unthought of ways to teach literacy may be developed. I can only reiterate that the research today may merely reflect the current limits of pedagogical imagination and the failure to do enough basic investigation of reading processes that might in fact suggest new approaches to literacy.

Spelling

Instead of making spelling instruction a separate strand of the curriculum, I suggest that it be treated first under the two-way literacy program and continued later in several ways to be mentioned below. An early, intensive instruction in sound-letter correspondences should establish a strong spelling base. Rehearsing of spelling knowledge should come through dictation and the constant effort to write original sentences. I agree with the Spaldings

---

[17] "An Exploratory Study in Reading on the First Grade Level Using a Combination of Trade Books and their Corresponding Phonograph Recordings," Wilma Jean Pyle, 1964, unpublished dissertation, Wayne State University, Detroit, reports an experiment in which children who read while listening scored a year higher in reading over children who only listened.

[18] *Reading Research Quarterly*, Volume 2, No. 1 (Fall, 1966).

(*The Writing Road to Reading*) that practice spelling books are a waste of time because pupils either memorize individual words, when rules of regularity could apply, or simply copy. I would not, however, advocate the Spaldings' practice of having pupils keep notebooks of spelling rules.

The main issue is that, aside from knowledge of prefixes and suffixes, which are included in many literacy programs, there is very little that can be taught that should not already have been taught in the initial presentation of the sound-letter relations. Most *irregular* spellings have to be memorized one by one. What new knowledge will help students *figure out* how to spell a word? As I see it, the problem is either in loss of attention or in loss of memory. That is, either the learner misspells a word he knows how to spell, which is frequently the case and can be corrected by proofreading, or else he has forgotten some phonic principle for regular words or the "look" of some irregular words. How students continue to learn to spell once the literacy program is over thus resolves itself *mainly* into the question of reinforcing attention and memory. To this we should add, however, the fact that some minor spelling patterns, concerning small groups of words, are omitted from some literacy programs and may need to be pointed out by the teacher to individuals who have trouble with them.

My recommendations aim to develop self-correction and self-diagnosis. Students take responsibility for spelling, but the teacher sets up processes that make this possible:

1. The teacher occasionally classifies for a pupil the *kinds* of errors he is making and thus teaches him how to diagnose for himself. Some errors can be corrected by referring to the phonic regularities of the literacy program or by mentioning some rarer spelling pattern not covered in the program. Some errors stem from faulty pronunciation, and some can be corrected only by memorizing the word. The main point is that students do not all make the same sorts of errors; each wants to improve *his* spelling. The group process for handling the writing leaves the teacher free to circulate and make such individual diagnoses (see page 207 for an example). This is far preferable to special spelling programs, which not only are tedious and time-consuming, but do not deal in a specific and timely way with just what each pupil needs. Such a shotgun approach necessarily teaches much that a given individual already knows and fails to single out what he does not know. From teacher diagnosis that becomes self-diagnosis, the learner can reduce a host of errors to a manageable number of corrective actions.

2. From the very beginning, pupils point out errors to each other in the writing groups when they exchange papers. Proofreading in groups teaches each individual to proofread alone.

3. Pupils should use dictionaries. The value of the dictionary is slight if pupils are seldom asked to write original sentences. If a program calls for abundant original writing, however, the dictionary becomes a major help

in learning to spell, because the pupil is constantly trying to spell out what he has to say, to grope actively from speech to letters.

4. The visual memory of words seen repeatedly in reading helps to standardize pupil spelling perhaps more than anything else after literacy training. Many adults are not sure of a spelling until they *see* it. Copious reading, then, is an important key. Three factors are critical here: If a very *small* vocabulary is incessantly repeated, as in the conventional basal readers, pupils simply do not become visually acquainted with enough words. And if sight learning of whole words is preferred over early, synthetic phonics, visual memory is apt to be less precise about the letters within words, that is, the exact spelling. An early focusing on the spellings of individual sounds should make the visual memory of even irregular words more acute and thus increase the benefit to spelling of reading. Finally, if skill builders, spellers, workbooks, and lockstep readers are thrown out, children will have more time simply to read a lot individually — with, I wager, remarkable results for spelling.

5. On occasions when a whole class is writing about something that will elicit a vocabulary in common, as in recording sensations at the same locale, mutual problems of spelling can be worked out in class discussion. The pupils are told to spell phonetically those words that they are not sure how to spell. Then afterwards the teacher asks for words that many had trouble with. Correct spellings are furnished by other pupils or by the teacher if necessary, and the teacher remarks briefly on why the phonetic spellings were incorrect: the word is totally irregular, or it is assigned one regular spelling rather than an alternative one (*reins,* not *rains* or *ranes*).

6. The teacher can dictate words or sentences for spelling practice, and go over them afterwards to point out reasons for misspellings. But this should be a last resort. During the literacy program, and for a while following it, pupils can stay fairly involved in dictation, but the older they get, the leaner their interest and motivation become. For spelling practice, composition may be less systematic but is probably more valuable and efficient in the long run. (See also the sections on taking dictation, starting on pages 137 and 176, and the remarks on page 134.)

Punctuation

Defining the Learning Problem

Punctuation is like spelling in that it translates speech to print. Learning punctuation also involves perceptual pairing and applies equally to reading and writing. As with sound-letter relations, the task is to match some graphic symbols with some voice qualities — in this case, some things like commas and periods with some other things like pitch and pause. It helps to think of two kinds of punctuation, oral and written. Pre-school children and illiterate adults can talk all day and have no punctuation problems, because the voice indicates the segments of speech in meaningful ways. The issue of writing punctuation is how to transcribe certain significant voice qualities such as stress, pitch, and juncture (the interaction of which I will call somewhat inaccurately but conveniently "intonation"). The issue of reading punctuation is how to translate commas and periods back into voice qualities.

Punctuation is not part of grammar. It may reflect grammar (syntax), but only because intonation does. Above all, good punctuation is a set of signals showing the reader how to read the flow of words as the speaker would say them. It should be presented to pupils in this way, not as rules. The auditory principles that underlie the rules are simpler to understand, more profound, and more accurate. All the rules do is overgeneralize the relations among sense, syntax, and sound. "Separate clauses by commas" merely echoes the fact that a partial drop in intonation, together perhaps with a pause, *usually* separates them. But you have to understand "clause" to understand the rule. Moreover, the rule is inaccurate because it is rigid. Educated writers often do not separate clauses with a comma if the clauses are short and if no ambiguity results. What the rule describes is not always true of what we do, and what the rule prescribes is not always indicative of what we should do. What we should do is punctuate with pencil as we do with voice. And that is a simpler principle to follow.

In these early years, children will seldom need to do more than use:

1. A period for a full stop (indicated by final fall of intonation).
2. A question mark for an interrogative intonation.
3. An exclamation mark for emphatic stress.
4. Commas for series (indicated by a special suspended intonation).
5. Commas separating clauses and setting off words, when the sustained intonation is interrupted by a partial drop.

The main problem by far is breaking the flow of words into sentences. Defining a sentence as a complete thought is futile; not only children but linguists and philosophers as well do not understand what a complete thought is. It could be a word, a phrase, a sentence, a paragraph, or an entire book. I believe the only way a sentence can be defined is by vocal segmentation, the sense of closure conveyed by a complete intonation contour (which of course expresses the intuition of syntactic completion). Children know a sentence when they hear one, and this operational definition is what teachers should utilize. Often a pupil mistakenly puts a period and capital in the middle of a sentence even though he would read the sentence correctly. This results, I believe, from being confused by directions about how to punctuate. But the more common mistake is the failure to segment the word flow at all, a failure that frequently persists — needlessly — into junior and senior high school, causing dreary hours of proofreading by a long chain of teachers. The problem is not that difficult. That it persists is testimony to the inadequacy of the rules approach and the complete-thought definition.

The chief hurdle to punctuating well is not being aware of what one hears. Children hear and produce intonation with ease — in fact, with such ease that they are almost totally unconscious of what they are hearing and producing. The features of intonation — stress, pitch, and pause — are especially important cues to meaning when one's vocabulary is limited. Even when he does not understand the words, the child can tell from vocal cues much of an adult's meaning and intention. It is fair to say that children are at least as responsive to intonation as adults, probably more so. But in order to punctuate with periods and commas as they punctuate orally, the pupils will have to raise their intuition to the level of awareness. A combination of several techniques will do this.

Procedures

In the first place, explain that when we talk, **our** voices rise and fall, pause and go on, lean hard on some words and lightly on others. Illustrate: "He likes candy," and "He likes candy?" Which is the question? How can they tell? Ask the difference between "I live in the white house," and "I live in the White House." How can they tell? Then say, " 'At night I sleep.' That is a sentence. My voice rounds it off and you can tell it is finished. This is a sentence too: 'Get your clothes.' And so is this: 'What did you eat?' Now, suppose I say, 'At night I sleep —' Is that finished? Why not? The whole sentence is 'At night I sleep with my teddy bear.' " Go on to pair off "Get your clothes —" with "Get your clothes off the bed," and "When did you eat —?" with "When did you eat the pie?" Make up other finished and unfinished sentences and ask them which is which. Then they can make up some pairs. In other words, through comparison, attention is focused on the vocal distinctions we make when we talk and listen.

Relate oral speech to print by saying, "But there is no voice in a book. How are we going to know how to read the words the way the person would say them? When we write, how can we let our reader know where our sentences begin and end?" This is the place to illustrate the use of periods, capitals, and question marks. Later, commas are introduced the same way.

Occasionally, when reading aloud as the children follow the text, tell them to notice how your voice follows the punctuation. Make a point of emphasizing pauses and intonation. When they read aloud remind them to "read the way the periods tell you to." Punctuation is constantly depicted as signals to guide the reader, to help him recreate the silent voice behind the words.

When they are writing in groups, tell the scribes to read aloud to their groups what they have written and the others to say where the periods and capitals go. Before passing on a group composition, the pupils test sentences in this way. Individuals writing alone should pair off, read their papers to each other, and check the segmenting. The writer understands that he is to read so that his listener can follow most easily; the listener says where he thinks the periods go. Of course, children just learning to read often read aloud haltingly, without being able to create the same intonation contours they would if speaking the same words in conversation. But a pupil reading his own writing does not have to decode the words one by one.

Sometimes a passage from a book or from pupil writing can be projected without punctuation, read aloud by the teacher or a pupil, and punctuated by the listening audience on their dittoed copies of the text. This is frankly a quiz with right answers, but it can be pleasant enough and will help beginners a great deal. For humor, project ambiguous strings of words that will inevitably be misread. One of my daughters, a five-year-old cracking her first primer, was reading to me one evening the sentence "Call the dog, Janet" but ignored the comma and read instead, "Call the dog Janet." She sensed the contradiction between her reading and what the meaning should have been, but could not put her finger on what was wrong. She merely paused and looked quizzical. I pointed out the comma and said that it meant the sentence should be read like *this,* and read it properly. She burst out laughing. When she had subsided a little, she explained the difference in meaning to me, read the sentence both ways several times, recalled the joke two or three more times, and broke up again each time.

Chapter 6

Reading

Though treated here as a separate topic, for convenience, reading is not, in this curriculum, deemed a specialty, to be isolated in scheduling or taught by a specialist, except perhaps for remedial decoding.

Since I do not undertake in this book to recommend titles of reading selections for the different grades, my remarks about reading will be necessarily general. In Chapter 2 I described an approach to reading that excludes some practices that one might ordinarily expect to find under the heading above. Here I would like to recommend some classroom procedures for handling the reading and some principles for selecting material. In most cases, the remarks are meant to apply throughout elementary school and even, where obviously relevant, to the years beyond.

Classroom Procedures

THE TEACHER READING ALOUD

The teacher should read large quantities of stories and poems to children. Before pupils can read much themselves, this practice is of course a necessity if their appetite for literature is to be both nourished and satisfied. It also makes reading a common part of everyday life and shows many children of non-reading parents what books are all about and what pleasure can be associated with them. And it puts the teacher in a giving position. While receiving this gift, the children become possessed of the urge to do themselves what the teacher does. In this respect he becomes a model to emulate. His continuing to read to children who have themselves learned how to read serves to show what good oral reading is like — how it recreates a storyteller's voice, how it brings out moods and feelings and meanings, how it follows cues of punctuation and typography. A very important part of reading to readers is having them follow the text with their eyes as they hear the teacher translate it into voice. The pupil can hear all aspects of the print brought to life — letters, typography, and paragraphing. Even in the upper elementary grades the teacher should periodically read, especially when the text contains a number of new irregular words, but also to maintain a good oral model.

CHILDREN READING ALOUD

The problem of the "reading circle." Children should read aloud so that they can hear the writer's voice in their heads when they read silently. The classic problem, however, concerns how each individual can have an ample opportunity to do this without boring his classmates, who, in the conventional reading circle, have to wait for him to figure out words haltingly but have no motive to do so because they have in their hands the same text he has. The halting can be somewhat resolved by asking the pupil to read a sentence silently before reading it aloud. And the motive to listen can be strengthened by asking the listeners to close their books while the reader carries the story forward. But these dodges do not resolve the real dilemma, which is that serial tutorial is being carried on in a group; the group cannot justify itself, and exists only because the teacher lacks time to coach each child individually. This managerial problem has arisen partly from a condition of the old basal readers, namely, that the slow introduction of words pretaught by sight entailed such a tight control of vocabulary that all children in a group had to be reading the same text together. A class was dependent on a single, graduated reader series through which all children marched step by step but at different rates according to the groups they were in. There is nothing inherent in learning to read that requires such a procedure.

When one child reads aloud to a group of classmates, he should do so because he alone has the text and they are not familiar with what they will hear. In other words, they constitute a real audience that he is entertaining, and they listen to hear what the book says, as when the teacher reads. But doesn't this already presuppose good oral reading? In a certain measure, yes. That is, the reader should have had some previous individual coaching, and, more immediately, he should have rehearsed his reading of the particular text for the day. My recommendations aim to make just these things possible.

Individual coaching. During the phase of beginning reading, children come up to the teacher and read aloud to him one at a time while the rest of the pupils are reading silently or doing other work. This practice stands in lieu of the conventional reading circle and is rendered feasible by other practices to be mentioned shortly. By taking a certain number each day, the teacher can hear all pupils once or twice a week. The procedure is that the pupil comes up and reads aloud some poem, short tale, or perhaps only a passage, that he has already read silently. The session is presented in the spirit of "now *you* read to *me*," a spirit that is easier to sustain if the children are reading from different books, and if time permits each to read a whole short selection. The coaching part consists of letting the pupil know if he is reading too softly or indistinctly, failing to follow punctuation, or misunderstanding the sound value of certain spellings. If the reading is very halting, the teacher should diagnose the problem: Is the child's decoding ability still poor in some respects, so that he has to puzzle out painstakingly? Is the text too difficult for him as regards either the amount of irregular spellings or the sophistication of the content? Sometimes the teacher may want the child to read a fresh text on sight, to determine how well he can do without a prior silent reading. Suppose a child reads inexpressively. Merely saying that he does and adding a directive to "put more expression into it" is not very helpful, and may even lead to contrived vocalizing. It is better to ask the reader what he thinks is the feeling under the lines, or the mood of the story situation, then to ask him to "make me feel that" or to "bring it to life the way you do when you're dramatizing a story." Convey the idea that you want to be read to in the same way he likes to be read to. Of course, this "read-to-me" spirit can be easily destroyed if the coaching is delivered in a severe fashion. The diagnostic remarks and suggestions should be perceived by the child as truly helpful for his own purposes, some of which relate to his role, discussed farther on, as reader to other children.

Choral reading. A social activity that children like very much is reading aloud in unison, as a chorus. Supported, and sometimes corrected, by the voices of the group, each individual can hide in the herd and let himself go. Better readers can carry along the less able ones, though it is also true that the latter can mumble uncertainly through, and that is why the individual coaching is necessary. Nevertheless, shaky readers can be bold, make guesses when they are not sure, without becoming personally exposed, and hear whether their guesses are right or not. Choral reading is, of course, one occasion when having a common reader is useful, but the teacher can also project texts overhead. These texts should have strong rhythms and cadences and varied and interesting "phrasing" (in the musical sense). Poetry is excellent, and songs especially will help teach phrasing and rhythm, since the melody usually parcels out word phrases according to musical phrases. Some of the books mentioned later in this chapter not only afford many good selections for choral reading but make particular suggestions to the teacher about how each one might be read, indicating which lend themselves to reading in "parts" or sub-choruses. Breaking the class into groups that alternate reading voice parts is, in fact, an especially pleasurable and instructive variation of choral reading. (What are the textual cues for each group?) It prepares for reading play scripts and remains popular among older children too. Generally, choral reading supplements the individual sessions by providing additional practice in sounding texts aloud. Both will undergird the following practice.

Individual reading aloud to a small group. Children take turns reading poems and stories to four or five other children to whom the text is either unknown or ever welcome. The main point in any case is that one pupil shall entertain others who shall constitute a real and expectant aud'ence. This practice presupposes that children are reading from different books, and that a large variety of single copies are indeed on hand. Since the kinds of literacy programs I have recommended make individual reading possible in the first grade, there is no reason why pupils should all have to read the same texts. By reading to each other, they can all become familiar with a wide range of children's literature and begin the exchange of reading experience that is to continue in all the later years. The audience has a motive to listen because it does not know the text or, at any rate, does not have it before them. The reader has a motive to read fluently and expressively because his group is dependent on him for entertainment.

The procedure is to divide the class into groups of four to six as for other small-group activities and to direct each child to bring to the group a book from which he is going to read *something he has already read silently.* During silent reading periods, they are told to choose and, in effect, rehearse one selection for the group meeting. Then they take turns reading their selections, not necessarily all in one session. Explain that, without interrupting the reading too much, the listeners may let the reader know if they are having trouble hearing well, and may let him know if he has made an obvious mistake. After each finishes, the listeners may ask the group about things they did not understand or talk about the content of what was read. These sessions, in other words, may provide some feedback to the reader and also launch discussion of texts. Whether the groups should or should not comprise children of mixed reading abilities is something that trial must determine. My suggestion is to try mixing them first, so that abler readers can help the less able. As group process whereby pupils teach each other, the practice merely establishes in reading the same learning method employed in speech, drama, and writing.

But the success of this practice depends on a reinforcing coordination of all the reading activities, silent and oral. Choral practice and individual coaching by the teacher take place concurrently with reading to the group, in a long-range sense, and silent reading of different texts precedes, more or less immediately, each group session. This means a silent and an oral reading period virtually every day (for which time is freed by doing away with phonic drills and rehearsals and "skill-building" or "comprehension practice"). The teacher might schedule each day the meeting of all but two of the reading groups, always leaving free eight to twelve children (the members of the two "fallow" groups) who will come up and read individually to him. Or he may prefer to have individuals read to him during the silent period so that he can sit in on groups during the oral period. Choral reading can be more sporadic and presents no scheduling problems, since the whole class is involved.

So far as I know, this particular set of activities for dealing with reading has not been tried on a regular and thoroughgoing basis, but I think it may solve some important problems. In some such manner children must be allowed to receive individual help and at the same time to practice reading aloud in an authentic group without inflicting boredom on listeners and without inflicting on themselves, if they are slower readers, the painful embarrassment that often makes them want to avoid reading altogether and for good.

DRAMATIZATION AND DISCUSSION

To these practices we should add dramatic work and small-group discussion, which, although treated elsewhere in this book, play a considerable part in learning to read. Their essential relationship to reading is that through them reading texts are elaborated and further explored for implications. It is from reading that dramatization and discussion draw a large part of their content. And they furnish a major answer to the question of what to do with a text after reading it silently.

The frustrating issue for the teacher is that silent reading is not directly teachable. The child is alone, and what goes on in his head at that moment depends greatly on what learning has *already* taken place, though we shouldn't forget that self-teaching goes on during sheer practice. But what he does with his silent reading — afterwards — becomes part of the learning that will precede, and transfer to, his next session of silent reading.

The traditional practice is to pose questions to the pupil about what he read, comprehension questions designed to find out how well he understood (test) and to make him think more about it (teach). The latter is what is important, of course — to invite him to relate facts and draw inferences he may not have while reading silently, and therefore to help him do so the next time he reads a new text alone. But it would be hard to find a child who does not resent the inevitable quizzing, by the teacher or the printed questionnaire, on what he has just read. He has enjoyed the story and now he must face the music, endure the commercial, pay the piper. Has anyone attempted to estimate the damaging effect of this on children's will to read? In rat-and-pigeon psychology, this administering of a pain after a certain act would be called "negative reinforcement," when it is intended to discourage the act. Indeed, how many *adults* would read if they had to face a battery of questions afterwards?

In order to dramatize or discuss a text, pupils have to think about the meaning of it and follow out implications. Enacting a story or poem is translating a text into voice, movement, and space. Characterization, sequence of actions, mood, setting, build-up, and climax have to be grasped in order to be rendered by the children. Disagreements in interpretation have to be discussed. Inventing details of action and dialogue and extending stories are based on implications and potentialities of the text. They help pupils render future texts in their own minds.

Small-group discussion of texts should take off from children's own questions and spontaneous comments, as allowed for in the reading groups, or take off, in the trained, topic-centered groups, from subjects the pupils have drawn from common reading. Asking the group for help in understanding some point in the text should become a natural habit. There are some things a pupil *knows* he did not grasp; he should have plenty of opportunity to find out what he missed, and perhaps even why he missed it. Comparing reactions and interpretations is also of vast importance, for it allows the reader to discover other things he has misunderstood *without* knowing it. It also shows that his reaction or interpretation may not be the only one justified by the text. Comparison itself often starts good discussion, because each child can refer to the text to support his reading of it. It is in this way that textual examination should occur. The teacher may suggest sometimes that members of the reading groups take turns reading aloud a single poem or story and talk about the varying renditions. This discussion, too, may cause them to look back closely at the text.

A possible procedure for the small groups trained especially for topical discussion is to bring to the meeting their copies of something read in common, agree on one or two things in the selection they want to talk about, and then start discussion. Or, during the conclusion of one session, when the group is settling on a topic for next time, they may propose something in their current reading.

INDIVIDUAL SILENT READING

A final kind of talk about reading matter can occur in groups assembled expressly for the purpose of exchanging experiences in the individual reading program. So far I have assumed such a program but not described it. It consists essentially just of providing books and time for children to read a lot on their own, making their own selections from a diverse array in the classroom or library, and signing them out to take home voluntarily. After the literacy program, children ought to read considerably more alone than in common. But instead of awarding a gold star for the meritorious service of having read a book, or rewarding the pupil for his efforts by making him write a report on it, the children should meet once a week or so in small groups to show and tell about what they have read. The function of this, they are told, is to let them familiarize each other with the books available and to give others an idea of whether they also would want to read them. (Some books may be brought from home and exchanged on loan.) Each takes a turn showing and telling about his book. The others are to ask whatever questions they want. Some of these may be factual questions about the content, and some may be evaluative questions calling for a judgment. In either case, the reader may be prompted to think more about the book without feeling quizzed by an authority figure.

Finally, children do not always have to do something with what they have read. They should be allowed to read just for pleasure and the pursuit of interests. Sharing is important, but so is solitary rumination.

SPECIAL MEASURES TO INCREASE EFFICIENCY

At the beginning of the preceding chapter, I defined reading in a deliberately narrow way — as decoding or word recognition — in order to exclude from the definition whatever is not *unique* to reading. The purpose of this strategy was to clarify the problems of learning to read. Now I would like to qualify that definition so as to broach the problem of increasing reading efficiency once word recognition has been mastered.

Visual processing of words. What the definition needs is something about the visual assimilation and mental strategies that go on during reading. The proficient reader does not give equal attention to all words or to all parts of words. He does not need to. There are many cues of word structure, syntax, and sense that make it unnecessary to process every letter, word and phrase in the same way. In a very real sense, we do not see everything in a text even when we "read" every word of it. For example, proofreading for typographical errors is very difficult because we unconsciously "fill in" the obvious — the letters we know are there because of how the rest of the word is spelled, articles and prepositions we know are there because nothing else could occupy certain slots in the sentence. This means that if errors exist in these obvious positions, we will miss them. Familiarity with the text makes proofreading even more difficult, because we fill in even more. For another example, the cloze procedure of deleting some letters and words from a text does not prevent readers from getting all the meaning of the text — provided that deletions are of *redundant* items, that is, of items that are dispensable because their information is conveyed equally well by other cues. If more important items are deleted, however, the text will become ambiguous or cryptic. Compare:

_ole_ant
tol_ra_t

Surely the letters deleted in the first were more essential, while those in the second were more redundant. Compare also:

I would _____ found it difficult _____ believe.
I _____ have found it _____ to believe.

But redundance is relative to the knowledge and experience of the reader:

> Give _____ this _____ our _____ bread.
> Marx's theory of historical _____ derives from _____'s
> concept of thesis and _____.

Scanning and guessing, in short, are integral to proficient reading. Swiftly, automatically, we attend to critical cues and infer what is in between. As we are reading along we constantly corroborate inferences by matching them against our ongoing interpretation. Occasionally, when something doesn't seem to fit, we "regress"; we flick our eyes back to a word or phrase and discover, for example, that what we took to be *importing* was actually the less common word *imparting*. It is useless to object that this is mere skimming or sloppy reading; it is what every proficient reader does, including those whose comprehension is best.

Differences between visual and auditory processing. Actually, not all of this perceptual scanning and mental processing is unique to reading. When we listen to someone speak we attend in the same selective fashion and have no more need to "hear" every syllable, in order to understand everything said, than we need to "see" every syllable when reading. Both seeing and hearing partake of the same general data-processing system. But there are differences too. One is that reading involves eye movements. Another is that reading concerns arrangement in space, whereas speech concerns movement in time. We can assimilate spatial information faster than temporal information — read faster than listen. These two differences are related: *how* fast we can assimilate visual information depends on how we have learned or not learned to move our eyes during reading.

Eye movements. A number of oculomotor studies have determined that reading consists of a series of fixations that last about a quarter of a second each, regardless of the reader's speed. About 94 percent of reading time passes in fixation. The rest is spent moving the eye from one fixation to the next. Time is lost, of course, in sweeping back to the left margin and in regressing. Since nothing can be seen during movement, only during fixations does true reading occur. Comparison of the eye movements of fast and normal readers shows that the fast reader fixates less often and regresses less often. The number of fixations, however, depends on how much area the eye takes in at each fixation and on what spatial pattern they create in moving over the page. It seems that the very fast reader moves his eyes in irregular fashion, which, I interpret, means that he fixates on critical textual points that he has learned to scan for, wherever these may occur on the page. Since we are told that four words represent the maximum area spanned in one fixation, very fast readers who comprehend well could not possibly be catching every word. By good scanning, they must be getting the maximum benefit of redundance. To this add the fact that the most rapid readers move their eyes vertically down the page, swinging to left and right in a smaller arc than do normal readers. They do not waste time sweeping from right margin back to left, like a typewriter, then moving all the way out to the right again. The vertical movement undoubtedly also enlarges the span of each fixation into a circle so that they catch words above and below the line of type fixated on.

Breaking early reading habits. How do habits of eye movement come about, and should they be changed? This is where the second difference between reading and speech must be considered — the difference between visual and auditory processing, spatial arrangement and temporal order. When first learning to read, children have to relate print to speech in order to recognize letter combinations in a book as familiar vocal words. Moving at first from one word to the next, they sound out words in succession just as one utters them in speech. Thus they learn the horizontal, left-to-right convention of reading and thereby learn at the same time the habits of eye movement that characterize the normal adult reader. This initial learning intensifies the habit of vocalizing while reading, and this habit, too, persists into adulthood, in the form of subvocalization. Thus the reading speed of normally proficient readers remains bound to the slow temporal order in which words are successively spoken. The advantage afforded by visual processing — the more rapid assimilation made possible by spatially presented information — is mostly wasted.

Both practical experience with fast readers and such considerations as I have just surveyed have led some reading experts to conclude that normally proficient adults read much more slowly than necessary, and that good school education should include the breaking of habits learned in beginning reading — namely, subvocalization and regular, horizontal eye movement. If they are right, as I believe they are, then a valuable kind of instruction has been much neglected. Educators have been justifiably wary, however, about believing the claims of speed-reading methods. The issue is whether one trades a gain in speed for a loss in comprehension.

The bugaboo of comprehension. Up to a point, the argument that fast reading increases comprehension makes good sense, for the accumulation of actions, images, or ideas that occurs as one reads has more effect and meaning for the reader if continuity is strongly sustained. Undoubtedly, some children read too slowly to comprehend well. On the other hand, when speed-reading proponents claim to increase rate without impairing comprehension, they run afoul the same problem that bedevils standard reading tests: Is there any really satisfactory way to measure comprehension?

Most teachers and school administrators have a much greater faith in standard reading tests than do either reading experts or testing experts, who are aware that the measuring of rate and comprehension is tremendously relative to the type of reading material and to the reader's purpose. The reader's purpose in turn determines how he reads — for detail, for main argument or story, or selectively for certain facts or points. A tester, however, must *assume* a certain reading motive and prepare questions that test the kind of comprehension matching the motive he has assumed. If the test is complex enough to allow for all possible reading purposes, then what is one to make of the scores, the meaning of which would vary according to each individual's motive in reading the texts about which he was questioned? Comprehension questions are of course designed to discover whether a reader has understood certain facts, points, or implications. A reader may miss some of these but catch others he was not asked about, because his purpose, emphasis, or interpretation lay in a different direction from that of the test maker. But let us suppose that any student taking a reading test has for motive the desire to score high, so that he assumes responsibility for total comprehension of small facts, main continuity, and all sorts of possible inferences. Then wouldn't a comprehension test covering all these matters give a valid index of his reading efficiency when combined with a test of reading rate? Or is it testmanship that is being tested? One junior high school student told me that during her elementary years she learned to take SRA comprehension tests, and score high, without even reading the passages — by looking first at the questions, which follow a pattern, and then by picking answers out of the texts! In sum, reading speed is dependent for significance on reading comprehension, and reading comprehension is dependent for significance on a host of factors that have not been accommodated and may never be satisfactorily accommodated in testing procedures.

Methods for increasing speed. Partly because the measurement of comprehension is fraught with unreliability, research on speed-reading methods is controversial and inconclusive. Also, some experiments indicate a loss of comprehension for students given a speed-reading course and some indicate that rate is substantially increased without loss of comprehension. These experiments usually involve college students and compare a speed-reading group with a control group when both groups are taking a common reading course. One experiment compared the four main speed-reading methods with each other. These methods were Tachistoscope, Controlled Reader, Controlled Pacer, and Paperback Scanning. All four were reported to produce higher rates and greater flexibility than normal without loss of comprehension, but the book-scanning method excelled over all three others,[1] which scaled down in this order — Controlled Pacer, Controlled Reader, and

---

[1] Leonard Broom and Allen Burger, "Effectiveness of Four Methods of Increasing Rate, Comprehension, and Flexibility," *Journal of Reading*, Vol. 11, No. 5 (Newark, Delaware: International Reading Association, 1968). This volume also contains a compact bibliography, "Ten Important Sources of Information on Speed Reading," by Allen Burger.

Tachistoscope. But the reading expert asks immediately, "What kind of comprehension test was used?" As the authors point out, the test covered only details.

The book-scanning method bears resemblance to the Wood Reading Dynamics Method, a well known commercial course that has increasingly gained the serious attention of reading experts, most notably of Russell Stauffer and his staff at the Reading-Study Center of the University of Delaware, which is certainly the best source of information and advice for teachers interested in reading speed and efficiency. The Wood Method teaches readers to move the eyes rapidly down the page while pacing with the hand. In order to break the habit of subvocalizing and of making numerous fixations, the students scan and turn the page at a rate far too fast for comprehension, then they slow down and practice scanning at a rate still higher than their usual speed, until the new habits of visual processing make good comprehension possible. There is more to the method than this, but these are the main ways it breaks the habits of beginning reading and allows eye and mind, not oral speech, to determine the speed of assimilation.

At the University of Delaware School of Education, the Wood Method has been much explored. Some of the staff have learned the method, taught it to students, and given outside teachers an in-service course on it. Various pieces of experimental research have been conducted, there and elsewhere, to determine if the Wood claims of greatly increased speed with no loss of comprehension are true. William Liddle conducted the most authoritative such experiment, with University of Delaware students, and found that reading rates were tripled and quadrupled in the experimental group but that this group scored lower on comprehension of fiction than the control group and lower also on comprehension of non-fiction in two of the three sub-tests (lower on "facts" and "Inferences" and the same on "Critical Reflection.")[2]

It would be very unfortunate if this finding confirmed the common prejudice that any effort to increase reading efficiency, including the Wood Method, is necessarily shallow and will produce mere skimming. Besides the uncertainties of measuring efficiency, I would point out here that the students in this experiment may simply have been pushed too far in order to achieve rates that tripled and quadrupled their initial speed. The fact remains that the overwhelming majority of adults are held to the speed at which they learned to read, even though their early reading habits are no longer functional for them. This is an absurd state of affairs, especially in an era of information explosion that requires adults to assimilate huge amounts of print. And it is this state of affairs that has prompted so many professional people and university students to seek out commercial courses that will do for them what schools never did. The problem of reading efficiency is one that schools must deal with. This does not mean that people *should* read fast

[2] "An Initial Investigation of the Wood Reading Dynamics Method," unpublished dissertation, University of Delaware, 1965, summarized in *Dissertation Abstracts*, Vol. 27 (September, 1966), p. 605-A.

but rather that they should be *able* to read fast when they want. The principle of flexibility — reading different texts in different ways for different purposes — is a principle now well established among many reading experts, but it will remain a hollow conviction if schoolchildren are stuck with their original habits and thus have no real options.

Recommendations. In view of the unsettled problems described above, it is difficult to make recommendations as definite as one would like about reading efficiency. But despite inconclusiveness, I strongly urge teachers to become acquainted with the Wood Reading Dynamics Method, which seems to be the best contender so far, and to try it with pupils whose mastery of word recognition makes subvocalization and short eye movements no longer necessary for them. (Russell Stauffer has suggested starting the Wood technique with able sixth-graders.) It would be very helpful for teachers to look at *Speed Reading: Practices and Procedures*,[3] especially "Uses and Limitations of Speed of Reading Programs" by Miles Tinker, who affirms, among other things, that book-scanning is equal to or better than methods employing machines. Tinker also points out that ineffectual eye movements do not cause reading problems; oculomotor behavior is flexible and adjusts to whatever perceptual and mental way of assimilating one chances to learn. My recommendation is that the way of assimilating print represented by the Wood Method be made available from the later elementary grades on, without pushing for immoderate speeds and pending further research and development in reading efficiency.

Practically, it seems necessary either for teachers to take a course at one of the Wood schools or for in-service training to be arranged for groups of teachers. Either the Wood Institute or the Reading-Study Center might help make such arrangements. At any rate, I know of no manual that enables the teacher to read about the method and then apply it. The basic technique, however, of scanning down the page at exaggerated speed, using the hand as a pacer, then slowing the speed and practicing regularly at one's maximum rate of understanding is a technique one might with discipline master well enough to teach to others.

Remedial Reading

The general view taken in this book on "non-readers" or "poor readers" of the later grades is that these children's problem results either from an inadequate decoding instruction or from personal characteristics such as low intelligence, faulty perception, poor motivation, or emotional disturbance that are *general* learning problems not confined to reading only and therefore not treatable as only reading problems.

[3] Volume X, March, 1962 (Newark, Delaware: Reading-Study Center, University of Delaware.)

As to the first, *Words in Color, Phonovisual,* and *The Writing Road to Reading,* like most independent phonics materials, are intended to be used, and have been used, to teach remedial reading or beginning reading to illiterate adults. (In fact, before creating materials for primary school, Gattegno developed his method while teaching older illiterates of different languages how to read.) A key feature of remedial work seems to be a decoding emphasis, usually explicit phonics instruction, even in schools where the initial literacy program does not show such emphasis. Chall's survey of clinical studies indicated that special focus on sound-letter pairing is a considerable help to children with a specific language disability. Such spokesmen for the Orton Society as Anna Gillingham have long asserted (along with the disputed theory of brain-lobal cross-dominance) that the synthesizing of separately presented letters and sounds affords the most effective help for those children tending to reversal and having subnormal auditory and visual discrimination. It is difficult to escape the implication that pupils who get this early will not wind up in a remedial program a few years later. If they do, the best remedy seems to be one of the literacy programs cited above, a proposal that is all the more feasible as they are virtually independent of graded reading material. Thus for remedying both poor initial instruction and some personal characteristics referred to as a specific language disability, a synthetic phonics course seems in order.

But, as I hope I have stressed enough, phonics itself is no panacea, because a mastery of decoding does not guarantee that a child will want to read, will pay attention to a text, or will get meaning from the ideas in it. Here we are into general learning problems of motivation, conceptual development, and emotional health that must be remedied by a variety of means that are treated in this book in other chapters — the opportunity for plentiful oral speech and dramatic expression, involvement in *making* books, the playing of logical games, and the general emphasis on meaningful reception and production of language. Moreover, the classroom procedures for handling reading proposed earlier in this chapter would be most helpful to problem readers of later grades. Far from being a luxury for the elite, for example, individual reading selections may be most important for the poorly motivated or less successful reader. Freedom from fear, individual coaching, help from classmates are all remedial aspects of the practices recommended. Being read to while following a text and participating in choral reading are easy, pleasantly social activities, appropriate for any age, that will ease problem readers into the more difficult solitary act. For especially arranged help under a remedial teacher, individual reading while listening to a tape of the text may well turn out to be the most effective single method.[4]

---

[4] Arthur Blumenthal and others, *Decoding for Reading* (New York: The Macmillan Co., 1968), is a remedial program consisting of 16 long-playing records designed to accompany some read-along books, but these recordings contain considerably more than just the text of books. In "Reaching the Culturally Deprived," *Saturday Review of*

Conventionally, however, poor readers whose problems go beyond decoding difficulties — if indeed the distinction is drawn — are made to undergo the sort of dull, mechanical course that actually requires the *most* motivation, confidence, and maturity to get through. They submit to "practice readers," "word study" workbooks, "skill builders," spellers, and so on. Remediation that consists of relentless drills and comprehension questions is based on a false assumption that the underlying problems are reading problems, whereas the problems are ones that *manifest* themselves in reading as elsewhere. For these children reading should be more, not less, fun than for others. Remedial reading specialists I have talked with in good school systems admit that they do not believe much in their own programs and are relieved to hear someone say what I have been saying here. But they do not feel free to admit this publicly, nor do they feel sure of offering alternatives.

As much as possible, poor readers should not be segregated. Part of the snowballing effect of reading failure stems from this segregation and its consequent effect on self-esteem. Abler children, moreover, should be tapped to help the less able. But special attention can be given within a heterogeneous class by taking poor readers aside for phonics work at the board and by coaching individually while the class is engaged in silent reading or in reading to each other in groups. Most of all, perhaps, poorer readers should be allowed to choose what they want to read, whatever the level and whatever the taste. When testing is absolutely necessary, it should be done as indirectly and humanely as possible, and other pressures should be removed.

If these recommendations for remedial reading essentially do not seem to differ enough from those for the regular reading program, it is because the latter has been designed to prevent reading problems. As in any other matter, the best remedy is prevention. But lest this seem too cavalier to those teachers into whose hands fall children with serious reading problems, let me say that the low-level technical approach has been tried for a long time and found wanting. A broader, more humane approach that eliminates fear and excites interest will be of most help. Where the technical avails is in solving a technical problem, namely the arbitrary conventions of letter symbols. The best advice can only be to filter out the true decoding problems, by listening to a child read aloud alone, and to remedy them as early as possible before they compound into despair the general learning problems that must be handled in broader ways. For the latter the whole human being must be considered.

Selecting Reading Material

From what has been said so far, it is clear that a classroom needs to contain books chosen for three purposes — for the teacher to read aloud, for

---

Literature (February 19, 1966), Terry Borton has described a successful way that he had disadvantaged students read literary texts while listening to homemade tapes of those texts.

children to read individually, and for children to read in common. The only necessity for buying class sets of the same book is to facilitate choral reading, group discussion, and dramatic work. On the other hand, some reading series, mainly of the supplementary sort, can be purchased simply as anthologies from which selections can be read either individually or in common. One principle here is that when sets are bought, it should be for their content, not for their method, unless a series contains the desired literacy program, for after that is over, the "method" is not something that can be embodied in textbooks. It follows that after the first few months of school, textbooks and trade books are in even competition, since the content is what counts, though some books aimed at schools, which I will mention, do have helpful suggestions to the teacher for oral reading.

MATERIAL TO ACCOMPANY THE LITERACY PROGRAM

Reading material is of two sorts — phonetically controlled texts that the children can read by themselves on the basis of the sound-spellings and sight words presented to them so far, and uncontrolled texts that the teacher reads to them, which are limited only by what the children can understand and take pleasure in.

Phonetically controlled reading. *Words in Color* contains some reading matter of the first sort, and the Foundation Program of the Open Court series contains some of both sorts. But *The Phonovisual Method* and *The Writing Road to Reading* do not include early readers, and teachers may in any case want to supplement whatever program they have chosen. Two good, phonetically controlled series for these first few months are the Dr. Seuss *Read by Yourself Books* (Boston: Houghton Mifflin Company) and the *Follett Beginning-to-Read Books* by Henry Lee Smith, Jr., and others, (New York: Harper & Row, Publishers). Both of these begin with the short vowel sounds, which is a point to remember (the Open Court series begins with long vowels, and *Words in Color* with short). The problem with phonetically controlled texts is that their order of presentation is meant to match a particular literacy program. On the other hand, they all feature *regularity* of spelling, and the farther along the child is, the less difference the order makes.

Material for the teacher to read aloud. The teacher needs to have on his desk one or two large, varied anthologies from which he can pluck any kind of poetry or prose that seems right for the class and the moment. The bible of this sort is *The Arbuthnot Anthology of Children's Literature,* edited by Mary Hill Arbuthnot (Chicago: Scott, Foresman & Company, 1961), a revised edition combining three of the author's previous anthologies. It is an omnibus for all ages. *Anthology of Children's Literature,* edited by Johnson, Sickels, and Sayers (Boston: Houghton Mifflin Company, rev. ed. 1960), and *a Golden Treasury of Poetry,* edited by Louis Untermeyer (Boston: Beacon Press, 1959), are also excellent omnibuses. The other books that I will mention below could also be purchased for children to read alone after the period of phonetically controlled texts is over. If ordered in sets, they would be good for choral reading and for reading aloud in parts.

Along with Northrop Frye, I feel strongly that much of the first reading matter should be poetry. The three R's of poetry — rhyme, rhythm, and repetition — teach children a lot about individual words and patterns of words, and they do so in delightful and memorable ways. This very frank bias is reflected in the following recommendations. A very popular book of songs and poems is *A Rocket in My Pocket,* edited by Carl Withers (New York: Holt, Rinehart & Winston, Inc., 1948). A more recent and very lively collection of poems is Stephen Dunning's compilation, *On the Gift of a Watermelon Pickle . . . and Other Modern Verse* (Glenview, Ill.: Scott, Foresman, 1966). *Voices of Verse,* edited by Flynn, MacLean and Lund (Chicago: Lyons & Carnahan, 1933, 1944) is a series of poetry anthologies graduated for different ages. So is *Let's Enjoy Poetry,* compiled by Rosalind Hughes, (Houghton Mifflin, divided into Grades K–3, 1958, and 4–6, 1961). This series stresses oral reading, the poems being grouped according to how they can be read (chorally, singly, a-line-a-child, two-part, three-part, with emphasis on rhythm, with refrain lines) and accompanied also by helpful suggestions to the teacher for handling each. Both of these series have good selections but do not include much modern poetry. An excellent volume for both selection and helpful presentation is *The Sound of Poetry,* by Austin and Mills (Boston: Allyn and Bacon, Inc., 1964) (which is followed by a volume for the intermediate years, *The Reading of Poetry,* by Sheldon, Lyons, and Rouault, 1963). This pair of books is more up to date and also contains very good suggestions for oral reading. The *Sounds of Language* readers I have already mentioned. They contain prose and poetry and many very good asides to the teacher about the oral possibilities of each selection.

I do not mean that these are the only good books for the teacher to read aloud from, but among them a teacher could find about any kind of selection he might want to read. Also, several of them, as indicated, will teach the teacher himself a great deal about oral reading; instead of discussing the art myself, I refer teachers to the books indicated, which can demonstrate it with illustrative poems. These books, moreover, are good candidates to consider when ordering singles and sets for the general reading program.

PRINTED MATERIAL AFTER THE LITERACY PROGRAM

Publishing sources. Three main sources of general reading material are open — trade books such as any parent might buy for his children to read at home; hardcover, graduated textbook series; and paperback books sold to children through school by such distributors as Scholastic Book Services.

The textbook series in literature may contain some editor-written material and some unsignalled abridgements and alterations of original works. Some of these amount to good anthologies but should be examined closely. Two especially good series are *The Umbrella Books,* selected by the Association for Childhood Education (New York: The Macmillan Co.) and the *Wonder-Story Books,* by Huber, Huber, and Salisbury (New York: Harper & Row, rev. ed.). The first contains much folk literature and the second contains many selections by first-rate creative writers. As noted before, *The Open Court Basic Readers* are excellent except for some editor-written sections. The book services rarely publish material for the first time but rather reprint trade books in school editions or anthologize already printed selections. These services are very useful for individual reading because they distribute trade books through schools at low prices.

Principles of selection. It would be foolish to attempt to survey either text or trade books. But some principles of selection may serve as a guide through the welter of choices. The first is that *content should be more important than anything else.* In literature, this means the highest quality creative writing, old or new, that children like. In social studies or other subject areas, it means the most up-to-date and best written books doing justice to the subject as defined by leaders in the area. The second principle reinforces the first: *do not adopt a package series just for the sake of the pedagogical paraphernalia it contains, or for the sake of some particular continuity.* The paraphernalia attempts to work over the content in ways better left to group processes, and the continuity can only concern some schematic or thematic irrelevance. (A sequence based only on generally increasing maturity and proficiency is a different matter.) The third is that *children's reactions must play an important part in selection.* Individual reading, of course, implies pupil-selected books, but for choice to be real the classroom must contain a large number of single copies of works that have passed the test of previous children. When large investments are to be made in hardcover sets, samples should be tried out first under conditions such as are outlined in this chapter. What do children say about books that have to stand or fall on sheer content — when children can talk spontaneously about them and thus reveal what they really got from them? In sum, teachers can apply Principles One and Two when screening down, but they can apply Principle Three only after observing their pupils' reactions. And all three principles do indeed throw text and trade books into a healthy competition.

THE CHILDREN'S OWN MATERIAL

Children following the curriculum in this book will pour forth an abundance of writing. They will be reading each other's productions constantly. Sometimes these productions will be in unfinished form as groups collaborate on a writing project or as workshop members exchange papers for reactions and commentary. Sometimes they will be printed and distributed for voluntary reading, or projected before the class. This reading matter will in a general way be automatically controlled for maturity of content and expression and for vocabulary and sentence structure. Expressing children's feelings, perceptions, and imaginings, it will interest children. It is home-produced for home consumption. What it lacks is what the best adult talents of the ages have wrought and what only greater resources of language and experience can bring to writing. It is only for this reason that published materials are needed at all. Otherwise, a reading program could be mounted with nary a book in the classroom, with nothing more than what pupils created themselves. This statement will not seem plausible until after the writing program has been unfolded in the following chapters.

What will the children write for each other? Picture captions, cartoon strips, songs, poems, stories, journal entries, jokes, riddles, telegrams, directions to follow, eyewitness accounts, personal recollections, personal essays, fables, editorials, and original nature booklets. Surely this constitutes a formidable reading program. Children will read generously in each mode of writing because doing so is entailed in group process. This material does not replace the vitally needed, rich input from the maturer culture, but it virtually doubles each pupil's reading practice, and it builds a bridge from his local world to that cultural legacy he meets in published books. As my reader continues through the remainder of this book, most of which appears to be devoted to composition, he will not forget, I hope, that every writing assignment is a reading assignment.

Chapter 7

Writing Out

Rationale

The kinds of writing treated later — writing down and writing up — are reality-oriented. Writing out, on the other hand, gives full play to the inventions of imagination and expresses inner psychic material.

What Stories Mean to Children

Children, of course, love to hear and tell stories, but we seldom think about why they do. My own theory is that storying is a child's way of thinking about nameless inner things, and that his thinking differs from ours mainly in the categories he establishes and in the symbolic ways he names them, not in the basic processes of logic. He is unable to acknowledge and designate his subjective categories of experience, and he does not yet possess either the vocabulary or the linguistic structures to classify and postulate *explicitly*. Nevertheless, through stories, he manipulates classes and formulates propositions.

To illustrate, let me translate into adult thought and language a very popular children's story, "The Three Billy Goats Gruff." An ogre tries to eat up anyone who crosses his bridge to graze on the pleasant slopes beyond. Between us and the attainment of our desires lie frightful dangers that we cannot go around. The smallest billy goat encounters the ogre at the bridge and persuades him to spare his life in favor of eating the larger goat to come. The second billy goat gets by the same way, and the third tears the ogre apart (into a satisfying number of small pieces). The three goats reach and enjoy the pasture. If you're weak and helpless, a child, you can refer the danger to Mother, who, if she cannot cope with it, can refer it to Daddy. *Some* "big person" will come along who is capable of overcoming the forces of evil and ensuring that you get what you have to have without being destroyed in the process. The small are backed up by the mighty, but you may have to make shift with a stratagem of your own. And you have to play on your size, not deny it. (This sagacious advice is perhaps the main statement.)[1]

I believe it is the important meaning that underrides the story that makes "The Three Billy Goats Gruff" so popular. Children's fascination with stories cannot be entirely explained by the love of excitement and adventure, for these exist independently of stories. A favorite tale, such as an animal allegory, satisfies the desire for novelty and excitement but at the same time organizes experience in reassuring and resolving ways. Characters, objects, and events are types, classes, and categories of experience in disguise; a sequence of events postulates something about these categories. The fact that the meaning is unconscious, the categories veiled, the propositions implicit in the action does not make storying any less an act of thinking than adult cogitation. I make this point not to put children's fun in a solemn light but to remind teachers that children do all of their serious business in a play form. That is to say, it is a great mistake to regard their addiction to stories as mere childish pleasure-seeking to be catered to until they have sobered up enough to reflect on life. They are already reflecting an enormous amount; we can't *stop* them from doing it. All adults have to do is recognize the function of their fun, and honor stories as a genuine mode of thought. Adult fiction too embodies ideas; it too presents types and symbolizes inner experience that we cannot name and think about explicitly. Novels have a "logic of the events," and the ambiguous word "conclusion" applies to the climax of both stories and syllogisms.

The Need for Stimulants

Inventing, however, is actually difficult for children if they are merely told to "make up a story." They need definite stimulants and frameworks that prompt the imagination. Their original stories are recombinings of familiar stories in more or less new ways. My impression is that their originality is much greater in painting and modeling than in creating fiction, perhaps because language is more public and standard than art media, and also because their language stock is more limited anyway. The second issue is that *writing* a story, rather than merely telling it, calls for additional motivation. Third, writing restricts the children to a shorter length than telling, because they can talk longer than they can sustain a written story. The following recommendations attempt to provide easy starting points, tie writing into honest motivation, and allow for the necessary brevity.

[1] To this interpretation my wife adds this very just observation: "But the child doesn't just identify with the little goat; he can successively identify with all three in turn and 'grow' to handle the situation directly rather than passing the buck."

Recommendations

YOUNGER CHILDREN DICTATING STORIES TO OLDER CHILDREN

A general suggestion for getting story writing under way: have older children, from the fifth or sixth grade, take down the stories of kindergartners and first-graders as they dictate them. Exchange halves of classes with the other teacher and pair off the mixed pupils. (See page 180.) The point of this is to enable the younger children to spin out a story fluently without having to worry about the mechanical problems of writing and without having to limit themselves in length. Seeing their words rendered on paper helps establish a tie between vocal speech and writing. For the older children this gives practice in transcribing speech. The procedure permits a lot more dictation than a teacher could handle alone.

Here are two pieces dictated by less mature first graders during their first months of school:

CATHERINE'S STORY

When I sleep with my brother, he wets his bed. He's only three. When he wets his bed, I go up with my brother Ronald and he wets his bed and he's nine years old. When I sleep with my sister, she doesn't wet her bed. She's twelve years old. When I sleep with my sister, she's seven years old, she doesn't wet her bed. When my brother, Charles, sleeps with my mother and daddy, he wets his bed again. When I get up in the morning, I eat all my breakfast but I can't have oatmeal. When I have a stomach ache, I don't eat my breakfast.

CHASE

One time me and my sister in the dark and then she ran ahead of me and I ran home because I was afraid. Then my mother said, "Why did you run home?" I said to her, "She ran ahead of me towards the store." Then when she ran ahead of me, I had to go back down after her. When she was at the store, I was at the store before her. Then she didn't know what to say to me but "go home." She wondered what I was doing down there at the store. She said, "Who sent you down here?" And I said, "My mother did." Then we walked home together through the dark.[2]

Though these two "stories" are not made up, they illustrate how dictation can catch the child's spontaneous composition of high-interest material, expressed with a fluency and maturity of language that he could not yet maintain in writing.

After he has been helped by the older child to read his own dictated story, the younger child pairs off with a partner of his own class and each

[2] I am indebted to Eleanor Grubb of the Cochituate Elementary School, Wayland, Massachusetts, for these two dictations.

reads his story to the other as the other follows along with his eyes. This fosters cross-teaching of reading.

Writing Captions

A simple point of departure for writing stories is to make up phrases and sentences to print beneath one's own drawing or painting. Children's pictures usually encapsulate a story or have the makings of one. Probably the best practice is to keep on hand a stock of homemade caption strips of the right size to be scotch-taped to the bottom of the art paper. After a painting or drawing session, tell the pupils to get a strip and write on it what their picture is about. The children then assemble in small circles to look at each other's pictures and to read the captions. Members of the circle take turns holding up their pictures, and each picture is talked about.

As the children break into groups the teacher directs them, when each picture is exhibited, to look at it, read the caption, ask questions, and talk with the artist about it. Many captions will need further explaining because not everything is in the picture, and because things the caption refers to may not be evident to the other children. The point of this discussion is to let the children elaborate orally what the caption summarizes in writing. Give them time at the end of discussion to expand their caption in writing, to include more explanation of what action precedes and follows the picture, and to answer in writing the questions they were asked.

A variant of captioning is to write below the picture what the figures in it are saying. Demonstrate first on the board how the speech follows the character's name and a colon. A variant of the whole process is for the pupils to hold up their uncaptioned pictures before the group, one at a time, and let the other members write on a slip of paper a caption for what they see in the picture. The artist concerned gathers the slips and reads them aloud; the fitness of each caption is discussed. Afterwards, the artist reads his own caption, and his colleagues compare what he intended with what they saw. This also brings out different story possibilities suggested by the same picture.

A further step is to draw a series of pictures (on a roll of paper) that tell a story. This might be introduced, on the occasion of a single drawing, simply by asking the children to draw a succeeding picture, something that "comes after" the first one. At a subsequent time, direct them at the outset to draw a series of pictures like a cartoon strip. In fact, if the teacher selects and projects a few cartoon strips containing dialogue that the children can understand, the children can follow these as a model and create talking pictures by encircling the words of dialogue and connecting this "balloon" to the speaker. Captions are also added. This combines dialogue with narrative and joins both to visual sequence. Gradually the word-picture ratio is reversed until the text is primary and the drawing secondary (without, of course, appropriating all their art work for this purpose). After the children are used to writing on and under their pictures, tell them to write a story sentence first — a caption for an action — to illustrate that, and so on. Children who have a hard time getting an initial idea can be put together briefly in a group to stimulate each other first, following some prompts by the teacher: "Imagine a place, a bridge, a dark woods, or a broken down house; then imagine somebody in that place. Is it an animal or a person? What is it doing?"

Both single pictures and series can serve as ideas for dramatic enactments. While discussing pictures in groups, the pupils can select one that they would like to act out. Besides providing material for drama, this practice exploits drama as a means of further elaborating stories. Elaborating is a major issue in children's story-making because the length they can write seldom does justice to a story and forces them to oversummarize. The difference between dead and alive stories depends partly on the ratio of summary to elaboration. Whereas the length of children's writing cannot be forced, their written stories can be spun out by discussing and enacting them.

Reversing the relationship now, acting can serve as a point of departure for story writing. I recommended in Chapter 3 that group story-making be followed by enactment. Rotating roles and acting out the story several times creates varying renditions and encourages departure from the original idea. Each child can then render his personal version in writing. The directions are simply to "write down the story the way you like it best." Of course the writing should follow hard on the heels of the acting, while the story is still hot. A very particular and practical reason for this writing — which should be announced in advance — is to pass the stories on to other groups for them to enact. This also feeds new story ideas into each group.

LITERATURE AND WRITING

Imitating forms. Children need impersonal forms into which they can project feeling without knowing that they are doing so. The material of folk literature furnishes one kind of public medium. The technical forms of poetry and song offer another. David Holbrook has put the point well in giving an account of his work with children's writing.

> ... I felt the only way to achieve this expression of feeling was by using as stimulants poems, passages, and themes which the child already recognized as means to the depersonalizing of his individual emotion — a way to that third ground which is a meeting-place between the "mind" of a community and his own. Such a depersonalized world, I have tried to suggest, exists in the sea-chanty, the folksong and the game-rhyme. It also exists in such poetry as the Chinese poems translated by Arthur Waley. The fairy tale provides it, and so too, I think, do certain other conventional types of chil-

dren's story — the story of exploration, for instance. And, it seems to me, even the wild western may provide a "half-serious, half irresponsible world" where self-identification may be indulged in, and painful feelings tolerated in an unfamiliar setting.[3]

In his work with children's writing, Holbrook has presented them certain poems, songs, and chanties that have a strong and simple pattern of metrical beat, refrain, or incremental repetition. The children read these in parts, dramatize them, and talk about them. Having absorbed the forms, they fill in the forms with their own words. They are asked to write a poem, song, or chanty like the one they have heard. The popularity of limerick writing attests to the feasibility and attraction of the idea.

I would like to recommend Holbrook's practice and at the same time take the opportunity to say that any program calling for pupils to produce must also give them a lot. Imaginative writing wells up from a source constantly enriched by an inflow. A teacher who would like his children to write should let them take in an enormous amount of folk literature from books and records. Not only do they absorb images and ideas that they can recombine in their own expression, but as they internalize the rhymes, rhythms, and other formal patterns, they are absorbing in a peculiarly effective way the vocabulary, locutions, and language structures bound to those patterns by association. Rhyme in particular is helpful for reinforcing phonics instruction; when the child sees and writes words of the same sound, occupying the same final position and receiving the same rhythmic stress, he has a particularly vivid opportunity to notice the different ways a certain sound is spelled and the different ways a certain spelling is sounded.

Borrowing the content. The content of literature is a less direct sort of stimulant. That is, instead of being directed to write a poem or story about such and such a character they have just read about, the children simply soak up from literature many characters and settings and story ideas that they can recombine when stimulated more specifically by some literary form. Through improvisation, however, they can extend some favorite stories in groups by borrowing characters and settings for which they invent new actions.

Oral reading as springboard. In connection with this intake of folk literature, two practices seem to me to be of great potential value in teaching reading along with writing. First, write out a poem, for example, on a transparency and project it before the class. Moving an opaque sheet of paper

---

[3] David Holbrook, *English for Maturity* (New York: Cambridge University Press, 1965), p. 112. Consulting this book would be valuable for teachers of all grades. Besides making the case that creative writing educates emotion and develops the whole child, he has compiled helpful lists of records and books containing folk songs, chanties, and poems for children of a wide age range.

down the transparency, line by line, either read the piece expressively and rhythmically, perhaps a couple of times, or play a recording of the piece and pace it by revealing the lines one at a time as they are sung. (Rhyme patterns, the refrains of chanties, and the incremental repetition of ballads ensure the recurrence of words in a manner certainly more interesting than vocabulary drills.) After reading or playing the piece a couple of times, ask the class to read it or sing it in chorus from the projection. This transfers reading from teacher to children. Now, when rhythms and repetitions are still pounding in their ears, and images swirling through their heads, send the children to paper to write their own nursery rhyme or ballad or limerick. They can brainstorm at first in groups, composing together as a scribe records. Then, when older, they can compose alone. A transition from collective to individual writing may occur naturally as group members think up variations on a common theme, using each other's ideas as stimulants.

Song Writing

Music can suggest words by means of technical cues having little to do directly with the mood or meaning. A sequence of stressed and unstressed notes in a musical phrase, for example, can evoke a parallel sequence of stressed and unstressed syllables in a verbal phrase. I was awakened one morning by hearing my five-year-old daughter singing, to the tune of "Happy Birthday," "Tapioca to you. Tapioca to you." With only slight distortion, she had fitted into the stress pattern of the notes for "happy birthday" the two troches of "tapioca." While concentrating on form, the child lets slip a content. Pauses, staccatos, the steep intervals between notes, lengths of phrasing — all elicit words and word clusters as well, perhaps, as images and ideas of actions. Such cues set up free thought associations, which determine the chain of ideas.

Inaugurate song writing by having the children sing a familiar short song together, then asking them to make up new words for the tune. Perhaps for a while they could collaborate on the lyrics in small groups, one offering a line and another adding to it or suggesting an alternative. A scribe could write down on a transparency the lines they decide on. Transparencies are projected one at a time, a member of the group that composed the song reads or sings it as others follow the written words, then the whole class sings the new lyrics.

Later, individuals write their lyrics alone, and the teacher introduces melodies that the class does not necessarily know. Seated at their desks, the pupils listen as the teacher plays phrases of the tune on a piano or flutaphone, or plays a tape of a previously recorded tune. Play a phrase at a time, and, while they are writing, repeat phrases and sections a number of times. When they have finished, tell them to entitle their song. Some of these lyrics too are projected, read, and sung by the class. Copied off the transparencies onto paper, entitled, and signed, the title of the original tune written below, these lyrics are compiled into individual or class songbooks. Thus, the purposes of writing are both immediate and long-range.

WRITING ABOUT PICTURES

Assemble a large collection of provocative photographs cut from magazines. Let each pupil choose one that he would like to write about. "Say what you think is happening in your picture. Make up a story from (or about) what you see." Role playing may be invoked: "Pretend you are that person (animal or thing) and tell what you are doing or what is happening to you."

RIDDLES, PUNS, AND JOKES

There is an oral folk culture among children embodied in such things as riddles, puns, and jokes that they take pleasure in passing on and thus would enjoy writing out in their own words. Inspired by these, the pupils can then make up their own.

Since jokes and riddles can perfectly well be shared orally in class, the purpose of putting them on paper or transparencies would be to circulate them more widely than can be done by word of mouth. The class compiles a book of them or puts them onto two or three transparencies, and these are exchanged with other classes. Whereas a book can only be read aloud to the class or put on a table for individual reading, transparencies carry this additional advantage: the teacher can use them as high-interest texts for a reading practice he can oversee, either reading aloud as the class follows visually or silently revealing a line at a time by slowly uncovering the transparency, to keep punch in the punch line. For riddles, pause before the answer and ask for guesses; then let the children read whether they were right or wrong. Since some jokes are based on a homonymous pun, the pupil writing the joke has to choose which of the homonyms to write down; you can ask the class what the other one is. (This game is called Sneaky Phonics.)

General Remarks on Writing

CREATING THEIR OWN BOOKS

Compiling books seems to have a very deep and widespread appeal for children. Exhibiting and reviewing their products gives them great satisfaction. Whatever they write beyond notes should be pinned up, projected, enacted, and compiled. As much use as possible should always be made of pupil writing. Papers should not end up on the teacher's desk. The child needs to feel strong reasons for bothering to put what he has to say on paper.

Pinning papers up for display, printing them for distribution, discussing them in groups — all provide motivation. All such broadcasting and preserving makes the abstraction of writing gratifyingly physical and social.

The principle underlying many of these learning activities is that children should in large measure write their own literature. Too many children think of themselves only as "consumers" and not as users of language. As creator one is more appreciative and discerning about others' creations. Moreover, when children write, they read more, they become more involved in language, they get caught up in cycles of giving and taking words that gather momentum and accelerate progress in both reading and writing.

THE WRITING WORKSHOP

Much of the writing at this age is composed by groups, as explained in succeeding chapters. In this case, members of each group revise sentences as they are proposed, and proofread them after the scribe has written them down. Out of collective composition develops the writing workshop, of which much will be made in this curriculum. Instituted to handle individual composition, it works like this: the class is broken into groups of three to six and directed to pass around papers they have just written, to read them, and to talk about them. The purposes are to provide each paper with peer reactions and to prepare it for printing. Pupils respond spontaneously to each other's writing and also make suggestions for changes, including but not dwelling on corrections of spelling and punctuation. Marginal notations of a proofreading sort are made, but at this age most other comments and suggestions are exchanged orally. These groups have dictionaries available to help them resolve uncertainties about spellings, and the teacher is available to help generally. For now, the responding to content and manner is left to the children themselves. Many other activities however, will influence their responses to and suggestions about each other's writing. What comes out in these group sessions will be the spontaneous reflection of much other learning experience, such as reading in literature, dramatic work, and punctuation practice, to name only a few. Although I will have occasion later to say more about the workshop, the reader may note for himself, as he reads on, a number of practices occurring outside the workshop that will sharpen the responses and suggestions that children will make within it.

THE TEACHER'S ROLE

In my view, there is no need for the teacher to write comments on pupil compositions or to grade them. For one thing, some of the writing at this age is composed by groups. For another, punctuation and spelling are not taught by marking papers. The teacher should give some help *during* the writing, by consulting, and, in a general way, *before* the writing, by means of other activities. As for grades, I suggest making general assessments of pupils' work by observing it closely — a procedure that the role of the teacher in this program makes more feasible, since he is free to pass among the groups, where he can both observe and respond to the work of his pupils. The printing of papers allows him to review conveniently the writing of different children. Of course, any teacher should have the right to remark on pupil writing, if only to encourage or appreciate, but I feel strongly that children should begin their careers thinking of the class as more the audience than the teacher, who should avoid making himself the source of evaluation. His paramount mission is to make group process so effective that children can teach each other.

Chapter 8

Writing Down

Writing down is the recording of ongoing events. It refers to note taking and transcribing. The child writes down what he perceives as he is perceiving it. What may be written down divides into two main categories — perceptions of outer things like sights and sounds, and perceptions of inner things like thoughts and feelings. A specialized kind of sensory data, moreover, is human speech. Thus vocal sounds make up a special subdivision of external perception. Three kinds of writing ensue from these categories — sensory, recording, dictation, and calendar keeping. All three go on concurrently, but I will take up sensory recording first.

Sensory Recording

My experiments with the following assignments were done in classes combining fourth- and fifth-graders, but the teachers there concluded that the activities should be moved down to the first three grades. They felt not only that younger children could do them but that they should, so that teachers in grades four to six could count on this background and thus launch their pupils into the fuller kind of sensory recording treated in Chapter 13. Sensory recording in grades one to three is distinguished from that in grades four to six by three differences: (1) the younger pupils record stimuli in school instead of outside; (2) they begin by recording one sense at a time instead of all at once; (3) they make fewer decisions about what to record. This principle of progressing from the more structured to the freer framework accords with other sequences recommended in this program and with the consensus among elementary teachers that smaller children need stronger guidelines for unfamiliar activities. Isolating the senses creates a small focus, to train observational attention and to eliminate choices between senses.

MOTIVES FOR OBSERVING AND FOR WRITING OBSERVATIONS

Even more than adults, children look *for* and listen *for*. Looking and listening for their own sake are rare and sophisticated. Though an infant's attention is diffuse, we all begin very early to tune in and out, to select according to our desires and fears. To say that children have a great curiosity and live in close touch with things in nature is not to say that their observation is pure and even. By school age their behavior is seldom random; it appears so to us only because we do not understand their selectors, the psychic focal points around which they are organizing the world. What I am getting at is a motivational issue: adults' efforts to train children to observe objectively are somewhat at odds with the child's reasons for looking and listening, which relate to private concerns. We should honor his more primal motivation by selecting stimuli likely to engage his attention, while at the same time directing him to focus where he might not have of his own accord, so that he may achieve some autonomy from his drives and observe more objectively what lies around him.

In other words, when we focus pupils on something, what motivation other than sheer obedience can we count on that will keep their attention where we have directed it? Excitation is one. It is true, however, that sensory excitation is to some extent a pleasure for them in itself, and that the range of attention is relative to the amount of anxiety a child feels about his desires and fears as he goes seeking and avoiding. The pleasure in games is another motivation, but too often we teachers rationalize ill-motivated exercises by calling them games even though the children do not perceive them as such. When we add to observing the *writing down* of observations, the plot thickens.

A general problem of writing at this age is: why write it when you can say it? To whom would the child be writing? And for what reason? Why do adults ever write? And why record? Why not just observe? Let us grant that elementary schoolers in general have a competence motive — to learn to do and become good at all sorts of crafts and skills valued by their social world and practiced by adolescents and adults. The competence motive is based on every individual's need to think well of himself, enjoy success, achieve things, and strengthen ego and identity. But, like game motivation, it can easily be abused, and when children discover that they have worked hard at something that is not "real" after all but just a teacher's invention for his own purposes, they feel cheated and resentful. This is a great source of cynicism among students of all ages. The younger the children are, the more willing they are to do something just because some adult asks them to. Although this compliance seems to simplify the problem of motivation, when looked at another way it means there is less check from the pupil against teacher irresponsibility. Truly absurd teaching practices could go off without a hitch, and the wish to comply could be relied on entirely even when more mature motives should be emerging and getting exercise. Unconsciously, moreover, pupils can defeat assignments even when they wish to comply, and attention in particular is notoriously hard for the conscious will to control.

These considerations, which may seem over-subtle at first, were prompted by experiments and by ensuing discussions with the teachers. That is, the pupils' response to my first version of the sensory recording assignments indicated that, even when the writing came out well, the teachers had to rely far too much on compliance. There was not enough pleasure and purpose. I could too easily envision these children in junior and senior high school still doing writing chores out of obedience, perfunctorily and not very profitably. So, while conditionally accepting the game, compliance, and competence motivations, I decided that sensory recording posed a special difficulty that could be solved only by embedding it in another activity for which motivation was assured.

To observe objectively and to write down observations for their own sake asked too much of the children, even in fourth and fifth grades, when the assignment was thus baldly presented. Second- and third-graders soon lost interest when asked on unrelated occasions to observe animals and merely say what they saw. But when they kept animals in the class for several weeks, cared for them, lived with them, and experimented with them, they not only observed them closely but they talked constantly about them, and wrote more about them than the teacher could have hoped for.

The lesson I learned — and this is why I have dwelled so long on this whole issue — is that a familiar, pleasurable, and well motivated activity can provide the context that will in turn motivate a new, different, and more advanced activity. With good gearing, motor power can drive an action that at first glance seems too remote. If objective regarding and recording are entailed in fulfilling a more basic and subjective intent, then children become engaged in it and learning occurs. These considerations of learning motivation, and the principle of engagement, will apply to other and future assignments, especially in the least natural domain of discourse — writing.

Posting these remarks as an introduction to sensory writing, I will turn now to two activities based on game and competence motives only but not, I believe, abusing them. These activities will prepare for much more extensive sensory recording, which henceforth will be assimilated into long-range projects, described in Chapter 9, Writing Up.

THE RECORDING OF SOUND

Pre-writing practice. Focusing on sound can begin in simple relaxation periods. "Rest, close your eyes, and listen. Relax completely and hear as many sounds as you can." After several minutes: "How many *far away* sounds do you hear?" Afterwards ask the children to list orally and compare the sounds they heard. Such a five-minute session should occur outdoors and in other places about the school as well as in the classroom.

With this background of listening and of saying what they have heard, the class can proceed to writing down the sounds. The stimuli may be either natural sounds around the school or ones taped by teachers elsewhere. Since school sounds will be limited, tapes would increase the range considerably. Also, when the children do not know the sources of the sound, an interesting game can be made of identifying the site where the tape was made and the actions producing the sounds.

Differences between sounds and sights. The isolated sense of hearing differs from sight in two ways that are obvious and yet not often considered. The experiments made me think seriously about these differences. One is that sound *must* issue from actions whereas sights *may* be and often are of still things. For a sound to be produced, something must happen, whereas what one sees may be action but it may equally well be static, a still-life. Hence sound falls into a sequence of happenings, and a record of them automatically becomes a story of sorts. (This movement in time makes part of the difference between music and painting.) Second, since hearing alone gives us very limited information, we are forced to *infer* more than we do when looking. Usually, of course, we synthesize hearing and seeing to get the facts, but even by itself seeing informs us more fully than hearing and therefore requires less inference.

These two differences help to define the recording of sound: it is action-centered, and it involves some guessing. Both are qualities children like. But, further, it can teach chronology and interpretation. For the latter, tapes are obviously better, since children taken on location to record receive a lot of information about the setting and possible actions even though their eyes may be on their papers during the listening period. Another advantage of taping is that setting and actions can be chosen for their particular interest to children. It is important, however, not to jam the tapes with sounds but rather to capture a series of distinct sounds that enables the children to distinguish them and that gives them time to write.

Writing down sounds. After the stage of listening without writing, place the class in the sound locale or play a tape to them. A home-made tape might present a short and simple sequence such as someone going out a door, whistling for a dog, placing a bowl down, and patting the dog while he eats. Distribute overhead projector transparencies and grease pencils to the children. Tell them that this time they are going to try to capture on paper what they hear, by writing it down in a short form. "Short form" means that they do not have to use whole sentences and keep repeating "I hear . . ." They are going to "take notes," an expression that will be used a lot and that relates to their work as scribes. To save time, they may write single words and short phrases. Tell them not to worry about getting down everything but to capture as much as they can; tell them also not to worry about spelling but to make good guesses. The latter is especially important, since one purpose of the assignment is to activate their knowledge of sound-letter relations through the effort to spell words they can pronounce. Recording should probably have an upper limit of ten minutes.

Discussing the order of recorded sounds. Immediately afterwards, or upon returning to the classroom, lead a discussion with the whole class of what they wrote. (After about the first two sessions, once a model has been established, this discussion is relegated to small groups.) Project one of the transparencies and say that they are going to put together a sound story from their notes. "Probably no one person could note all the sounds by himself, and some of you may have heard things that others didn't hear. So we will fill out the recording together." Read aloud the sounds on the transparency, then ask, "What other sounds did *you* hear?" As these additions are enumerated, write them on the transparency. But *where* do they go — before and after which other sounds? This leads not only to establishing chronological order but also to distinguishing it from simultaneity (sounds occurring together), and from repetition (recurring sounds). Discussing these temporal matters naturally entails using corresponding verb tenses and aspects — perfect, progressive, and repetitive ("keep"). Help the class set the record straight, writing on the transparency the sound events in order of occurrence, placing simultaneous sounds side by side, and inserting repeated sounds at points where the children agree that they occurred.

Discussing the form of notation. A second issue for discussion concerns the form of notation. Whether this should be brought up on another occasion is perhaps something for the teacher to decide in the light of his pupils' maturity and readiness. At any rate, looking at the transparency being projected, remark that some words tell the thing making the sound (*bell, airplane*), other words tell the action (*scraping*), and other words describe the sound (*click*). Sometimes a phrase may combine these (*bells ring, foot scraping, click of metal*). Point to the words that exemplify these different ways of recording, and remark that this pupil used all of one kind, or mixed them, or used more of one than the other. Put on another transparency and ask them which ways of noting *that* pupil used. Then direct them to look at their own recording and notice what they did. Finally, ask them which kinds of words do which things best. What do you want to know — the object involved, the action causing the sound, or what the sound is like?

The point, of course, is that recording, or note-taking, forces us to sacrifice some information for other information; things have to be left out. Also, the basic parts of speech are focused on in this way without being formalized —

nouns, verb forms, and sometimes adjectives (*loud banging*). *Foot scraping* comes closest to a sentence, having subject and predicate elements; it is the kernel of a kernel sentence. These two points are related as the practical matter of which kinds of words have which advantages for recording which kinds of information. This they discuss by means of particular items projected before them. I am not sure how far discussion at this age can pursue the matter — certainly not far at one sitting — but the teacher should set it before the class so that small groups will carry it on as far as they can. Later recording, for a specific purpose, will require choosing among alternative ways of noting that will yield different kinds of information.

A fine opportunity exists here to increase and refine vocabulary. While comparing variant wordings, children can discuss whether *bell* or *buzzer* is the best word for the sound source, whether the bell *rang* or *tinkled*. Sometimes only one child may know the correct name for something heard (*air conditioner*), but that name is then made available to the whole class. And the teacher can supply vocabulary.

Correcting spelling. The third issue the teacher deals with before the class is spelling. I place it at the end of discussion so that the children will, in their minds, place content before mechanics, but it will be a natural concern of pupils acquiring the competence of matching their oral vocabulary to written symbols. During the earliest sessions, make it clear that you expect misspelling and that they are going to help each other learn to spell by trading knowledge. Children do not, of course, misspell the same words or have trouble with the same phonic problems. Since they are recording the same sounds, however, they will be trying to spell a number of words in common. Ask them which words on the transparency are misspelled and what the correct spellings are. Since pupils will be generally expected to get spellings from each other or the dictionary, instead of relying on the teacher, supply only the spellings no pupil knows and only for words common to many of the recordings. Instead of writing these on the board, spell them orally so that the children will write them from the spelling, not merely copy them on their recording. Your spelling out gives them the sound particles and their own writing gives them the visual whole. (The literacy program is assumed to be over at this point.)

Recording on paper in groups. After two or three sessions, paper replaces transparencies, the class breaks into about five groups, and tapes become the only sound source. The groups are directed to do essentially what the whole class has done before except that now they have the general mission of guessing where the tape was made and what was going on there. Whereas the school sound recording drew only on compliance and competence motives, now game motivation is added. One child in each group is appointed as leader.

He is to read his list of sounds, ask his colleagues what else they heard, and write additions onto his paper. Again they discuss when the sounds occurred in relation to each other. Since they did not see the objects and actions producing the sounds, which in most cases could have been made in different ways, the effort to determine which items in a record are the same or different sounds will naturally cause the pupils to discuss differences in how they named them. They may discuss which names are best and which assume more than they know (words for sounds are safest, words for actions less so, and words for objects least). If one child challenges another's item *wheel turning*, he is questioning not just the other's wording but the amount of inference he made. But all he says is "How do you know it was a wheel?" Is that the same sound as someone else's item *clicking*? To answer that, they have to check where the two items came in the sound sequence.

In other words, merely comparing their recordings carefully ensures discussion of several important relations of words to things. This is basically their task, but of course the teacher cannot put it in that way. He has to recall to them the earlier discussion he led and state distinctly what they did then — collect everybody's sounds, put them in order, and find out what different words they used for the same sounds.

The second mission, the children are told, is to help each other get spellings right. They are to ask each other for spellings and then to pass around papers to check quickly for misspellings of words that the authors thought were correct and therefore did not ask about. If they are sure of how to spell a word that they see is written wrong, they are to change it and tell the author. Words that none know how to spell are looked up in a dictionary or saved for the teacher, who circulates among the groups helping with discussion problems and also with spelling, to the extent of answering questions about whether a spelling is right or not, referring to their sound-letter training when appropriate. While offering this kind of consultation about spelling, the teacher makes it ultimately the pupils' responsibility.

When the class is reunited, the leaders are asked to report what their groups decided was the locale and action of the tape. The climax of the game element in these sessions comes when the teacher tells them what is happening on the tape. (Clearly, some skill is needed to tape a sound sequence that is neither too easy nor too difficult to guess.)

As with all assignments in this program, the purpose is multiple. Though focused on rendering the sense of hearing into words, these sessions give practice also in reading, talking, reasoning, and writing. Seen simply, all note taking at this age merely provides one sort of occasion for children to write informally and fragmentarily before they are ready to write connected pieces comprised of whole sentences. It is a realistic kind of discourse for which isolated words and phrases are quite appropriate. The audience is the author himself and the members of his working party. This kind of writing can be contrasted for pupils with other kinds of writing, perhaps having other kinds of audiences, for which full and connected sentences are appropriate.

RECORDING THE SENSE OF TOUCH

General procedure. Recording tactile sensations also operates on essentially a game motivation. Place a lot of tactually interesting objects, recognizable when *seen* by these children, in five bags and give a bag to each group. One child reaches in and feels one of the objects, without seeing or revealing it, and says aloud what he feels — the shape, texture, consistency, and so on — but without *naming* it even if he thinks he can identify it. The others of the group write down what he says as well as they can keep up with him. (For examples of this kind of writing, done by fourth- and fifth-graders, see page 180.) It should be explained that each person may miss some things the "feeler" says, but that the group as a whole will probably be able to piece his words together later. "Just write down key words." These monologues are usually brief.

Afterwards, the group drafts a composite account of what he said, that is, a tactile description of the object, and this will be read before the class later so that the other groups can try to guess what it is. There will probably be time for only two people to be "feelers," but the others can get their turns on another day. Before the groups break up, they are allowed to see the objects they described from their bags but keep the secret within the groups. Their pleasure then is in seeing if the rest of the class can identify the object when one of them reads the description of it. In addition, these descriptions will be put together as a kind of riddle book and exchanged with those in other classes. These purposes are of course explained in advance.

To compose the description, one pupil reads to the group what he wrote down on his paper; the others make additions and, with the help of the speaker, settle on a rendering. Besides help with spellings, the teacher makes one specific suggestion: if the description so far composed repeats "It is . . ." and "It has . . . ," explain that these sentences can be combined by using series (a series of adjectives for "It is . . ." and a series of nouns for "It has . . .") and that commas are used to separate items in the series. Say that this shortening will make it possible to read a lot of riddle descriptions before the class and will save space in the books. This is the first step toward the economy of predication that results from combining several short sentences into one elaborated sentence ("embedding," in terms of transformational grammar).

Purposes. Children can learn several things from this activity besides verbalizing their sense of touch, which of course is learning one way to describe. As stenographers, they are taking dictation. As drafters of something to be read to the class and to be passed to other classes, they are composing and editing. As guessers themselves of what each object is, they can learn, by their absence, how names simplify identification and, conversely, how much can be said about a thing that does not appear in the name. Difficulty in guessing an object relates to the low sensory level of tactile information; ease in guessing relates to how *telling* the particular details are, whether the details mentioned are characteristic of many objects or of only a few, and whether these details combine to evoke the whole of the object. These matters could become a discussion topic either in the "feeling" groups or in small discussion groups given a set of riddle descriptions from another class and asked, of each piece read, "What makes this easy (or hard) to guess?" By way of summarizing that discussion, the question can be asked in a general way: "What makes some touch descriptions easy and some others hard?"

By third grade, pupils can probably be paired, one partner feeling and the other taking down what he says. Then they draft the description together and reverse roles.

Taking Dictation

Much more will be made of speech transcription in grades four to six than now. But besides the two forms of it already mentioned — taking down letter sounds and words dictated by the teacher during the literacy program, and taking down tactile descriptions by classmates — another sort can be undertaken during these years. The children transcribe whole short sentences dictated by the teacher.

Teacher Dictation of Short Passages

Choose interesting sentences that tell a story or have some other continuity. Use suspense to make dictation fun. The slow unfolding of a text makes the punch line of jokes more effective. A riddle contrasts question and statement intonations. Poems too are excellent for dictation if the ends of poetic lines correspond to the ends of sentences; otherwise, the two kinds of termination are at odds. Texts may be selected from booklets of pupil writing as well as from books. Before dictating the text, announce that you are going to read a sentence at a time. Choose sentences at first that have no internal punctuation. This means that every segment dictated will implicitly define what a sentence is. All they have to do with punctuation is put in capitals, periods, question marks, and exclamation marks. Although this sort of dictation is an important way of teaching the sentence, the emphasis is on spelling, the activation of word memory and phonic knowledge.

Whenever the children are ready for it, the next step is to dictate sentences having internal punctuation — half-drops and slight pauses for commas. Choose passages containing constructions the pupils themselves are starting to use in their own writing — series, offset phrases, perhaps some subordinate clauses. Since each sentence must be read off as a whole intonational contour, some children may have difficulty retaining the entire sentence in their minds until they can write it. Allow for these limitations of retention and writing speed by choosing rather short sentences and by repeating them.

Function of teacher dictation. I confess to some mixed feelings about dictation. Though confident that it will help a great deal to reduce the purely transcriptive problems of their own writing, I think it holds a limited interest for children. Compliance and competence motives, and some measure of game motive, may keep it interesting for a while, but the older the child, the weaker the motivation. Also, I hate to see children spending very much time copying when they could be composing. So I suggest that teachers play up the other ways by which the speech-print equivalence may be taught — reading aloud, listening and following the text as the teacher reads, choral reading, and perhaps most of all, doing genuine writing in collaborative groups. To the extent that these activities fail to clear up transcriptive problems, however, dictation may be in order. If spelling is coming along well but you feel that internal punctuation needs strengthening, ditto an interesting passage without its punctuation, read it aloud, and have the pupils write in the commas and periods on their copies. (For more about this procedure, see page 177.)

It is important to make clear that the whole point of teaching spelling and punctuation through dictation is to separate transcription from composition, in accordance with the principle stated earlier. When really *writing*, children should feel uninhibited by concern for spelling and punctuation, drawing spontaneously on what they have learned about these things in other contexts. (One such context is group proofreading, which *follows* composing.) Children should be encouraged to write any words, use any sentence structures, that come into their heads. The teacher does not write corrections of mechanics on their papers. Composition should *reflect* skill in spelling and punctuating; it is not the place to *teach* that skill. And we have to remember that, if children read and write a lot, spelling and punctuation gradually become more correct anyway, even without specific teaching. Children writing freely whatever they are capable of saying will make many more errors than those writing only what they know they can transcribe correctly. It is far preferable to give dictation than to spoil the writing flow by inducing fear of error.

Calendars and Letters

Noting down inner perceptions takes the form of brief entries in a homemade, personal calendar.

Procedures

The children cut up sheets of light-colored paper into squares about seven by nine inches, punch two holes along the nine-inch edge, and place enough of these leaves onto two notebook rings to equal the days of the oncoming month. With crayons or colored felt markers, they write at the top of each leaf the month, day of week, and date. This repeated writing of the names for the days and months should ensure their learning to spell them.

The children are told before they make the calendars what they will do with them. A few minutes each day will be set aside especially for them to make entries. These can be of two kinds — reminders for the immediate future and remembrances of the immediate past. The children turn to the leaf for today, look to see what they have written on it before, then write down on future leaves what they or their family are going to do. (Looking back prompts memories.) Then, on the leaf for today or yesterday, they note things that they did then, or that happened then that they would like to remember later. Explain that many adults write notes to themselves on a calendar so that they will remember things they have planned to do; the notes usually say what, when, where, who, and perhaps other things. Show them how to write times and distinguish the halves of the day — 6:00 A.M., 5:00 P.M. Then say that some people keep a diary of what they do and what happens around them so that they can look back later and recall what went on. This is like writing a real day-to-day story in pieces.

The children should understand that the calendars are theirs, that they will keep them at the end of the year, and that the teacher will not look at them unless asked to. They write for themselves, in whatever way the words come, not being held to complete sentences or to dressing things up for the teacher. They may draw decorations and illustrations on the calendar. Remind them, however, that if they do not write clearly, they may not be able to read their entries later.

Purposes

Keeping calendars helps to develop an objective sense of time, which in turn facilitates kinds of thinking based on it. Planning, tying events together, continuity, cause and effect, cyclic regularity, and the consistency of the self all relate to the public concept of time. Chronologic is, after all, a form of logic. This is not to say that it should replace the child's subjective sense of living in a timeless moment, to which he has a right and which has an existential reality not to be supplanted. Being practical and official, calendars are an appropriate learning to associate with the *public* concept of time. (Children's spontaneous stories, on the other hand, should not be brought into this association by imposing chronology on them.) We know that a serious difficulty among severely underpriviledged children is that life seems chaotic; there is no continuity, order, progression, or relation among events. This is true both of how they live and of how they talk about life. The result is both an emotional and a cognitive deficit; security and sense of self are weak, and temporal and causal ways of thinking are limited. Such children especially would benefit from calendar keeping.

But mainly, for all pupils, keeping calendars is writing practice of a real and well motivated sort, a variant of recording that can serve in turn as base for other writing. Differences are the future-oriented aspect, the more personal subject matter, and the necessarily more summary nature of the notes, which capsulize rather than actually record. In a sense, however, calendar keeping *is* an ongoing record — of what is passing through the child's mind during the five or so minutes. (Recording of thought streams will be pursued later.) Also, calendar keeping accompanies nature journals during the same years and lays a foundation for personal diaries recommended for later.

WRITING CALENDAR ENTRIES AS LETTERS

Periodically, the pupils are told that they may write a letter to someone telling what they have been doing recently, using their calendars as reference. I am uncertain how long the period should be — a whole month or less — and the teacher may want to let different children write at different times, perhaps awaiting individual urges. At any rate, they decide first whom they want to write to, then read through their calendars and pick out events that they want to tell that person about and think he would like to hear. Then they write a newsy letter covering many things or dwelling on only a few. The teacher demonstrates on the board the form of dating, greeting, and closing, and the address positions on the envelope. They bring to school a stamped envelope and the address of their party. After reminding them that the postman cannot send their letter unless he can read the name, street, and city, the teacher tells them to address their envelope and ask a neighbor if he can read it. They post their letters in a mailbox replica made for the classroom and understand that the teacher will put them in a real mailbox; or if possible, they walk with the teacher to a mailbox near the school.

Besides motivating the writing, the letters provide an outside audience, and one at whom the content is especially directed. Of course, once introduced, writing letters need not depend on calendar keeping; the children may be asked occasionally if they would like to write a letter and then given time for it and help with it.

Chapter 9

Writing Up

"Writing up" refers to final writing that takes off from talk or notes and results in something complete for an audience or an overall purpose. As such, it digests other work and takes on a more public form requiring whole sentences and connectedness. It occurs in long-range projects such as I have only alluded to so far but will now treat in more detail. I can see two main kinds of projects, both lasting several weeks.

Burning Issues

The first kind of project is like the campaign against stealing and must necessarily be stated in an open and general way, since the subject comes from the pupils and the exact stages of the procedure will vary according to their intention. In Chapter 4, "Speaking Up," I described the process that two classes of second- and third-graders went through in order to determine the reasons for stealing and to propose remedies. It remains only to dwell a little on the part of the project involving writing up. The publication called *Beta-Gram* that the one class produced consisted of eight kinds of items or articles arrived at by small- and large-group discussion from which notes were made. Each child drafted an article, which the members of his group, acting as an editorial board, read and criticized for content and mechanics. These were rewritten and one or two from each group were chosen for printing. The audience and purpose of *Beta-Gram* were clear in the children's minds. A less desirable aspect, perhaps, was that not all articles were used.

What distinguishes this project is the writing up from discussions rather than from observations. The only facts involved were common experience and the questionnaire. This sort of project stems from feelings about moral or social matters and aims to treat these concerns in a tangible form. Such a campaign might germinate in one of the small-group discussions if the topic hits on some "burning issue" that the children want to pursue by other means than talk. "Other means" will not always entail writing but often will. (One class in the stealing project did posters.) The *Beta-Gram* that resulted from the experimental project is reprinted below. Since the contributions were screened, these generally were the best.

BETA SURVEY

As you remember Beta had a worksheet. It asked if you lost a pen or pencil this week. Then it asked how you felt about it. Some boys and girls said:

1. I feel badly because I don't have anymore.
2. I feel badly because I don't have anything to write with.
3. I don't feel badly because I have plenty left.
4. I feel good about it because I didn't lose any.

It also asked if you ever stole a pencil or pen. This is what some people replied:

1. People steal mine.
2. I found it, no one was around so I kept it.
3. It's not fair to the owner.
4. I wouldn't like it if somebody took mine.
5. I know it is wrong.

The worksheet also asked if you know a way to stop the stealing. There were lots of ideas. Here are some:

1. Put a mark on the pencils or put your name on it.
2. Have the children bring their pencils in a pencilcase.
3. Make them go to Mrs. Bears if they steal.
4. Keep them after school if they steal.

WHAT TO DO WITH LOST PROPERTY

If you find a pencil, troll, doll or anything of that sort give it to the teacher. When you lose something tell the teacher what you lost. If you find something put it in the lost and found box.

TALL TALE!

Bonnie Smith had lots of pencils stolen so she decided to find a way so people would not steal her pencils. She was talking about it in class. One of the boys had an idea. She decided to do it. She went to the store and got mouse traps. If someone tries to steal her pencils her fingers will get pinched.

The End

A Tall Tale

One day when I was in my room at school I herd the teacher yelling at Gurtrude Mcfuss for stealing a pencil. He "said" Gurtrude *why did* you steal that pencil?" But she would not say he did it. But finally she did. The teacher made her stay after for stealing and for lying "But when she got home she got in worst trouble. She went to bed with out any dinner That didn't help She just lying and stealing. She kepted going to bed with out any dinner and staying after school. Finally she learned she lesson. And thats how Gurturde Mcfuss learned her lesson. Never Steal!

If you don't want your toys or pencil's taken follow these simple rules:

1. Don't bring toy's to school unless necessary.
2. Keep your things in a box.
3. Give valuable things to your teacher.

Punishment for Robbers

This just might happen to you! If you steal pencils you will get into trouble. You may not get allowance for three weeks. You may get a spanking so watch out! Don't steal!

Wanted Posters

If you find this girl you will be rewarded 20¢

[Picture of one Pamela Cookie]

Beware she is a pencil thief. If you find the five pencils that she took you also will rewarded with 10¢. Bring her to 9–A They are all red pencils.

Advertisement

Beware! If you steal pencils, you better stop it now! But keep this in mind if you might start, don't steal anything! If you don't steal, keep pencils in safe places. And If you steal — at least tell the truth. If you find a pencil — don't keep it but give it to the teacher.

A Tall Tale

Michael Byrne had to stay after school for stealing four pencils and he had to stay after one and a half hours. He had to tell his mother and father on the telephone what he did. When he got home he had to do work. He got a beating. He had to go to bed at six-thirty.

Join the Good Citizens Club

To join the Good Citizens Club you have to have an application. It has to have your name, date that you joined, age, and homeroom. When you join the club you should do things that are good. You help people if they can't to it. You also do things for other people. Good Citizens never take things that belong to others, Bring the application to room 9–A

```
NAME _____

DATE _____

AGE _____

HOMEROOM _____
              Your Application, Good Citizen Club
```

LOST AND FOUND PAGE

A leather comb case.
It is brown.
If found return to 6–A Eva Arsenau.

Orange pen that writes red. If found
return to Tommy Harvey. Room 1.

Nature Study

The second kind of project stems from observation of living things selected by either teacher or pupil. External reality, not inner concern, is the point of departure. You may say, "We are going to observe how a tadpole grows into a frog, and keep a record of its growth," or a pupil may bring in a pet that the class wants to keep a journal on. One thing leads to another. I will describe more fully an animal project devised in one of the classes participating in the campaign against stealing.

ACCOUNT OF TRIALS

I mentioned before that the group of second- and third-grade children did not become very interested in the animals until they began to live with them and care for them. Then they were so involved that a project not only crystallized but proliferated in many sub-projects. There were rabbits, gerbils, guinea pigs, and rats. The children observed and wrote descriptions of the animals (without, I should add, having had the sort of literacy training in punctuation and sound-letter relations advocated in this book):

APPEARANCE

She has a long tail. She has little pinkish eyes. Her ears are curled a little. She has long teeth. She has long whiskers.

Appearance

Puddles is brown with a little white line on her head. She is small with little pointed ears. Her eyes are brown.

Appearance

Cleo is brown, black and white. She is fat and she has big feet. She has four toes and she runs around in her cage all the time.

Ogden is brownish. He has sharp teeth. He is nice. His Eyes are black. His tail has hair on it.

How he Looks

Ginger is a rabbit. Ginger is black and white. Gingers eyes are blue. Ginger has four toes. Ginger is cute. Gingers toes are white. The bottom of her back front paws are brownish gray.

Snowball

Snowball is white with red magic mark on her head so we can tell her from Whitey. She has long teeth. They are yellow. We have given her wood and meat t make her teeth shorter.

They made comparisons:

Snowball compared to puddles

They are different in color. Puddles has longer ears than Snowball. Snowball has a longer tail. Puddles has to be fed by Danny with an eye dropper.

Comparing Rabbits

I am comparing Puddles to the other rabbit but puddles is smaller and than Ginger who is older, But both of them are cute. Ginger is the other name of the rabbit. Ginger is black and white. Puddles drinks from from an eye dropper But Ginger eats lettuce.

Snowball

I compared Snowball the rat with Danny's baby rabbit. Snowball is bigger than the baby rabbit. Snowballs teeth are bigger than Dannys baby rabbit's. The rats eat a lot of food a day. Danny's babby rabbit gets fed by an eye-dropper.

They told where the animals came from:

Where Cleo came From

Cleo is a ginney pig. Cleo was born in a house. Cleo is 2 years old. Richard Parrish brought Cleo into school. The End

Where aminal came from.

Ginger and Sniffles came from West Acton. Ginger and sniffles are 4 months old. Ginger and Sniffles a my pet rabbits Ginger and Sniffles live in a very big cage.

Where Whitey came from.

Whitey came from a lab in Wilmington Mass. Mrs Glassmen got her. We've had Whitey 5 weeks. When we first got Whitey. She weighs four oz and now she weigh's eight oz.

Snowball

Snowball came from a Labratory and Mrs. Glassman gave Snowball to our class. We feed her meat and lettuce and carrots and all most any, thing. She needs a Clean cage.

Where Puddles came from.

She came from a side of a garden. Everyone was touching about a half a dozen rabbits. You know that if you touch a rabbits, the mother will go away.

Ogden

Gerbils are from a desert climate. Ogden came from a gerbil farm. Then Miss Hoffman   was nice enough to bring it to Franklin School.

They told how the animals behave and how they have to be cared for:

The Desert animals

The gerbils name is Ogden. A gerbils cage is not cleaned often. About once a mounth. They are so clean. They eat sun flower seeds.

Caring for Cleo.

You have to hold her firmly. She eats celery, carrots and lettuce. She doesn't eat meat. We have to let her out of her cage so she can get exercise. She is fun to play with.

Ginger drinks water and eat rabbits pellets. She is cleaned once a week. She has exercise every day of the week and she chases other rabbit too. She plays games like tag and house with the other rabbit.

You clean whitey's cage every day. You feed whitey two time's a day. You let whitey ran through the maze. We are teaching the rat's to ran through the maze   whitey sometimes forgets the way to ran.

PUDDLES

She has to be fed often. Danny feeds her with an eye dropper.

TEACHING SNOWBALL

We have a maze. a rat starts am one side and is suppose to turn the corner. snoball is learning. But over the wekend she forgets

After the teacher wrote the first entry of the journal on a lined sheet and pinned it to the bulletin board, they took turns writing entries:

March 30, 1966
Cleo was to stuborn to come out of his cage. All she did was crawaled under newspapers. And messed up the cage.

whitey pedoon my hand and pam put white in a pisc of popor and snowbal did number to on debby hand The ene

April 4, 1966
Cleo was near the back black board. Cleo has no exercise. He was curious about his surroundings. He was eatting the papper I put on the floor.

April 5, 1966
Cleo would'nt come of. But at take us two miutes to get cleo out.

April 12, 1966
10:7 Snowball and Witey was resing. Cleo was on the pice of wood Then he was in the right hand eating the rabbit pelits.

Tue. 29
We got are rats. and we wher quiet. And our sturburn guine pig cleo would not come out of his cage. and when we got him out of his cage he wen't all over the room. and his cage was as messy as could be

One interesting report from the teachers was that the project stimulated many children to write who had been "non-writers" before, that is, pupils who had, because of difficulty and poor motivation, already begun to feel that writing was not for them.

Later, each child kept his own journal. In addition, they took the animals home on weekends and wrote an account of the animals' activities so that the rest of the class would not miss anything. They looked up related information. They visited the science museum. They ended by teaching rats to run a maze and keeping a journal on this experiment. Some of these ideas originated with the teacher, most with the children. The "project" was really a complex of activities thought up along the way. Teachers experienced in improvising this way can start with only an inspiration and not plan very much. This is ideal and undoubtedly the best "teaching method" in veteran hands. But many teachers will need at least a base plan from which to depart until they gain assurance.

RECOMMENDED NATURE PROJECT

A simple structure for an observation project is the physical development of some growing animal or plant. Bring in a bird or reptile egg, a newborn mammal, larvae, or tadpoles. Explain that the class is going to care for the creature and watch it grow up, but do not describe the course of growth in advance; their discovery will make it more fun. Tell them the food, temperature, and other requirements, and arrange a caretaking routine. Since waiting for an egg to hatch[1] or an animal to reach a new stage may leave little to observe at times, it is best to have a couple of things growing at once. Observation need not be daily if little is happening. With planning — and luck — the teacher can have the children record special events like births, moltings, and metamorphoses. And they can observe at times when particular events are taking place, such as the feeding of ladybugs to leopard frogs. Nature study should not be just cute — it can include preying and mating. The cycles and relationships in nature will teach the most and provide the most interesting material for recording. The child is rare, if he exists, who is not entranced by watching a caterpillar become a butterfly.

An alternative to growth as a project structure is the complex workings of social insects. It is possible to buy "ant farms" that have a transparent wall for observing. Or teaching animals to run a maze, by a reinforcement schedule of feeding, would provide an excellent structure.

It is in this way that sensory recording becomes integrated into projects. The stimuli are living things that interest children and that can be brought into class — animals and plants of all sorts. For this age the more the subject moves the better, although once involved in a project children do become motivated to observe small changes from day to day, if, say, they are growing certain plants, culture molds, or crystals. Since the foundation of science is observation, noting down sensations places pupils in the basic role of the scientist or naturalist. In fact, the children are told that they are going to "be" scientists and do one of the things scientists do.

Focusing on single senses. In order to focus on one sense at a time, choose a subject that naturally features one sense. For example, all one can do with underwater creatures in a tank is *watch* them; fish or seahorses would be good subjects. Or have the children watch the subject on one occasion and feel it on another. Observation of animals is mostly visual except for occasional sounds and smells. But of course mixing senses in a recording is ulti-

---

[1] A hatcher costs about $5. *A Sourcebook for Elementary Science* by Joseph and Victor Hone (New York: Harcourt, Brace & World, Inc., 1962) contains helpful information about caring for animals as well as suggestions for science projects.

mately desirable; the only reason for taking them one at a time is to increase acuity by focus and to simplify the task for beginners. We know from the experience of blind people that blocking out some senses increases the keenness of the others. We also know that asking younger children to write down all of their sensations is too vague and bewildering. Although silent movies and still photographs isolate vision, they are not practical. Children cannot write while they watch a film. And photographs are not only static, they present *simultaneously* an infinite amount of detail and therefore too many arbitrary choices of what to note down.

After working with isolated senses, tell the children to observe everything they can about their subject — to feel it, smell it, and (when safe) taste it as well as look and listen. While visiting one third-grade class that was recording what happened to candle flames when various things were done to them, I noticed that several group papers contained sentences beginning with *if-* and *when-* clauses, which appear rather rarely in the writing of children this age. Then I realized that it was their physical manipulations of the candles that were causing these sentence constructions: "If I put a jar over the candle, the flame goes out," or "When we throw alum on the flame, it turns blue." This is typical, I believe, of the organic way in which experiencing and thinking should lead to increased language complexity.

SPECIFIC PROCEDURES

Whatever the subject or the sense being focused on, the procedure is to let the children observe and record for five or ten minutes, in small groups or as a class body, depending on which is more practical for the subject, then to discuss their notes in groups of four or five. The function of the notes is, first, to remind each pupil of what he observed so he can "compare notes" with his colleagues and, second, to provide specific words, phrases, and observations for a group write-up of a collective recording. A scribe writes down on his paper what the others dictate to him from their notes. They discuss which items overlap, which wording of an observation is better, what the order of actions was, and which spellings are incorrect. Presumably, disagreements will arise about what was seen, interpretations of what was seen, and accuracy of color, shape, movement, and so on. Then, as the scribe writes on a fresh sheet of paper, they compose the account by suggesting and agreeing on sentences, an operation that involves discussing where sentences should begin and end, which words are capitalized, and perhaps other problems of mechanics. As the teacher passes among the groups, they call on him for help. The goal of this collaboration is to produce a full record of their observations, written in continuous prose.

Making books. The children are told at the outset that they will keep a journal and make a book. In effect, they will be writing their own science texts. The book will be on an individual animal or plant, or on a group of them. It will include the journal, a summary of the journal, drawings, and perhaps other pupil-created material. The first few times such a project is done, the journal and the book are group-written. By third grade, say, each individual can do his own.

A suggested program for the book collaboration goes like this: After observing and taking notes, the pupils collate their individual notes in small-group discussion, then write together their journal entry for that day (including the date). Weighing growing animals can provide additional data. Since a lot of the same words are used over and over, these can be gradually added to a long-standing list on the board, which pupils can consult for vocabulary and spelling. The entries are accumulated in a previously prepared booklet cover. Some observing sessions can be devoted to drawing pictures of the subject while watching it. These drawings can be dated and captioned to explain, for example, what the animal was doing at the time, and added to the booklet. At the end of the growth period or at some other appropriate time, each group meets to read over its whole journal and write a summary of it. Members of the group take turns reading entries and showing the drawings.

The process at this point becomes one of topic-centered discussion, the topic being something like "What are the changes Spot has gone through since he was born?" They discuss changes in appearance, behavior, feeding habits, weight, etc., referring to the journal for evidence. If the journal is about an ant farm, one would not expect the topic to get at development but at generalities in behavior: the routine operations and labor divisions of the colony. One would expect such a journal to record similar behavior on different occasions, so that gradually a general picture builds up. Thus the topic might be "What different kinds of ants are there and what does each kind do?" The journal might be summarized by asking several such questions and by writing up each separately. Discussion can serve to catch the gist of the journal. A scribe notes the ideas as the summary is going on, and the group rewrites these notes into the summary to appear at the end of the book. They check spellings and discuss where sentences should end.

Either teacher or pupils may have other ideas for writing to go into the book, perhaps arising out of some projects inspired along the way. Making the book not only motivates the writing part of the project but also fixes what they are learning and develops abstractive abilities. To avoid repetition of projects, teachers of kindergarten through grade six should work out a sequence designed to cover important kinds of knowledge.

Chapter 10

Playing Games of Language and Logic

Writing Telegrams[1]

The children are asked to write a message limited to 15, 20, or 25 words, depending perhaps both on the children's ability and on the complexity of the story situation surrounding the message. "You want a friend of yours to stay overnight with you. You send him a telegram inviting him and telling him what he should bring with him. You have to tell him all the information he will need, but you also want to keep down the cost of the telegram. Each word costs a nickel." Besides bringing arithmetic into the game, weighing the cost against the adequacy of the information sets up a requirement that a minimum of words should convey a maximum of meaning. Another situation concerns a message to Grandma cancelling an invitation to visit because a sister is sick.

When these two situations were tried out in the second and third grades at a private school with classes of 15,[2] the children were eager to write the messages and spontaneously began a discussion about the kinds of personal articles a friend would or would not need for overnight, and about whether the sister's sickness was contagious or posed some other obstacle to Grandma's visit. When tried out in the second and fourth grades of an urban Boston school serving very disadvantaged Negro children, the researcher, who was not a teacher and did not know the class, ran into several difficulties, most of

[1] I am indebted to Anita Rui for the essential idea of this and the following game, and for the account of trials with both. Under the auspices of the Teacher-Researcher Project of the Harvard Research and Development Center in Educational Differences, she tried the telegram game in urban Boston classes.

[2] Lesley-Ellis in Cambridge, Massachusetts.

them resulting, as she reported, from her not having prepared the pupils sufficiently. These children needed to learn first what telegrams are, and to have the whole session paced more slowly — two problems the regular teacher could predict and solve. Also, they had been so thoroughly enjoined in their earlier career to write whole sentences that they could not adjust easily to the idea of telegraphic writing. Children used to sensory note-taking, however, will not be surprised. Indeed, one value of the telegram game is to present another but different writing situation in which word economy is an issue. The situation is different because telegrams are addressed to another person, not just to oneself, and therefore must communicate. (Teachers who may be concerned, understandably, that the game will encourage the writing of non-sentences should see the following assignment.)

The telegrams are read aloud and compared, or projected if written on transparencies, the latter being preferable since it affords reading practice and several telegrams can be viewed at once, for comparison, by overlapping the transparencies on each other in staggered fashion. The children should have a chance to see how a number of their fellows dealt with the problem of information versus economy and to discuss loss of intelligibility, adequacy of information, and unnecessary words. In so doing, they can learn the risks as well as the advantages of stripping down language. As the Boston trials showed, children who are forbidden to write anything less than whole sentences may become *unable* to adapt writing to other needs.

Expanding Baby Talk

This unusual and very successful game was inspired by the research of the Harvard psycholinguists Roger Brown and Ursula Bellugi, who have been tracing from its early stages the language acquisition of a boy and girl by transcribing their conversations with their mothers. A critical feature of such conversations, they have found, is the mothers' expansions of their children's utterances. Here are some samples from Brown and Bellugi.

Child	*Mother*
Baby highchair	Baby is in the highchair.
Mommy eggnog	Mommy had her eggnog.
Eve lunch	Eve is having lunch.
Mommy sandwich	Mommy'll have a sandwich.
Sat wall	He sat on the wall.
Throw Daddy	Throw it to Daddy.
Pick glove	Pick the glove up.[3]

[3] "Three Processes in the Child's Acquisition of Syntax," in *Language and Learning,* edited by Janet Emig, James Fleming, and Helen Popps (New York: Harcourt, Brace, & World, Inc., 1966), p. 12.

PROCEDURE

Copies of some of Brown's and Bellugi's transcripts were used as scripts and acted out by children at the two schools where the telegrams were tried (the second and third grades at the private school, third and fourth grades at the urban school). They read the mother's and child's parts, adding some gesture and movement. Then they were given some of the child's utterances similar to those in the sample above and told to fill them out on paper in the manner the mothers had done in the dialogue. They read aloud their various expansions and compared them in discussions. The ambiguity of a child's utterances, which a mother can expand rather accurately from context, can lead, of course, to very different sentences when pupils expand them without knowing the context. As Brown and Bellugi point out in regard to the samples above, what the child omits are mostly functor words — auxiliaries, prepositions, verb forms, articles, and pronouns. In other samples, inflected endings indicating number, possession, and person are also omitted (*He go out. Daddy brief case.*). The pupils, of course, do not all assume the same subjects of the action, times of the action, relations among objects, and so on.

PURPOSES

In expanding these utterances and comparing expansions, the children may learn, generally, the risks of telegraphic speech and therefore the value of whole sentences and, specifically, the importance of functors and inflections and the ambiguity their omission creates. Moreover, they can grasp intuitively the relations between full and incomplete utterances and how these relations depend on certain "parts of speech," although these parts should not be named. Finally, lower-class Negroes who characteristically omit many of these functors and inflections may become aware of their own speech traits and of the resulting ambiguity (ambiguity at least for speakers of standard dialect). The game could then be a tactful way of helping them to expand their home-learned speech. Alternating this game with telegrams opens up a two-way street between expansion and abridgement so that the pupils can move *deliberately and awarely* between potential sentences and actual sentences, being limited to neither and able to choose either, according to their purpose. "Sentence fragments," we note, have nothing to do with this two-way process, since these are almost always lopped-off phrases or clauses (*Into the town. As soon as they left.*) that result either from poor punctuation or from reading too many Volkswagen advertisements.

This game went very well with both the private school and urban school children. Why it had such appeal is interesting. They seemed to enjoy very much feeling superior to the smaller children, being able to do more with speech than this "younger generation" can. Perhaps they liked being a baby again and at the same time being more than a baby. And of course the mother-child relationship is intrinsically interesting to them. The dramatic and story element is fortunate also; in fact, the game can inspire playlets and stories if the children are asked to write their own mother-child dialogues, or to take their expanded sentence and make a story around it.

A practical difficulty with the whole idea is in obtaining authentic transcripts to use. Since publishers are not loath to supply more material for schools, a strong enough demand would undoubtedly inspire them to print such dialogues. Pending this possibility, someone in the school system might tape a few conversations between a mother and her 18-month- to three-year-old child, or a mother in the community might make some up out of her experience. Incidently, this game, like some that follow, illustrates how similar some language research activities and some school learning practices can be. If more ventures were launched similar to the Teacher-Researcher Project at Harvard, under whose auspices the telegram and baby talk games were tried, each party would probably find the other a source of helpful ideas for his profession.

Scrabble-type Games

A regular scrabble board might be used, after the teacher has explained the rules of the game. The children play in groups of three or four, but if the waits between turns prove too long for some children, pairing might be better. Among other things, the game affords practice in using the dictionary, since the players must frequently consult an authority to find out if they are spelling a familiar word correctly or if a certain combination of letters creates some actual word or merely a phonetically possible word. A regular dictionary could go with each game board (special children's dictionaries might not contain enough unknown words). The game is, of course, one way of learning spelling and vocabulary. A less obvious feature is that trying out various letter combinations can reinforce phonic understanding and flexibility in assigning possible sound values to letters. For example, given the letters T–H–A, one child might add an N to form THAN, whereupon another might think of further adding K to form THANK, a move that would change the sound values of all four preceding letters.

Anagrams

Children who do not seem ready for scrabble (the crossing constellations of letters sometimes restrict rather severely the possibilities for further words) might begin with the simpler anagram type of game. The children are paired off and given a deck of homemade cards each of which bears one letter on one side, the more common letters occurring on more than one card. One child makes a word by picking up cards and forming a "hand" out of them. Then he shuffles that hand and gives it to his partner to unscramble into the original word. If the partner forms with the hand a real word other than the one intended, he must recombine the letters until he gets the intended word. Then partners turn about. Or the children might play the game as straight anagrams in the first place by trying to make up words that can become other words merely by transposing letters (re-ordering cards).

Unscrambling Words

Anagrams is based on combinational possibilities that can be extended to whole words or even sentences. One child writes a sentence on a strip of paper, cuts the strip between words, shuffles the words, and passes them to his partner to unscramble. Amusing possibilities can occur, of course, that the writer did not intend, and the scrambling has the appeal of secret codes. Children would, in effect, be playing with the syntactic possibilities of the language and with the syntactic ambiguity of many words that might be either nouns, verbs, or adjectives. The point of the game might be to get as many additional sentences as possible out of the set of words that forms an original sentence.

Unscrambling Sentences

Starting with a whole paragraph and unscrambling a mixed set of sentences leads to logical issues concerning which sequences of sentences can "make sense" and which cannot. The original sequence might sometimes be a story, sometimes a set of directions, sometimes something else, thus creating different logical problems. Although the point is to reconstruct the original sequence, the learning occurs in the trying out of different sequences and deciding which ones make sense. In watching his partner try out combinations, the writer can see alternatives to his original sequence that are equally logical.

Sentence Building

Again playing in pairs, one child makes up a sentence by placing word cards in a sequence, then his partner attempts to add to that sentence with other cards, then the first child tries to build further, and so on, the object being to make as long a sentence as they can. Thus:

> Bobby plays ball.
> After school Bobby plays ball.
> Every day after school Bobby plays ball with his friends.
> Every day after school Bobby plays football with his new friends.
> Every day after school Bobby plays football with his new friends until his mother calls him.
> Every day after school Bobby plays football with his new friends until his mother calls him to come eat supper.

This is at once an intriguing game and a very important practice in sentence expansion.

The word cards may be manufactured ones or ones that children have made or asked the teacher to write out for them. Since their private stock of word cards may contain only nouns, verbs, adjectives, and adverbs, they will encounter the need for other sorts of words — prepositions, determiners, and conjunctions. If provided with plenty of blank cards or slips, they can write new words on them as they play the game, and these additions can be added to their stocks for use on other occasions.

Purposes

The fact is that all such combinational games are at bottom logical. The differences among playing with letters, words, and sentences are in the hidden premises involved — whether these premises are spelling rules, syntactic rules, or the rules of common sense. Essentially, trying out the possibilities allowed for by the various rules develops meaningful choice, which in the case of whole words and sentences opens stylistic and rhetorical possibilities as well.

For similar creative games of word- and sentence-building, see Gattegno's *Words in Color* (page 89).

Checkers

Checkers, too, is basically a game of logical possibility. Deciding which moves to make on the board is a concrete way of syllogizing: "If I move here, then he may move there, and then I jump this man." Move A and move B are premises, and move C is the conclusion. In playing these games one learns to predict, to extrapolate from the actual to the potential. Furthermore, one has to displace himself to the opponent's point of view, to play the role of the opposition (a feature of nearly all adversary games, including baseball): "What would I do if he made the move I am considering making?"

I believe that children's powers of thought — to turn over alternatives permitted by the rules, and to go beyond an egocentric point of view — can be considerably advanced by allotting them time to play checkers. While it can be argued that such games can be played at home and not in school, the fact is that in many homes parents would never think of introducing such a game to their children, and even if they did, the likelihood of a child's finding an equal partner in the home is very slight. Pitting oneself against a parent or an older sibling is not ideal, whereas school can provide matches with peers. Since the games could be purchased with some of the money now spent on unnecessary textbooks, the only other objection I can imagine is that the children would be having fun in school when they should be working.

Card Games

PURPOSES

I am concerned, first of all, with the logical ability to group different instances of a thing in order to form a category. Most conventional card games, and most children's card games, are based on categorizing. One makes "books," for example, by putting kings, threes, or hearts together, or, in small children's games, by putting lions or tightrope walkers together. It is interesting that researchers in psychology frequently use cards — mostly of their own devising — to study thought processes, especially concept formation and concept attainment.[4] Whereas concept attainment is the inferring of a previously established category from instances of it, concept formation is creating one's own categories by grouping instances according to one's choice of which attributes are to be the criteria. Teachers would presumably be concerned with both, with the child's grasping of conventional concepts and with his forging of his own categories of experience. And we may assume that experience in attaining conventional concepts will help him make explicit the concepts he forms on his own.

The second purpose of card games is to develop the ability to range concepts in some relationship to each other. One way of ranging is to place them over or above each other in the manner of classes and their subclasses. Another way is to place them in a successive order, or series, such that each "adds something" to the one before.

Hand in hand with the growth of concepts goes the growth of vocabulary. Although most expansion and refinement of vocabulary occurs in discussion, reading, and writing, this is the place where it may be presented systematically.

For these purposes I propose that children learn to play card games with decks especially created for schools. Since the possibilities of card games for classroom use could itself take up a book, I will merely sketch some of these possibilities and hope that enterprising teams of teachers will pick up the suggestions and work out particular decks and game rules through experimentation, making the decks in class at first, and then, when satisfied with results, proposing the more difficult decks to publishers (good illustrations are especially necessary).

CATEGORICAL GAMES

The earliest type of deck could consist simply of picture cards for children to group according to identical pictures, the object being to complete the

[4] See, for example, a *Study of Thinking,* by Jerome Bruner, Jacqueline Goodnow, and George Austin (New York: Science Editions, 1962).

most "books" or to go out of the game first by completing books. This kind of game could precede reading. Its main function would be to teach card playing itself, for the following purposes, and to associate it with classifying.

The next stage would be a deck of labeled cards bearing *non*identical pictures of animals, plants, vehicles, and other things in such a way that each picture card would be an instance of one such category. Each book would be a set of instances. Prior labeling of the pictures would not be necessary to the game but would merely be a form of sight learning of words. But the relation of subclass to superclass could be explicitly taught by placing the word *bus* beneath the picture of a bus and placing the word *vehicle* above it. Thus, all vehicle cards — airplane, bus, car, cart, etc. — would be individually named according to subclass and yet all would bear the name of the class concept that subsumes the subclasses. Such labeling might not be necessary to play the game, but it would help the child to range his concepts explicitly in a hierarchy. For new concepts, more abstract categories, and more finely discriminated subclasses, this double labeling would most likely be really necessary to play the game. Making books according to categories that are new to the children would probably be far enough to go with categorizing at this age. Many different decks would be rotated among pupils, each deck introducing new concepts and vocabulary.

SERIAL GAMES

Another cognitive feature of conventional card games is serial ordering. A very simple game like *War,* where players match single cards to see who has the highest card, presupposes knowing how to count serially. In fact, such games could be used to teach the higher numbers if special decks were made covering the tens, hundreds, and thousands. A further step along this line is to represent numbers arithmetically, as seven-minus-five or eight-plus-four instead of two and twelve; when players match cards to determine which is higher, they must first figure out the number of their respective cards. I am not merely digressing here into the teaching of mathematics, for there is continuity between mathematics and English, the bridge being logic. "Set theory" in math, for example, concerns the formation of classes, the grouping of items that are in some sense similar; the attributes criterial for a category can be quantitative or qualitative. Though most easily exemplified by numbers, serial relations do not have to be numerical; all that is required is a notion of "higher than" or "more than." Consider jack, queen, king, and ace. Social, royal, governmental, and military rank could be represented in a deck of cards, or series of figures or geometric shapes in which each item adds a "new wrinkle" to its predecessor, or chronological series, or series by size.

The earliest form of serial card games would be one-to-one matching of card after card until one player has acquired a whole deck. Then the game is changed to a higher level of sophistication: five cards are dealt each player, discarding is required after each draw, and the point becomes to get a "straight" — five successive cards — before the other players do.

The subject matter of both categorical and serial card games can embrace mathematics and social studies as well as commonalities. It is the processes of categorizing and ordering that we are after. The virtue of teaching different subjects through the same medium is that the method itself correctly implies to the child that these subjects are related and that what relates them are these thought processes.

Part Two

_____

_____

_____

GRADES FOUR

THROUGH SIX

It is assumed that teachers of grades four through six will have read the preceding chapters on kindergarten through third grade. Many of the language activities to be proposed here are merely continuations of earlier ones in more mature form. For these continued activities I will suggest developmental modifications appropriate to this age. Teachers whose classes are new to the curriculum would need to give their pupils an adapted version of some previous assignments before proceeding with later assignments that evolve from them.

The classification of activities does not remain exactly the same as before, for several reasons. As writing becomes more differentiated, the three basic categories of composition in Part One — writing out, writing down, and writing up — now ramify into a larger variety of types. Since what I have to say about literacy has been said in Chapter 5, there is no separate chapter for it in Part Two. Pupils who have never had a course in sound-letter correspondences, or who read and write as if they had not, should be screened out and given one.

Since much of Chapter 6, "Reading," was meant to apply to all of the elementary years, it has no counterpart in Part Two. Teachers of grades four through six should refer back to it.

"Speaking Up" (Chapter 4) is discontinued for a different reason, which has been stated before: the account of small-group discussion for kindergarten through grade three applies equally to grades four to six, there being as yet insufficient knowledge to distinguish two stages of small-group method. *By no means, however, does this omission signify a diminution of its importance or practice. In lieu of further discussion of method, I would like at least to give a sample of discussion by some sixth-grade children and to refer to the research during which the discussion occurred.*

John Mellon and I set out to learn more about some of the factors at play in small-group discussion among children — the differences that age, group size, group composition, socio-economic background, topic, and leader role make in the thoughts and language of children.[1] *For one of our brief feasibility trials, preliminary to future, controlled experiments, we taped trios of children discussing four topics for several minutes each. These were single sessions conducted in school with children to whom we were strangers. Our purpose was to observe the close interaction that we believed the minimally sized groups would afford. There was no leader, and we experimenters did not participate in discussion except at rare moments to spur the talk from the sidelines. We used topics derived from earlier trials, which seemed to show that brief "cases" posing a problem worked better than other topics we tried. We made up a number of cases, one of which appears below. I based it on an old Chinese dilemma and aimed it at Negro ghetto children.*

Ellen was a young mother alone in the world with a small baby. Her husband had disappeared and she could not find a job. Besides, who would take care of the baby while she worked? She felt so bad about being alone and having no money that she left the baby on the doorstep of a nice-looking house and went to another town to look for work.

In that house lived a woman named Betsy whose children had grown up and left home. She and her husband took in the baby and cared for it as if it were their own. Betsy was pleased to have a child again and loved it very much. They named the boy Jeff.

After five years Ellen came back to town. She had got a job and then had married again. She went to the house where she had left the baby and said the child was hers and she wanted him back. But Betsy said, "You went off and left him, and now he's mine." Ellen said, "I didn't want to but I had to. He's my child." Jeff did not know his mother and clung to Betsy, not wanting to go off with a stranger.

How do you think the dispute should be solved?

[1] This research was supported by the Harvard Research and Development Center in Educational Differences and by the National Council

Three sixth-grade girls discussed it, as reproduced below. To appreciate the interaction process illustrated by this sample, one should note the stand that each girl takes at first toward the conflict, and then observe how these stands are modified as the three influence each other.

A: *Well, in a way, I think that, um, Betsy should'a kept the chile', because, um, because — well, my cousin — well, you know, she um, she had to go to 'dis school for bein' bad, an' she had this little son, so my aunt's keeping him — so, ah — she's back now, though — so, um, I guess she wanted her chile' back too, but my aunt still has 'im an' she's gonna keep him, but da' boy — he knows his mother — but, um, ah' don't think she should get him back, though, becus' she — she wouldn't know, you know, how to handle him an' be married an', you know, so I think that she, um shouldn't give 'im back. So I think Betsy should keep him.*

C: *I think that Betsy should keep him because she had raised 'im, an' she had — went off and left him there! She probably really didn't care about 'im until she found the job, or anything like that.*

B: *But — um, Ellen — but she had no other choice! The baby would'a starved! She didn't have no money, an' she went to, um, work to get the money to support the baby. And she remarried.*

C: *Yeah, but couldn't — she hadda' — lef' a note in the backa' da' — whatever she lef' him in — ta' tell the lady 'dat — just ta' keep him until she finds a job n' gets married, but she wasn't thinkin' right then. See, she just took an' lef' the baby right on the steps an' let da' lady take 'im in — she didn't know who it was at all!*

B: *Now I think that, um, the baby should take his choice — which one he wants to stay with.*

C: *Yeah — that would be —*

A: *Yeh. Better. But — But he already did. He was clingin' ta', um, Betsy, so Betsy might as well just keep 'im.*

(Pause)

---

of Teachers of English. A preliminary report on this first phase of research is forthcoming and will be obtainable from the Publications Office, Longfellow Hall, Appian Way, Cambridge, Mass. 02138.

A: *'Cause I think 'dat, um, if — 'cus the lady — she shouldn't
have left him with no one while he was so young. She
should'a — you know . . . .*

C: *And she really didn't know why she lef' 'im — de' only thing,
now, she wants to keep 'im —*

A: *Uh huh. So — an' Betsy supported him an' everything, so I
think dere' —*

B: *Well, I don't know —*

Adult: *Suppose you were a judge and the case was brought to you
and you had to decide.*

A: *Well —*

B: *Well —*

A: *I'd give it — I'll give it to Ellen, n' tell her that if she ever
does it again, then, um, you know, so — we'll just have ta'
send the baby to an orphan an', if she supports him well an',
you know, doesn't just keep remarryin' an', um, sendin' him
to different houses an' stuff — that, then, I — then I would
let her keep him. But if she does, you know, just does what
she did again, and then expects to have the baby back — then
I wouldn't give it to her.*

B: *Well, I think Ellen should have the baby — but if he would
get used to her, an' den' I would let her — let him see Betsy,
or visit Betsy — the one he was raised with. 'An let both of
them really have the baby — like, spend some time with Betsy
an' spend some time with Ellen.*

A: *But — but wouldn't it be harder —*

B: *I think —*

A: *— but then he'll think that Betsy was his mother, but once he
get's used to Ellen, then you could do it that way, you know.*[2]

    *A and C begin by stating that Betsy should have the child
because Ellen is unfit, whereas B defends Ellen, remaining un-
committed about the choice, which she proposes that the child*

    [2] For their cooperation I would like to thank principal Forrest Lewis
and teacher James Sullivan at the William Bacon Elementary School in
the Roxbury district of Boston.

should make. This solution, which bypasses A's and C's assumption that they should decide in favor of one woman or the other, prompts second thoughts. But it occurs to A that the child has already decided — a very neat objection. Then A and C return to their initial positions, having assimilated B's disagreement, and B returns to her indecision. At this point, feeling that they needed a new stimulus, I made my suggestion. I might have done better, but the effect of such an adult interjection is precisely what teachers should discuss together in reviewing tapes. A now reverses herself in favor of Ellen, conditionally. B is now inspired to offer a definite solution, one that allows for both women's claims. Though A objects that the compromise will confuse the child, she overrules her own objection by emphasizing the condition that the child should get used to Ellen before they both share him.

What this discussion illustrates, I think, is that the pupils have influenced each other toward greater complexity of thought. The initial simplicity, based on condemnation or defense of Ellen's character, gives way to the multiple-viewpoint approach to the problem, in which implications are brought out and ideas are amended. Peer interaction without significant adult leadership has wrought this change, though adult sponsorship of the discussion was no doubt an important influence. This exchange may be taken as a miniature model of how group language behavior can improve individual utterances. I see A's last remark — with its two but's *— as symbolizing the increased complexity of thought that group process induces in each of the members.*

Chapter 11

Acting Out

"Acting out" includes verbal drama and also pantomime, charades, "dance drama," and any other use of the body to imitate action and symbolize feeling.

Body English

Nonverbal expression remains important as a supplement to speech, a base for speech, and an alternative to speech. What should be explored are the advantages and limitations of both. One way to understand what speech can do is to withhold it: in pantomimes and charades, one sometimes fairly bursts to speak those things difficult to convey by movement and gesture alone. Conversely, body English can say some things with greater brevity and power. Some of the intention of the following is to relate words and deeds and, when possible, to translate from one to the other. In addition, physical action gives pupils a respite from paper work while at the same time enhancing it. Finally, some children issue from a relatively wordless world, which causes them to persist in uttering most meaning and intent through the body, whereas other children of this age are rapidly becoming verbalizers at the expense of physical expression. Both need a counteractive influence.

Guessing Games

After they have acquired some confidence and ease from earlier pantomime, pupils can put on their actions individually before classmates in small groups and let the others guess what these actions represent. The ideas for these actions might come at first from suggestions by others: each member writes in advance on a slip of paper something that one person could act out alone — such as "a woman trying to hang out wash on a windy day" — and these are shuffled and passed around. Writing the directions has a value, too: the author of a slip sees his words translated into action and gets a sure-fire indication of whether his written speech is understandable or not. Pupils are reminded of the possibility of getting their own directions to act out. In fact, this possibility prepares for making up one's own act impromptu, a practice to follow this one in due time. After the pantomime and the guessing have ended, the actor reads aloud the directions he received.

At some point determined by the teacher, one group plans and silently acts out a situation or scene before another group, which attempts to guess, when the skit is over, what happened. (For now, this is as far as spectatorship will go.) Planning consists of either collaboratively making up an action or selecting one from material already known. If the material is from a poem or story that the class is familiar with, the guessing involves the recognition of it in nonverbal form, and the acting is translating. If the material is original, the spectators' guesses translate acting into words.

In the case both of individuals pantomiming before a small group and of groups pantomiming before other groups, guessing should be held off until the skit is over, and disagreements over interpretation parlayed into discussion, after which the situation or scene is revealed, verbalized, by the actor or actors. Spectators are asked to say specifically which gestures and movements made them construe the action as they did.

Comparing interpretations can be a valuable way to treat inference — how we assemble cues into inferences and how it is that, witnessing the same action, we can infer different things. This uncovers the sort of hidden assumptions and subjective reactions that operate in our interpretation of real life. After comparing is played out, they turn to the actor's statement of what he was trying to do. Further discussion can then center on discrepancies between what was intended and what was inferred. (It is assumed that actors try to communicate, not mislead.) From the remarks of the spectators, the actor knows which gestures and movements communicated and which did not. This feedback can now become a joint effort to think about how the discrepancies could be overcome, the deeds better matched to the intentions.

Learning to act, learning to write, and nearly all other kinds of learning depend on ascertaining the effects of one's efforts. For the best functioning of such discussion, the teacher relies on the pupils' prior experience with small-group discussion, but establishes in advance the two phases as just described and sits in for a while with each group. For more intensive work with inferences, in fifth and sixth grades, check out the planning of the groups to insure ambiguity in the skits so that, for example, some spectators will say that a pantomime is about a hunter stalking game and others will say it is about a detective tracking a criminal. This work with interpretation relates, of course, to sensory recording, which necessarily entails mixing inferences with observations (hence the double sense of "observation"), and to the comprehension of literature, where too the best interpretation is the one that allows for all the cues, not just a selected few. In short, a guessing game is an inference task, and the art of the teacher is to help children to learn one while enjoying the other.

Written recording of pantomime, which extends the whole activity, is described on page 211.

CHARADES

The guessing game can also, within small groups, be extended into the more adult form of charades, the acting out of verbal phrases, titles, and quotations. That is, what the audience tries to guess are not the actions themselves but certain words that the actions merely evoke. This feature, of course, makes the game more sophisticated and more abstract, since actions must be linked with particular words for them, not with just any words for them ("steed," not "horse"), and often, via purely verbal associations such as puns, the right word is arrived at secondarily ("aunt" by brushing off an ant). Also, instead of holding off the answer until the end of a whole presentation, the actor makes the audience guess at each act, each word. This makes for audience participation and fast feedback.

Thus, the actor learns very soon if he is communicating. In fact, before he can continue he must adjust his body English until he does communicate. When he fails, he tries another action. At the same time, his audience must keep offering words until *his* feedback lets them know that they have hit on the one wording that will do. Both are learning communicative precision, one by trying out gestures and the other by trying out words. The audience develops flexibility in interpreting and in wording because they must offer alternatives — a wholly different "reading" of the action, a one-word synonym, or a variant phrasing. The essential skill required of the actor is to play on associations he and the audience share, associations between things and words and between some words and other words. A fundamental part of writing is knowing which associations are in fact shared and can therefore be counted on for communicating. The art is to evoke one thing by means of another. Private associations will not work. The best way to sort private from public, to put oneself in the place of the audience, to discover a common coinage, is by playing precisely this sort of game, verbally and nonverbally.

ENACTING STORIES AND MUSIC

Wordlessly acting out fables, fairy tales, poems, stories, and music can be coordinated with verbal dramas so that the very process of deciding which material should be pantomimed and which dialogued receives major attention. The teacher breaks the class into small groups, not necessarily of the same size, and directs each to choose some piece they have heard or read in class or written themselves. They make their choice by nominating several pieces and discussing whether these would go better with or without words. The pieces rejected as needing dialogue can be saved for verbal enactment on another occasion. Such discussion also leads into planning of the action, which is in effect an editing and adapting job. The advisability of having a director for each group needs experimentation. In any case, roles are rotated and different versions enacted and compared in brief intervening discussions. An adjunct to this activity can be the showing of several kinds of silent films — some pantomime, some not, some fictive, and some actual. The absence of dialogue makes these especially good for discussion.

The writing assignments will also provide considerable material for both pantomime and verbal dramas. These possibilities will be pointed out in passages treating sensory and memory writing and original stories and poems. Conversely, writing based on pantomimes will also be described.

The use of music with pantomime creates two differences. One is that the necessity of playing music for the whole class at once means that all children will be acting from the same stimulant at the same time. But the possibilities are still open to simultaneous individual pantomimes, simultaneous group pantomimes, or even a single full-class pantomime. Individual acting can proceed from the movement-to-music sessions described on page 39, which permit each child to give a bodily rendition of the feeling or idea the music elicits from him. Group pantomimes can be planned, just after listening to the music once or twice; or, if known story-music such as "Peter and the Wolf" is used, roles can be simply assigned; or, furthering the suggestion on page 41, grouped individuals can invent movements in relation to, say, three partners, the directions being to move as one feels but to stay aware of the others, share the group space, and let oneself be influenced (reciprocal influence adds a social stimulant to the musical one). This last, which was a culmination in kindergarten through grade three, could become a regular activity at this age.

The second difference between dance drama and pantomime is that the feelings stirred by music act as a more vague, more subjective stimulant than words, while at the same time the ongoing rhythm and melody create a series of quite specific stimuli that are readily translateable to movement. The actions of pantomime tend to mimic recognizable things, whereas dance drama tends to express less explicit inner things given form by the music. The same movements might appear in both, but whereas they would be patterned by music into regularities and continuities, under verbal stimulus they would be determined by situational or story ideas. There is no reason to distinguish the two kinds of body English, however, except to clarify for the teacher the differences to the pupil between musical and verbal stimulants. Although story-music bridges the two somewhat, movement to music offers more opportunity for personal spontaneity and therefore comes closer to free improvisation.

Verbal Drama

Although I have separated body English from verbal drama, because I believe they should be alternating activities done on different occasions, the point, of course, is to integrate them while distinguishing them. The relation of the two corresponds to their relation in scripted plays, where stage directions indicate nonverbal behavior, and dialogue indicates verbal behavior, both fusing into a total action.

ENACTING WITHOUT SCRIPTS

Dialogue enlarges considerably the range of material that can be acted out. This can include the majority of selections children read, not only folk and children's literature, but excerpts from geography and social studies. A lot of their own writing can be dramatized, and the recording of live conversations (page 181) will, in fact, supply actual play scripts. The procedure is the same as for pantomime and for enactment in the lower grades: the groups choose the material (separately or as a class), discuss adaptation and roughly plan the action, act out with no spectators, rotate roles, and discuss and change successive versions.

IMPROVISATION

Practices. Henceforth the term "improvisation" will designate only impromptu acting with dialogue. Crowd scenes involving the whole class are one kind of improvisation that would be especially appropriate to begin with. The teacher describes the scene — the midway of a fair, a street corner in town at a certain time — and lets students make up roles for themselves, suggesting some himself if necessary. Talk is encouraged. After a few minutes the teacher creates an incident, perhaps by capitalizing on some bit of action going on in one part of the scene. He might suggest, for example, that a "child" wandering on the midway begin to bawl because he is lost. How do the others react? By this means he can extend actions and sustain the scene, taking the students through a sequence suggested by their spontaneous behavior. Later, the students supply ideas from the outset.

For small-group improvisation the teacher proposes a minimal situation — a child has brought home a pet and tries to persuade his parents to let him keep it — or asks the class for one. Once they get the idea, the children will readily supply good situations for a scene. The class breaks into groups containing enough members for all the roles — no more than three or four —

and all groups improvise at the same time, rotating and doing different versions.

Teachers who, at my request, tried out improvisations in their classes[1] reported that their pupils did them easily and eagerly, as they had pantomime before. There seems to be no doubt that children love to act, and jump at the chance. At the time, moreover, the improvising was introduced abruptly and done right off before the class — not a good practice, since improvisation should be prepared for and should remain unwitnessed throughout elementary school except for the assignment described on page 46. One of the situations used in the experiments was "report card night at the supper table." To give an idea of how such improvisations go, I offer here a recapitulation of one written shortly after the performance by a no doubt untypically able girl who watched it.

An Interview with the Smith Family

The Smith family was seated at the supper table, because today report cards had been brought home by everyone in the family. Father said to Jill "What did you get on your report card, dear?" "Well – a, let Susan tell what she got first." And Susan replied back "Well father asked you so you tell him." Jill was not pleased with what her sister had said, but she said in a sweet voice, "Well – a, I got a pretty good mark in math, well it was (amiably) it was, a "d". Father couldn't believe his ears so he said "Say that again." And so this time Jill trembled a little as she said once again a "d". Then mother asked Susan what she got on her report card, and Susan sighed, and said "I too got a good mark in math, a "d" also." This made their parents very angry as they asked Jimmy what he got on his report card. He said "Well I got and a in math, in chemistry I um, I um burnt a hole in the floor." And father said in a stern voice "You may pay for that with your own money." The father asked John what he got on his report card. And John replied, "I got "a" in every subject." This pleased father very much as he collected the report cards. First he looked at Johns and he had 5 f's. And father said "I thought you got all "A's". Then he looked at Jills report card and said "funny you got a "B, c and 5 d's", father was very displeased. Then father looked at Jimmy's report card and said "Well I see you did get a bad mark in chemistry." And at last he looked at Susan's report card which read [Here there was a drawing of the card.] First father ripped all the report cards, and told John to pick them up and put them in the wastebasket, as his punishment. Next he told Jimmy to go to school and repair

[1] Some members of the Omega team (fourth- and fifth-graders combined) at Franklin Elementary School in Lexington, Massachusetts. I wish to thank the whole team for their invaluable experimentation with many of the assignments in this section of the book, and for their willingness to meet frequently after school for a whole year to discuss the trials. They have supplied most of the pupil writing printed in this part. Team members were: Margaret Clark, team leader, Barbara Palermo, JoAnne Setzer, Judie Daly, Abby Dratz, Mary O'Connell, and Carole Scharfe. Other researchers than myself have benefited from the excellent experimental climate created in the school by the principal, Ethel Bears.

the floor. Then he told Susan to make the beds every week. And at last he said to Jill in a mysterious voice "Hmmm what *shall* I do for your punishment." And finally he said "You shall take the rubbish out every night"! The End!

Not all situations have to be drawn from real life, but many of those proposed by the students of this age are.

Values. It is best to think of improvisation as a learning instrument, like small-group discussion, that can be used for many purposes. The point is not just to teach drama but to teach other things *through* drama. To take on the role of a parent or shop girl or manager is to extend oneself into another life-experience, perspective, and style of speaking. And, as in the skit above, noncommunicative uses of language are put on display — dominating, evading, etc. Improvisation puts a great emphasis on verbal interaction and on rhetorical ploys, on getting effects with words.

Improvisation is especially valuable in elaborating over-condensed stories. Most myths, legends, and folk tales that come to us second-hand are in summarized form, lacking much dialogue or specific movement. The dullness of such summaries is a big stumbling block to presenting these fine stories to children of an age to be especially appreciative of them but not yet able to read the elaborations of them in the plays and epics of great authors. But they provide good "minimal situations"[2] which children can expand and bring alive through improvisation. The teacher reads the summary, and the groups take as their situation the few sentences that recount a scene. Take scenes, not plots; groups can do successive scenes on successive occasions.

Since their own writing is limited in length, children's narratives tend also toward digests that need elaboration. Although the writing assignments recommended for this age try to head this off by keeping the length of time covered by their narratives commensurate with the length of their writing, pupils will frequently over-condense. Expanding these digested actions through improvisation will help them to see the values and the possibilities of greater detailing. Generally, an important relation in writing and literature is that drama elaborates narrative and narrative summarizes drama. Novelists work within constantly varying degrees of résumé, and cover a lot of story ground, whereas playwrights present the total action of only a few carefully selected scenes. The principle of abstracting is that one always trades a gain in coverage for a loss of detail, and vice versa. By improvising dramas from narrative sketches, and, conversely, by writing narrative summaries of improvisations, pupils can grasp this abstractive relation between these two orders of discourse.

The report-card skit had a theme: children's failure to comply with parental demands. I find that children's skits always do. Such themes are natural topics for small-group discussion when preshaped by preliminary dis-

[2] See page 44 for definition.

cussing of the skits themselves. If small-group discussion and improvisation are coordinated, a very powerful learning, I feel sure, will result, because ideas can be dealt with — again — in two modes, at two levels of abstraction. A topic is a distillation, in question or statement form, of particular instances of some theme, any one of which can be improvised. And discussion of improvisations distills themes into topics. In other words, by improvising the instances that come up in small-group discussion the pupils can go from generality to example, and by discussing the material of improvisations in small groups they can go from example to generality. (Material can come from literature, everyday life, and social studies.) This movement between abstraction levels is not only a vital issue in writing but a major educational goal.

_____

_____

_____

Chapter 12

Writing Down

Grades four through six are the time, I believe, when transcription should be learned once and for all. Of course this cannot mean a definitive mastery of spelling, simply because children will always be learning some new words for which the spellings have to be memorized. But certainly the segmenting of speech flow need not linger for years as a problem to exasperate both teacher and students; nor for that matter should the bulk of spelling remain a problem, for, after all, the growth of vocabulary beyond elementary school introduces only new words, not new phonic relations.

Principles of Teaching Transcription

A child leaving elementary school should be able to render graphically, with only a few misspellings, anything he can speak or understand orally. There is no aspect of transcription that his future development will make it possible to learn if it has not already been learned. Actually, a person's sensitivity to speech sounds and intonations is probably better in grades four to six than later, proponents of foreign language teaching at this age claim. This stage not only combines the good ear of the small child with the motor skill and phonic understanding of the older one, but it is the period of strong competence motivation, when children are still willing to master an ability somewhat for its own sake. By contrast, junior and senior high school students insist much more — and rightly, for their age — on meaning and content, and resent what they feel to be the nit-picking of fuddy-duddy clerics who are interested only in a hollow formalism, not in what you have to say. This attitude represents, in fact, greater maturity. A top priority goal of elementary school, then, should be to eliminate transcription as a problem so that the work of later years can be free to satisfy this riper motivation and can avoid alienating older students from writing as composition.

173

To teach transcribing is *not* to ride herd on mechanics. This is precisely why I suggest separating transcription from composition. Meaningful writing should be treated as such; the teacher helps with spelling and punctuation *before* composition takes place, and pupils can proofread each other's writing afterwards. Frequent printing of pupils' writing motivates proofreading and helps the teacher to associate spelling and punctuation with typography rather than with moral values. When either the teacher or other pupils misunderstand a paper because of transcriptive errors, however, this should be brought out in commentary or discussion as a matter of helpful feedback to the author of the composition.

A teacher who marks a paper up for mechanics almost inevitably establishes a value scale for pupils upon which transcriptive errors rank higher than content and composition. Only the future will tell us how much student writing has been made inferior by penalizing spelling and punctuation mistakes. Like the child who said she used the word "bar" instead of "trapeze" in a story because she was unsure how to spell the latter and didn't want to be marked down for it, most pupils adopt the error-avoiding strategy of using only words they are sure they can spell and sentence constructions they know they can punctuate. In the long run, avoiding risks can't possibly reduce error. Pupil strategy should consist of making educated guesses and of checking guesses later with the teacher, other pupils, or the dictionary. The teacher can, however, give personal diagnosis: "You have trouble knowing when to double consonants," or "You need to listen more for punctuation in the middle of a sentence."

With this as general procedure, we turn now to the transcriptive assignments themselves.

Taking Dictation from the Teacher

The goal is self-dictation, reproducing one's silent composing voice on paper, but it is very difficult to do this straight away. One takes his own intonation for granted, and becomes aware of it only gradually, from having to pay attention to someone else's in order to transcribe it. Also, taking dictation from another person gives a practice in spelling that is utterly unrelated to composition, and that at the same time ties punctuation to vocal cues.

In order to control the transcriptive difficulties and to focus on particular issues of spelling and punctuation, the teacher may need to give some dictation himself. (See page 138 for my reservation about the use of dictation and for suggestions on how to go about it.) The only justification for asking pupils to transcribe a passage verbatim is the felt need for work on spelling, for punctuation practice can be afforded much more efficiently in the manner described farther on. A language lab would be very valuable for transcribing prepared passages verbatim. A live voice or prerecorded tape dictates. A visual loop attached to the machine would enable each pupil to compare his transcription immediately with the printed text. Only those pupils who need the practice need go to the lab; the pupil can operate the machine himself and replay the parts of the passage he needs to hear again.

Punctuating Unpunctuated Texts

For segmenting the speech flow alone, the pupils can punctuate dittoed copies of an unpunctuated text as the teacher reads it aloud. This goes fast and is really only a variation of being read to; the pupils follow along on the dittoed sheet instead of on a projection, inserting periods and commas as they go by following the teacher's vocal punctuation. Afterwards, ask pupils what they put down and allow them to compare their transcriptions. High consensus helps to establish the more objective universals of punctuation, and allows individual pupils to note deviations of their own that may indicate areas of unawareness in hearing. Low consensus, or mixed response in places, can show the teacher which sorts of punctuation are difficult for his class. Let the disagreeing pupils justify their responses and then reread the sentences involved. If this brings no resolution, try to discover whether the problem is one of pause and intonation alone, or a subtler one involving logical options as well. As a humorous way to make a point, occasionally project a text that you have mispunctuated and read it according to the mispunctuation. For older students, I used to write on the board, "what is this thing called love," and ask them to read it aloud in as many different ways as they could and to tell me how each version should be punctuated. They thought of readings that had not occurred to me. Try it yourself.

As soon as it seems wise, ask the pupils to read pieces of their own writing aloud as the rest of the class punctuates dittoed copies of it from which punctuation is removed, first announcing that the pieces are not selected as either good or bad. These must not be picked as bad examples but on a rotation basis, so that every pupil's punctuation gets the benefit of class consensus and teacher attention. Pupils asked to read their writing for the class to punctuate are told to read without haste and in exactly the way they think their paper should be spoken. If members of the class have trouble punctuating the text, or disagree considerably, this provides a chance to bring the author's reading or writing more in line with his intentions, and to correct obvious intonational faults. His original punctuation can then be revealed and discussed.

Principles of Punctuating by Voice

Dissociating punctuation from rules and textbooks takes a lot of the mystery out of it. Replacing the foreign text with their own writing, and teacher reading with pupil reading, should thoroughly score the point that the authority for punctuation resides in shared speech habits and therefore in each person.

WHAT CAN BE HEARD

Let's put it all this way. Except for questions and exclamations, which are obvious, a drop of the intonation contour almost unfailingly calls for a punctuation mark. The issue is which one — comma, dash, semicolon, colon, or period? Even if he chooses unwisely, a child who puts *some* mark of punctuation there has fulfilled the first principle of punctuation — to segment the flow of speech. Whether a comma or a period is called for depends on the length of pause and on whether the intonation drops merely to a lower point, somewhat suspended, or all the way to the bottom for a distinct closure. (Read this last sentence aloud.) A true comma splice would occur only when a full drop was mistaken for a half drop; a period after a sentence fragment would occur when a half drop was mistaken for a full.

WHAT IS DIFFICULT TO HEAR

And yet punctuation is not completely objective. There is a margin of personal option, and it is true that some of the more sophisticated usages governed by logic are not necessarily audible. One cannot always hear, for example, when two sentences are joined by a semicolon or colon and when they are separated by a period. And one would be hard put sometimes to distinguish by ear alone a colon from a semicolon or a comma from a dash, or a series of commas from a series of semicolons. But these are the only four cases involving option and logic where voice may be an inadequate guide, and they can be explained, through illustrations, when they come up in dictated passages to which the class gives mixed or uncertain responses. For example, unless read together in careful contrast, the punctuation of the following sequences might be rather difficult to detect:

(1) *He sprang up, he looked over his shoulder, he sprinted off.*
(2) *He sprang up; he looked over his shoulder; he sprinted off.*
(3) *He sprang up. He looked over his shoulder. He sprinted off.*

MEANINGS OF THE SYMBOLS

The teacher can, however, compare the different punctuation marks to "rest" symbols in music, and describe them as a progression of increasingly larger breaks — comma, dash, semicolon, colon, and period — while remarking that the length of pause alone may not be enough of a clue to which of any two is called for, and that, furthermore, emphasis and meaning make a difference too. A dash is a kind of comma — but more emphatic. Like an arithmetical plus sign, a semicolon merely adds one sentence to another; this summing indicates closeness between their actions or meanings. A colon is like an equal mark: the sentences on either side of it restate each other. If illustrated, the practical purpose of using semicolons for a large series and commas for subseries contained within it is easy to grasp and remember. In fact, presenting sets of instances of each of these kinds of punctuation will do more good than lengthy explanations.

PUNCTUATION OF SINGLE WORDS

Another kind of logical punctuation that may or may not be audible is internal punctuation of individual words — apostrophes and hyphens. There is no way to hear the apostrophe of possession and contraction. It must be explained through instances. Hyphenation, however, can almost always be heard, because pitch is sustained through a compound word. Compare *He entered the second grade* and *He entered the second-grade classroom.* Write on the board some unpunctuated sentences that will be misread and cause a double-take: *He counted three toed sloths.* Ask the children what the problem is and how they think it can be solved. (Compare *three, toed* and *three-toed.*) Write an ambiguous sentence — *They saw many colored butterflies* — and ask someone to read it aloud. Can it be read another way? How would you show the difference to a reader? Ask them for examples of other compound words, remarking that two words that are compounded in one sentence may not be in another. After they are sensitized to the audible difference, make a statement to the effect that just as our voice joins the two words in speech, so the hyphen joins them in print.

Some capitalized words can also be distinguished by ear: *white house* and *White House.* Some remaining typographical equivalents of speech will be mentioned in connection with transcribing conversation.

I believe that such an account of written punctuation will cover all but the most abstruse of possibilities and will prove serviceable throughout the later years, even for options. Many teachers don't *want* to bring personal option into the picture, because it would seem to present punctuation as a subjective matter of "anything goes." But the virtue of an intonational approach is that the voice is a remarkably objective guide, indicating personal options in a public medium. That is, one does not punctuate as one pleases, one punctuates as one speaks. Most personal options can be heard. When they cannot, the few logical principles stated above will supplement vocal discriminations.

Taking Dictation from Classmates

Dictation occurs quite naturally in the role of scribe, as used in various discussion groups and working parties. Its virtue is that spelling and punctuation are practiced in a situation that does not at all smack of an exercise, since the point of the writing is to record ideas for later use. As notes, however, the writing will not necessarily be in whole sentences, nor will the speaker's words be taken down verbatim. But even abbreviated transcription has value, as I believe the papers below show. A boy in the Lexington Omega group (fourth and fifth grades combined) was transcribing what a partner said as she felt four objects in a paper bag. (This paper was done in the original tactile experiment before the teachers decided the assignment should be shifted down to the lower grades; see page 136.)

1ST   bumpy, shallow bowl, two small handles, little ridge around bottom

2ND   large bumps, shaped like a large egg, between bump feels like enameled wood, its smooth between bumps except at smaller end

3RD   like a dry sponge, smooth edge like crust on bread, shaped like a piece of bread only thinner

4TH   circle if you look at it from bottom, smooth. Shallow depression at top, small, feels like made of glass

Though he has reduced her sentences to essential descriptive phrases, by omitting "it has . . ." and "there is . . . ," he has reproduced with commas the intonation drops that ended the sentences. The result, incidentally, is series, properly punctuated, which could again be given predicates, only more economically, one for each series instead of one for each quality or item in a series. Note also that the girl used *five comparisons* in the effort to convey her sensations. This assignment is a realistic way to elicit similes, because the practical need for them is great. Below, a girl in the same group writes down what three "feelers" said.

Jill says, "It's smooth like a shirt and kind of short, It's hollow, It feels smooth, It feels as though it has string tied to it, It feels as though its kind of square, It feels as though it made out of suade, It has two long corners, Its kind of like a bag of candy, you can put things into it."

Donna says, "Its feels rough on one end, you can put your hand in it, I can put my fingers in it one by one

Stephen says, "It feels like its made out of rubber, It feels like a bunch of circles in it, theres it has deisigns on it, there is some string on it

The children in the experiment had had no experience with this sort of dictation nor with intonational punctuation. Many found verbatim transcribing difficult, but, as I think the teachers would agree, this would not be so if they were more used to it. The main problem is the speed of spontaneous speech. Dictation by the teacher or by scribes can be slowed down.

Taking Dictation from Younger Children

Another realistic transcription task is for pupils of this age to take down the dictating of first-graders. A common practice now of many kindergarten and first-grade teachers is to transcribe for their pupils, one at a time, their stories and other things they have to say. My suggestion is that older children take over the teacher's role in this case. Two teachers exchange halves of the classes so that the older and younger children can be paired off. What the first-graders say may be about all sorts of things, related to other current work or entirely individual; the content makes no difference. Explain that the upper-graders will write down and show them later what they have said, and that you will circulate among them, both to help prompt the younger and to help the older with spelling or punctuation problems. (Suggesting in advance that the latter too may need help will save face for them when changes need to be made in their transcriptions.)

There are advantages for all parties. The dictaters get a chance to see what their oral speech looks like when rendered on paper. They read it, they learn spellings, and they have the satisfaction of keeping the paper for showing to others. The attention and help of older children, the big-brother or big-sister relationship, the desire to emulate bigger people are all powerful learning forces not utilized often enough in schools. For their part, the older children enjoy being looked up to and having their greater capabilities seriously called upon. Since it is important that the transcriptions be accurate, the teacher, as announced, checks them over for spelling and segmenting of speech flow — preferably during his rounds, but later too if necessary. An enormous amount more dictation can be done in this way than when a teacher alone undertakes to act as secretary. Exchanging the papers among themselves afterwards affords more reading practice for the younger children, each speaker being able to help his readers to make out the words.

Dialogue Recording

In conjunction with transcription, and also as a specialization of sensory recording — the taking down of voice sounds — the writing of real, over-heard dialogue may begin now. One teacher in Lexington began this by writing down on the chalkboard, as the pupils entered the room, the various remarks and exchanges that she heard them make. Amused and interested by this, the pupils were then not surprised when she asked them, as home-work, to place themselves somewhere with paper and pencil and write down some live conversation. Of course, they cannot write as fast as people talk, but they can be told to catch as much of the conversation as they can, not to worry if they miss some things, and, if they have to, to recapitulate some of the conversation in their own words.

I reproduce here an Omega boy's transcription of a home conversation.

A shoe bag. Well this will do for you're junk. Weeell this will do. Larry I got you a few things! I want you *both* off those stairs! ! ! See what you did Tim! ! *I'm* going home *I'll* hide somewhere. whaaaah Tim do you want some Ice to chew on? Want some more? I got a cut at school too. I *almost* got a cut. Listen you thing. I'm going to hide somewhere. And I'll find you. wha-a-a. Would you like a cup uh chopped Ice? What are you doing overthere? What are you taking everything down for? Tim wanna play house. uh-uh. Timmy were not mad at you. Larry is this your homwork or are you *trying* to be funny? Larry, Larry, Larry, *Larry! !* It *isn't* any help to be a noodge. I got you something too. What's going on here? Its the filmstrip. The baby came over and ripped up all the cards. We made all these this one is like pin. Tip is pin, tin, grin, pin

These need not be done at home. As with other sensory recording described later, pupils are encouraged to go to different places where they think interesting "scenes" may be going on.

Certain problems arise as to who is saying what. This is the place for the teacher to help them to learn the typographical devices for keeping speakers' straight, such as quotation marks and paragraphing or colons after speakers' names. It is also an opportunity to relate vocal expressiveness to some punctuation usages that I have not discussed so far. Using projected papers for illustration, the teacher explains that dashes indicate interruptions (including self-interruption); suspension marks, a long pause within a sentence or, with a period, the trailing off of a sentence; and underlining, an emphatic stress on a certain word. Real dialogue also inevitably includes many opening and closing tag phrases to be set off with commas (*Well, he is going, isn't he?*) as well as cases of direct address, all indicated by the voice.

Ditto or project a transcribed conversation and let the class try to read it silently. Then ask them what problems they had. During this discussion interject whatever explanation they need of the punctuation usages mentioned above. Make changes on the transparency. When speakers have been straightened out, with the help of the child who recorded, ask some pupils to take parts and try to read the dialogue aloud. Sentence punctuation can be worked out when the readers show uncertainty or misread a line (the recorder is asked to speak the line the way he heard it). Tell the children that this session illustrates what they are to do in small groups, and that the purpose of clearing up the transcriptions is to provide copy for printing up and acting out.

When the class seems to have grasped the issues, after one or more sessions, direct the pupils to revise their transcriptions as best they can, then to huddle in small groups for collaboration. They test each other's dialogues by reading them aloud in parts and letting the transcriber listen for discrepancies between their reading and the original. When the dialogue does not run true, they revise typography and punctuation according to what they learned from the class sessions, calling on the teacher if they need help. Then the transcriptions are prepared for printing. Since these will be exchanged within and between classes, their goal is to permit strangers to reproduce dialogue from the page. To this end, they should use every device available — paragraphing, parentheses, quotation marks, underlining of stressed words, suspension marks (...), and dashes for interruption.

Below is another transcription of an overheard conversation, this time by an Omega girl who is obviously far more skilled in quoting and in taking down speech than most children will be on their first attempt or so.

"Whaaa Whaa" "ha ha" "That's right Kathy" "No!" "Ow" "Wait a sec, Kathy you have to go right to the a a um ironingboard. and I have to go the the the bed". "R-R-A-A-A-" " . . .Set go!" "Kathy won!" ". . .right there. . ." "Yah! !" ". . . now before. . ." "1,2.3 GO!" "Go Kathy!" "I won that time! I touched this before Kathy did." "You heard me I said. . ." "So now I have to run down with you. Wha Wha." "I have to touch these papers." On your mark, get set, GO!" "you forgot to touch these papers." "On your mark get set ur go!" "Whaa ow" "ha ha ha!" "On your. . .times places! One, two, three e-e-e-e-e-e-e-e-e-k-k-! Get out of here" "gaga gu .gu!" A-A-A-A-A-H-H-H" This sis sis sis sis sis sis say anything! Say it as loud as you can." Margie said go!" "a-a-a-h-h" "shush children!" "were just playing a game. Watch! Please Mommy let me" "Margaret you may go to your room." "What?" "Please," "allright you may go right to your room Come on!" "No-o-o." "those lucks, Lorie an Susan won't let me. "Me too!" "Now Kathy the first you are told to do something you do it. So many times I've had to yell." "Were having a yelling contest and the person who yells the loudest gets to pat Tinderbell about ten times." "Okay" "Ma-a-a Ma-a-a!" "Now who can say it the softest!" "Margaret won!" "Yeah" "Okay, Kathy won, Okay." "Children I have a better idea why don't you simply get out some paper and play a game." "Let's finish this first, Okay Nutmeg."

But even this paper could use a lot of mechanical revision for intelligibility and readability. The important thing is to make both the transcribing and the revising part of a well motivated and meaningful process.

After some transcriptions have been printed up and distributed, take one from another class, let the children read it silently, then make a game of guessing the time, place, situation, and speakers. What action is accompanying this dialogue? Then let them choose other transcriptions and act them out, improvising the action as they infer it and perhaps expanding the dialogue. On a subsequent occasion project a transcription and, after they have inferred circumstances and speakers, show them how to convert it into a play script, which will indicate the things they have been inferring. Write in speaker names, followed by colons, and insert action and setting parenthetically. These stage directions are in the present tense and are limited strictly to what can be seen and heard (being like a sensory recording). Then send the children to small groups to revise some new transcriptions of their own into script form. They collaborate in preparing these for printing. When copies have been distributed, they select scripts to act out within small groups (loosely, without memorizing lines).

Besides furthering their transcriptive ability, the recording of overheard conversation will prepare for writing plays and for reading the professional dialogues of fiction and the theatre.

The Use of Tape Recorders

I hope that teachers will go on to imagine and try out other kinds of transcription assignments than those I have outlined here. One particularly fertile possibility is for students to take down their own voices from a tape recorder. This enables a pupil to transfer the transcriptive process from others to himself, to his subvocal inner speech. Again, accurate self-dictation is the goal. Pupils can take turns composing on a single tape recorder, or if a language lab with recorders is available, go there all at once. They are directed to say into the microphone whatever it might be that they would otherwise have written. Afterwards, they listen and write down verbatim what they said. (Most school machines have an easily operated mechanism for pausing and replaying, a feature that gives this activity an advantage over live dictation.) If some children have trouble segmenting and punctuating their own speech, listen to their tapes and help them with either their speaking or their hearing. Next, they may make compositional revisions on the transcription. This should prove to be an excellent procedure for inducing awareness of how writing must compensate for the loss of physical voice, and for making the general transition from speech to writing. One Omega class verbalized their auditory sensations on tape, transcribed them afterwards, and made revisions on the transcription. At Ball State University, Anthony Tovatt and Ebert Miller have done preliminary experiments with ninth-graders composing on tape and revising; part of the inconclusiveness of their work so far, they speculate, may be due to the possibility that students should have this experience earlier in their career.[1]

If any part of the language arts lends itself to teaching by machine, the sound-sight correlations of transcription do. The more nearly mechanical the skill, the more mechanical devices are justified. I hope that future technology will provide us with an electronic spectrograph machine that, when a child talks into it, will enable him to *see* the stress, pitch, and pause of his intonational contours.[2]

---

[1] "Effectiveness of an Oral-Aural-Visual Stimuli Approach to Teaching Composition to Ninth Grade Students," unpublished paper given as a talk by Dr. Miller at an American Educational Research Association meeting in Chicago in February, 1966.

[2] I am told that Mrs. Jean Olson of Minneapolis has used an oscilloscope for this purpose. A series of television tapes prepared by her in 1966 showed speech segments very graphically.

_____

_____

_____

Chapter 13

Sensory Writing

The process described on page 148 of taking observational notes and individually keeping science journals should definitely be continued through grades four to six. All that one should probably expect to see change are the complexity of the observations, the fullness of the notes, and the finer matching of language to fact as vocabulary and linguistic forms develop. I leave the subjects of observation to the local collaboration of science and language arts teachers. What I will outline here are other kinds of sensory recording that are introduced into the program for the first time. Since considerable experimentation was done, at my behest, with this kind of writing, I will give a rather full account of it, not only to indicate its possibilities and problems, but also to turn over some general writing issues.

Account of Trials

AROUND THE SCHOOL

In casting about for in-school subjects other than animals or objects, the Lexington Omega teachers (of fourth and fifth grades combined) tried sending their students into other parts of the school, in this case into another classroom:

> I hear squeeking chires and writing of pencels, people walking. I see boys talking the teacher looking the flag flaping. A blue sky. An open window I smell the freash air. I see clouds in the sky. I here a door slam crash! I see the teacher talking to a child.

These ongoing notes were made by a boy of average ability who then revised the paper, without benefit of written commentary or correction:

> I came in the room and sat down. I heard squeeking chairs and people writing. Some boys are talking. The teacher is looking at someone. The flag is flapping in the blue sky. I can smell the fresh air through the open window. The little clouds ar in the sky foating very fast. Bang! A door just slammed shut. The teacher is talking to someone.

It is interesting to note the revisions that he made on his own.

One of the teachers' ingenious ideas was to bring a first-grader into class and let pupils record the child's actions as he went about making something from clay, pipe cleaners, and other materials. This by an able girl:

> Her name is Marisa. She's sitting down in the nearest seat to her. She's breaking the yellow clay into balls. She's a little shy. She's never been to Omega before. She isn't saying anything. Now she's beginning to have a good time. She's smiling a little. She's working very carefully. She looks around and smiles every so often. She's only using the yellow clay. She's very quiet. She's making some sort of figure. It looks sort of like a man. Now she's using the toothpicks and the scissors. She's feeling more at home. She feels more sure of herself. She's using all the colors of clay. Now it looks more like a person. She's putting an egg-carton hat on the figure. The only thing she hasn't used are the straws. The figure has feet, eyes, nose, mouth, hat, legs, and a few toothpicks and sticks sticking out of it.

And revised:

> The little girl came in shyly. She said that her name was Marisa. She sat down in one of the seats and started breaking the clay into balls. She worked quietly with the yellow clay. Then Marisa started to have a good time. Every once in a while she looked around and smiled. Marisa worked very carefully and started to make some sort of figure. It began to look like a man. Then she picked up the scissors and toothpicks and began to use them. Gradually she felt more confident and she began to enjoy herself even more. The figure looked more like a person. Then Marisa used all different colors of clay. She made a hat out of a piece of an egg carton and put it on her man. The figure really looked like a man then. It had feet, legs, nose, mouth, eyes and a body all made out of clay. It had a hat too. And she had stuck a few toothpicks and sticks into the man. Now, she is going back to her room. She is hurrying along. The only things she didn't use are the straws. She has enjoyed her visit to Omega.

Although not all pupils can carry off the assignment as well as the girl above, there is no question that if they can write at all they can do it. The issues, rather, for both of these assignments are these: What is the pupil's motive for doing them? (Why is he observing and what use can be made of his paper?) Are the time and labor involved in revising justified? One could argue that, though slight, the actual changes made are important compositional touches; that mechanical errors are corrected; and that pupils confront a critical shift in tense and point of view (the boy begins in the past but lapses back into the present whereas the girl sturdily maintains the new past tense). The revision, of course, puts an added strain on motivation. It might be helpful for my reader to compare the originals and revisions above and make some judgment on these issues before continuing.

The second assignment above differs greatly from the first in one respect. The events one records in a classroom are random; the observer takes potluck on his material. But the action of someone making something presents a selected and focused set of events that raises interest and motivation. I think that among our pupils the latter assignment was much more successful in this respect. The act of composition starts with a selection and focus of material, from which different writing issues ensue. This is a relationship that both teachers and pupils need to grasp securely. The novice writer can grasp it by having to make decisions about his raw material.

AWAY FROM SCHOOL

In our experiments we sent children out of school to record on location without telling them to pick a place where they knew some action would be going on, specifically some action they knew they would be drawn to. They went to nearby places with only mediocre motivation, and took their chances. Here are some observations done by slower children not inclined to write voluminously on any occasion. Tidied up after discussion:

I can see houses. And I can see a lightpost. I can hear the bird whistle. I can see a boy come down the street. A dog is drinking water from a puddle. That makes me very thirsty. There is hardly any smell.

I hear my mother talking to my brother. I see a bed, and a cat, then a picture. I smell fresh air and sweet grass. The sweet grass reminds me when school is over. I hear my father cutting the grass. It reminds me of my electric tooth brush.

Before revision:

HEAR	SEE	SMELL
Birds tweeting, seems like they're taking music lessons	Birds, small and cute Thorn bush, I wouldn't want to go in it.	Cold air, makes you shiver
Dog barking		Winter air, seems like winter
A highway, one great big noisy truck is there		Dirt, ice cold, damp

See seven chairs and see stove. I see the front door, people walking around, and some dishes in the room — making footsteps and hear somebody washing the dishes, hear radio going in the background. I hear talking in another room. I smell a little of the breakfast and I can smell some air that makes me think of food.

Also unrevised, but benefiting from "natural selection" (the first a girl, the second a boy):

Meow, meow, shhh, Nick is having kitties. Thump, thump, shhh, Nick is having kitties. Ohhh, I know, scratch, scratch, Nick is having kitties. Oho, what do you know, she had three kitties.

I watched my mother clean the table and clean the dishes. I heard my mother yell at my sister because she didn't help.

Clearly, an occasional poetic or laconic vignette issues from such casual observing, sometimes even an enviable bit of imaginative perception:

My Back Yard

It sure sounds funny how the wind goes through the trees. The smell of flowers blooming. The red pail lying in the grass. Our rope swaying across the air as if it was going somewhere. The wheel barrel like a ox pulls leaves. Trees are having buds. It's a beautiful night. The fence bending back in the wind. Our shed standing still there. I can hear the rabbits eating. I can see houses. I can hear the toad communicait. I can see our dog. I heared a bark from the yard. Our swing set trying to keep its balance.

Besides the French imperfect tense in *communicait*, what I appreciate in this boy's notes is the rendering of the wind — the rope swaying, the fence bending, the swing set trying to keep its balance — all in contrast to "our shed standing still there." The kind of finely noted evocative details that teachers fall all over themselves trying to get students to put into their writing are here — the red pail lying in the grass, the wheelbarrow pulling leaves like an ox (comparisons are rare in children's speech and writing), the sound of rabbits eating — and yet I don't feel that the boy was striving for poetic effect or trotting out his prettiest adjectives to "do a description." He was really experiencing the moment and translating it into words.

Formulating the Problems and the Assignments

But sticking one's thumb into a pile of papers and pulling out a plum does not prove the worth of an assignment. After we tried out, during the fall and winter, a variety of kinds of sensory recording — in school, out of school, isolating senses, combining senses — these following problems remained.

1. The speed of note taking often resulted in dry, abstract lists of words.

2. The obligation to stick to sensations caused the children to exclude thoughts and feelings that arose from the sensations and that actually would have made fine compositional material; the restriction seemed to devaluate the personal response and imagination.

3. When a whole class recorded at the same place, there was no audience for whom to write up notes and hence little motive for composing.

4. If pupils rewrote notes every time they recorded, they sometimes got stuck with dull material that they had no interest in writing up.

5. Furthermore, this practice entailed too much writing of a copying kind.

6. The assignment did not of itself stimulate similes and metaphors, which we all felt should enter into sensory writing.

With these problems in mind, and feeling a need to formulate the assignment as explicitly as possible for the final experiment in the spring, I wrote the following directions for pupils and teachers. These were mimeographed and distributed. The pupils kept their directions in a folder prepared for the project in which they also kept all the papers they produced in response to these directions. Both sets of directions are reproduced here as a base from which other teachers can make adaptations by their own lights and in the light of reservations I will make afterwards. Directions to the teacher are in parenthesis.

Record sensations at a locale away from school.

1. Choose any place away from school that you would like, go to that place with paper and pencil, and for fifteen minutes write down what you hear, see, and smell there. Think of what you write as notes for yourself later. These notes will not be graded but you will need them later for another assignment. Bring them to class. Don't worry about spelling or correct sentences; write in whatever way allows you to capture on paper what you observe in that time. You may also include your thoughts and feelings about what you observe. You may also want to say what things look, sound, or smell *like*.

(1. Two worthwhile issues can be raised and dealt with in the discussion of these first papers:

1. The difference between, and relation between, sensations and non-sensations, physical facts on the one hand and inferences, personal reactions, similes, etc. on the other hand. Both should be valued, but it is important for the child to be able to spot what he has mixed of himself with the environment. "Observation" thus takes on its double sense of "sensory data" and "personal reaction." With a dittoed or projected sample paper before them, ask the class what things in the paper might have been recorded by *any* observer and what things show traces of the particular

person doing the recording. The use of "loaded" words and comparisons could be brought out as well as just obvious personal statements. Also, compare two papers for the relative amount of sensory data vs. personal reaction; ideally, this would lead to the discovery that, given the time limit, a gain in one is a loss in the other. Then give back their papers and let them underline words or sentences that they feel convey non-sensations. As a check for them, let them exchange papers and have a neighbor underline what *he* considers to be non-sensations.

2. The *form* of the notes: word lists, telegraphic phrases, and whole sentences; amount of paragraphing and punctuating. Since these are notes to oneself, they should not be judged for correctness or intelligibility to others but only for their value as notes. Discuss the gains and losses of different forms of note-taking. Ditto or project two papers of contrasting form. What do you lose when you use just word lists? broken phrases? whole sentences? They should get some sense of which words are dispensable, which words or phrases capture a lot quickly, which suffer a loss of detail, and what the advantages and disadvantages are of longer phrases and whole sentences. (In general, lists cover a lot of items but lose the detail of *each* item, whereas full sentences modify, qualify, and elaborate single items but don't cover as *many* items.)

Students should be encouraged to develop a notation style that works well for them — that enables them to go for coverage or go for detail, to strike whatever balance they want. This should help with Assignments 2 and 3.)

Record sensations at a new locale or time.	2. Do as you did in Assignment 1, but this time change either the time or the place. If you went to an indoor place before, go somewhere outdoors now. If you went to an active place, go now to a still place. If there were no people where you went before, go where there will be people. Or you may return to the same place you went before, but go at a very different time of day, or when the weather is very different. Remember that you are to take notes of what you observe, see, hear, and smell and of what thoughts and feelings you may have about what you observe. If you have found a better way of taking notes since last time, use the new way.

(2. Discussion of these papers might center on two new issues, besides perhaps picking up the two earlier points if the students seem to want to pursue them.

1. Again with a sample before them, ask if the class can tell the time, place, and circumstances of the recording. How much can they tell of the mood of the observer and what he felt about the scene? Is there a main mood, impression, keynote, attitude, etc.? Does one sense dominate — sound, sight, or smell?

2. Try now to lead into the selection process of the observer. Get the class to imagine what things were *left out.* Ask the writer of the paper to recall what things he did *not* put down. Hand back all the class papers and ask everyone to look at his paper and compare it with his memory of the scene. Ask first the authors of the sample papers and then the whole class how they came to include some things and reject other things. If they say they put down the "most interesting" or "most important" things, ask how they decided some things were more interesting or more important. This more or less unconscious selection process is at the heart of composing; some awareness of it should help later with Assignment 4.)

Record sensations with some other pupils.

3. Do as you did in Assignments 1 and 2 but, before you leave class, plan with two or three other pupils to go somewhere at the same time. Decide together where to meet and when. After you meet, place yourselves at different points at that place (not too close together) and then begin to take your notes on what you see, hear, and smell. Again, included whatever thoughts and feelings you may have about what you observe.

(3. Read aloud or project all the papers of one group that had a common locale. Discuss what things all noted, what things only one or two noted, differences in physical vantage points, differences in inference and personal reaction or mood.

To prepare for rewriting, use this set of papers to confront the question: "What would you have to do to this paper (the sample before them) in order to make it understandable and interesting to other people?" See first what things they think of to mention without prompting. You may have to guide them a bit toward things they do not mention. Have them look at their own papers, ask the same question, and write some responses on the papers. Some possibilities are:

1. clarifying some of the wording or references
2. dwelling more on some things and less on others
3. cutting out some things and adding others
4. giving more or less personal reactions
5. rewriting to avoid repetition of the same words or monotony of sentence structures (finding different words and constructions).

These discussions of Assignments 1–3 should make possible some successful collaborating in the small groups (see pupil's Assignment 4 slip).)

Compose one of the foregoing papers.

4. You will be put in a group with two or three other pupils, and you will all help each other to select and rewrite one of your papers. So take Assignments 1, 2, and 3 to your group, and exchange all three papers for the three papers of someone else in the group. Read those three and decide which one could best be rewritten into

an interesting composition for the rest of the class to read.

Write on that paper some comments. Say why you think it has the best possibilities, and make suggestions about how it could be rewritten. Would you like to know more about some things he or she mentions? Could some things be cut out without a loss? Would you change the order in which he mentions things (put some things later and move others nearer to the beginning)? What suggestions would you make about changing the words and changing the way some sentences are written? If you see spelling mistakes, correct them. Try to be as helpful as you can; remember that the other person is doing the same thing for you, and that his comments will make it easier for you to decide what to rewrite and how to rewrite.

When you and your partner have finished reading each other's three papers and writing comments on them, you may talk about the comments. Then exchange with another and do the same thing again until you have been all the way around the group.

Next, look over the comments made on your papers and talk over with the other members of the group any questions you may have about what they said. You do not *have* to follow their suggestions, but knowing what they think should help you decide which paper to rewrite and how to go about doing it.

"Rewrite" means not only improving sentences but also making large changes — adding new things, cutting out old ones, and moving other things around.

Now rewrite, in whatever you think will be the most interesting way, what you observed at one of your three places. All of the finished papers will be read later by the whole class.

When you hand in your final composition, hand in Assignments 1, 2, and 3 with it.

(4. Discussion of the finished papers should feature comparison of them with the original papers from which they were rewritten. That is, ditto or project an Assignment 4 paper along with its predecessor and ask the class what changes the writer made, how he got from one stage to the next, and what purposes they assume he had for making such changes. For discussion pick two or three pairs that show different *degrees* of revision or different *bases* of revision.)

Results and Conclusions

The specific invitation to include personal reactions and comparisons did in fact lead to an increase in both. Teachers who talked up similes and metaphors a lot got more of them, but I felt that some of the comparisons thus elicited were strained. Teachers who emphasized imaginative freedom in rewriting for Assignment 4 caused many children to restore thoughts and feelings that they had while recording but did not note down. Asking the pupils to rewrite only one out of three recordings allowed them to choose the material of greatest interest to them and to their audience, and spared most children from being stuck with a dull set of notes. The very process of selecting the best set — through discussion, written comments by other pupils, and the author's own comparison of recordings — accomplishes a lot of the composing that one normally expects from written revision alone. The fact that each pupil recorded alone away from school gave more point to writing up an account of observations, since the class audience was being informed of something it had not been in on. When several pupils recorded together, for Assignment 3, the bulk of this audience remained to be informed, and the opportunity for comparing different versions of the same scenes added interest, I believe.

The strategy for handling the biggest problem of all, the note taking itself, requires longer explanation and involves some of the other problems.

Difficulties of note taking. Sensory recording seems to invite a lot of concrete data but actually requires great summarization and consequent loss of information. Sometimes the notations are disappointingly colorless and undetailed, and do not leave much material for later composition. But this is a *valuable problem.* Although it could be viewed as an unnecessary and artificial constraint, it is better viewed as a reality of any kind of recording. That is, *if* one's purpose is to take down external events, and *if* the means of recording is slower than the events (as writing certainly is), then it will always follow that (1) the recorder's reactions to what he sees and hears (his nonsensations) may lose priority to the stimuli themselves, and (2) language will necessitate a selective, summary notation. For the sake of certain gains, one takes certain losses.

These conditions inhere not only in the assignment but in the nature of recording as well. Since selectivity and summary are at the heart of information processing and of composing, this is an excellent difficulty that the constraints of recording impose. To exploit it for learning, the teacher should make the loss of information (both of reactions and of external details) a central issue of the assignment, in discussion and in composing Assignment 4. Solutions lie in sacrificing large *coverage* of everything that was observed for the sake of doing better justice to fewer things, and in reducing the speed of recording in order to permit more elaborated linguistic structures (modifiers, qualifiers, fuller phrases and sentences.) All this amounts to a real exploration of the art of note taking — how to vary attention, speed, and coding qualities in the light of considered gains and losses. The children can carry out this exploration in an operational way by experimenting with different ways of note taking, by comparing and discussing the results, and by finding out for themselves the advantages and disadvantages that different ways of recording offer for compositional rewriting.

IMPROVEMENTS TO BE MADE OVER THE TRIALS

I have several reservations about the directions reproduced on pages 189–192. To begin with, I instinctively resist formalizing assignments to that degree; the definitive look tends to mask uncertainties and to hamper the discovery of other possibilities. Also, some problems that became clear only in the course of trials were not allowed for in these directions, and some other matters that I would have liked to have put in would simply have over-burdened the project.

Engagement with the material. The first issue is that a lot more emphasis should be placed on seeking out scenes of action, or at least scenes of specific personal interest. Too often our more passive children simply went fatalis-tically to the nearest place, although many other children either instinctively selected a good place or else made a personally meaningful selection of events at a random locale. What should probably be avoided are mere landscapes and still lifes. They bore most children, who have not yet found how observ-ing leads to involvement and thus to interest. For novices, at least, more human and dramatic scenes would be better. But no one knows yet the effect of cumulative experience in recording over the years — whether or not the higher development of observational powers would increase interest in things of smaller note.

My concern about occasional flagging of interest and motivation may be unduly influenced by situational factors. By the spring these children had already had an excessive dosage of sensory writing, because the experimenting was all done in one year with one group (the school had no sixth grade at the time). The consensus of the teachers afterwards was that sensory writing should be spread over the years, and that the in-school recording of isolated senses should be shifted to the lower grades so that in the upper grades pupils would have already many of the skills and much of the perception to make more random observation interesting. Also, we inevitably, but perhaps un-fairly, compared the slow response to sensory writing with the quick, en-thusiastic response to memory writing, which has built-in advantages worth mentioning here.

A memory comes from within and is thus by nature personally meaning-ful. That is why it is remembered. One is already involved. Furthermore, a memory is something that has *previously* been recorded and so, at the moment of recall, exists already in a selectively digested form convenient for wording. This difference in coding helps us to understand the unique difficulties of recording: the observer may have no prior personal relation to what he wit-nesses; he confronts raw material that he must encode for the first time.

These truths are qualified, of course, by the fact that any observer brings to bear on what he witnesses his memories of similar things or perhaps of the same things, so that the "raw material" becomes immediately associated with past experience and hence assimilated to the inner life. This is precisely the gist of my reservation about the assignments as we gave them: they did not insure enough that what was recorded would engage the inner life and draw on personal associations. (A typical symptom of revised landscape recordings was, in lieu of personal meaning, a reliance on nature clichés and flowery language as a means of drumming up reader interest, the effort itself betraying the writer's own mild involvement.)

Purpose of the writing. But of course involvement and motivation stem from purpose as well as subject, and I think the mimeographed assignments lacked emphasis here too. Although the directions stated that recordings would be used later and that the write-up (Assignment 4) would be an account for the class to read, I think now that we should have given more purpose to all of the writing. This could be done by setting up the four assignments as a class literary magazine or newspaper operation. The pupils go out getting fresh material and shape it together for publication. The teacher can explain that just as a photographer has to take many pictures to get the one he likes, writers have to sift different material for some that will make the best reading.

In the experiments, we tended to reveal stages of the series one at a time because I was afraid that foreknowledge of what was to come would cause the pupils to record with too much of an eye to the next stage. But of course after the first round or so they knew anyway that they would rewrite, and this foreknowledge did not seem to spoil the recording; in fact it would have strengthened purpose and motivation.

Discussion of recordings as outlined in the directions would be combined with editorial deliberations. Since part of these deliberations concerns classifying items for the magazine as more personal or impersonal, discussing the degree of private response and objective account would be more natural and less academic. The same practical bent could be given to group experimentation with different ways of note taking, usages of language, and processes of selecting detail.

Revising. Characterizing the project in this more meaningful way may help to solve another problem. As we set it up, the rewriting (Assignment 4) entailed three versions of the scene — the original recording, the rewrite of it that was read and commented on by partners, and the final copy that incorporated the comments and corrections. A child this age is apt to find the third draft tedious, especially since it involves a lot of copying even if partners recommend several revisions. The more revisions, the more point to another draft, but not all first rewrites need much change, and of course sometimes the suggestions for revision may be meager.

It is hard to be sure of the best course here, because so many factors play into the revision process. Our pupils, for example, had had little experience in commenting on each other's writing. Our setting up of discussions about the recordings and of the small-group cross-commentary suffered from all the muddling through of a first trial, so that the insights and feedback that give revision its real reason for being were much sparser than I think they could be. (The teachers themselves did not write comments and corrections.)

Also, revising is notoriously resisted by students, even in high school. The original impetus for writing is over; their concept of revising (probably conditioned by conventional teaching) is to tidy up through minor adjustments; and the copying is dull and unrewarding. Many times I noticed that a pupil's final copy was not as good as the one before, because the pupil — even when he was able and well motivated — cut back and simplified his material to reduce the labor of the final copy. Ill-considered assignments of revision can actually make for bad writing.

Recommendations

Generally, my recommendations include the directions reprinted earlier but with modifications that should solve the problems that have been brought out. Greater flexibility and a better motivational frame are needed.

PROCEDURES

Solutions to the revision problem are of several sorts, all of which, I think, should be tried together. The principle underlying them all is that revision incorporating commentary should be justified by actual needs: it will provide final material for publication, and the amount of revision suggested will really require another writing. The first rewrite should be in pencil, so that if the paper stands well as is, except for minor alterations, these can be made by erasing and writing in. If much copying is involved, that is a sign that the amount of revisions do not warrant another draft. This means that some pupils will truly revise Assignment 4 — add, subtract, shift, and reshape — and some will stop with Assignment 4. There is no sensible reason for uniformity across the board; revision should be for a real purpose and not just to provide "clean copy," which, for that matter, the dittoed publication will provide (for folders, bulletin boards, parents, etc.). Children have too much honest writing to do to be made to spend time copying. Only in the wrong atmosphere, where children felt that the whole project was just a chore for the teacher's benefit, would the pupils who do an additional version feel any injustice. The whole point is that when the commentary from peers is good the motivation to make changes willingly is strong. And, as a couple of samples will show later, pupils' suggestions to each other can be very good indeed.

Putting together a publication, furthermore, motivates children to pursue their composing process until they have achieved a version they like. Also, those teachers in the experiment who emphasized the liberties one may take with material helped tremendously to promote well motivated revision. Once the concept of rewriting is extended well beyond the pupils' notion of tidying up, then a further draft becomes more like an initial composition, and a fresh impetus to write arises again.

Most of all, the success not only of revision but of any writing project depends on effective exploitation of the group process of discussion and feedback. Without marks and written comments from teachers, our children did a huge amount of high quality writing that came out at least as correct as their usual writing. Despite our weak and uncertain setting up of the group process, and despite the inexperience with it of both teachers and pupils, the pupil cross-commentary and collaboration loomed as a powerful learning method. But to ensure informed feedback, focused class discussion of writing samples is required, and to ensure helpful feedback, a climate of collaboration rather than competition, of pupil rather than teacher initiative, must prevail in the classroom. Since this group process will be a staple method of teaching writing throughout this program, I will try to define it more clearly here, drawing on the experience of trials in junior and senior high as well as in elementary school.

THE WRITING WORKSHOP

The teacher's main role is to set up and oversee a cross-teaching operation among pupils. Select and project sample papers from an assignment and lead class discussion of the samples until the issues the pupils are to focus on later in groups have been well aired. Afterwards, break the groups into threes and fours, direct them to read each other's papers and discuss them in terms of these same issues, then lapse into a secondary role as ambulatory consultant. Thus the problems inherent in recording — sensory data versus personal reaction, the form of note taking, personal selectivity, inference, point of view — come up under teacher guidance but are shifted then to the groups.

A simple keynote question about the projected samples, especially if it is a comparative question, will plunge the children into the issue without didactic hocus pocus: "What differences do you notice between the way this person took notes and the way that one did?" "What changes did this person make between this version and that version?" "Do you think you understand why he cut this and added that?" Or, to keep discussions related to the overall project: "You're the editors as well as the writers of the magazine. When you suggest changes to each other, you may have to decide whether you would like the author to play up his personal reactions or to stick more to straight reporting. Look at this paper. What are the things that tell more about the observer than the scene? What would you suggest to the author?"

Examples of issues for discussion. While remaining concrete and germane to the publication goal of the project, the issues raised this way can range among a lot of important semantic, stylistic, rhetorical, and linguistic matters. For example, comparing projections of two recordings made in the same time and place can direct attention to alternative wordings for the same thing. *Flower* or *blossom:* "Which is better, considering mood and purpose?" Comparing a telegraphic recording and a rewriting of it in full sentences leads to discussion of sentence elements and sentence expansions.

The conjoining and embedding of short sentences to form fewer, more complex sentences comes up for scrutiny as a matter of avoiding monotonous repetition. That is, in sensory recording the order of words follows closely the order of events and results in short declarative sentences that repeat the same words and begin with *now, then,* and *next.* A pupil who revises merely by expanding kernel phrases (*coat falling*) into kernel sentences (*I see a coat falling,* or *the coat fell*) ends up with a lot of repeated *I's* or *coats* and a string of data predicated in a string of separate sentences.

Although the heart of the matter is learning to build complex sentences by combining simple ones — a major linguistic development of this age — it can be broached as a practical matter of style. When projecting such a paper the teacher states that sensory recording carries a built-in problem of word repetition and sentence monotony and asks them how it might be solved in that paper. Some will suggest joining sentences with conjunctions like *after, while,* and *during.* This leads to subordination, at which point the teacher must make sure that their suggestions allow for proper emphasis as well as for style. If, for "The pole is breaking. He slid down the pole." someone proposes "While he was sliding down, the pole broke," suggest that maybe the author meant, "While the pole was breaking he slid down," or "After the pole broke, he slid down." The author is then consulted, as should happen often in these discussions. (Comparison of alternatives is so often the key to learning.)

As suggested in these dummy sentences, another natural problem common to the age and especially raised by the rewriting of recordings is the mixing of tenses. Many children get hung up between the present viewpoint of the recording and the past viewpoint of the revision and reflect this in a wavering of verbs between the two. And again, sensory recording offers rich possibilities for development of vocabulary. Some discussion should center on how things are named and include specific suggestions from pupils and teacher to the writer about other words he might use.

A final example concerns titles, another omission from the directions used in the experiment. Setting up a working title, perhaps to be changed in a final draft, helps the writer to think about the totality of his subject and about what he intends to do with it. All directions for compositions and drafts thereof should constantly remind pupils to entitle their pieces. Recordings themselves are obviously excepted, but as a lead into collaborative revision, the teacher might project a recording and ask the class to propose titles that would do justice to it. If the recording has a natural unity or coherence, proposing titles can bring it out; or if the recording is miscellaneous, the titles can suggest ways of reshaping that would build a unity from selected elements in it. If the composition is projected, the teacher may block out the title, ask the class to entitle it, then let them compare their suggestions with the author's original. This brings out discrepancies between intention and effect, such as misleading emphasis, which the class can discuss, or reveals matching of intention with effect. All such kinds of feedback are valuable and would be transferred to the group relationships.

Cross-teaching. And that is the teacher's function in group process — to create models of talking together and helping each other that pupils can put into operation in small units. It is harder and more fun than correcting papers. More writing can go on, and with better results. Instead of asking for a very occasional assignment, done in one shot, which a pupil is either able to do or not, which tests more than it teaches, and from which the pupil discovers afterward — too late — all the things he should have done but did not, the compositional process is now phased and externalized. It is subjected to feedback and correction along the way, provided in greater quantity and by equals in the game, not by authoritative superiors. Attention is on the actual learning issues, not on one's status with the teacher and on sibling rivalry. Errors are exploited, not avoided. Writing is learning, not being tested on a sink-or-swim basis. Final products benefit from learning and leave a feeling of achievement, instead of revealing ignorance and leaving a sour taste. But it is the teacher who has shown the children how to do this for each other. Out of his spirit he creates the climate of collaborative learning and helpful responding. Out of his understanding of language and composition, he focuses the issues implicit in the assignments and sets up model ways of commenting and proposing.

The chief obstacle to cross-teaching, I found, is the past conditioning of both teachers and pupils. There are no intrinsic reasons for this group process to fail. Any misleading of one pupil by another is tremendously outweighed by the increased writing practice, the constant and varied feedback, which no teacher could otherwise provide. And small groups tend to set misleading individuals straight. (One teacher paired pupils for the revision of the write-up — with, I must say, very good results — but the hazard of this practice is the loss of group consensus.) Our experiments showed, I believe, that the children instinctively spot some writing problems even without focusing; I noticed that they are especially good at catching poor punctuational segmenting, run-on sentences with *and,* unnecessary repetition, obscure phrasing, and failures to allow for the reader's viewpoint. What exacts good judgment from the teacher is deciding which issues he must raise himself and which ones they will confront anyway. Also, the raising of issues before the whole class must be related rather directly to the project goals and done with a light hand; ax grinding is out. More technical aspects of language and composition can be better taught when children are necessarily involved in them by the nature of the assignment. All the teacher does is help pupils see in the vague practical problems particular technical issues that actually constitute the problems.

SEQUENCE

Before illustrating some of these remarks with samples from the experiment, I should add a note on sequence. Assuming the sensory writing recommended for grades K–3, a project similar to the experimental one could be given once or twice each in grades four and five and twice in grade six. We have to allow for the fact that cumulative competence in both recording and revising would progressively decrease the necessity for many parts of the process described above, so that by fifth and sixth grades one or two recordings might suffice for gathering material, and most small-group work might proceed with much less preliminary raising of issues. To speak, then, of giving the assignment twice in grades five and six is simply to recommend two short projects of personal eyewitness reporting reduced according to whatever evolution further trials may indicate.

Discussion of Some Samples

Here is a fairly typical sample of a straightforward recording and revision of a landscape (done by a girl):

SEE	HEAR	SMELL
trees swaying	birds peep tweet	rich soil
grass	faint noises	fresh air
little bugs	from cars	
big gray rocks	bees buzzing	
branches shaking	dog collor shake	
a field of yellow	dog bark	
twigs braking	plane	
a tree house	leaves rustling	
birds over head	twigs fall to ground	

Listing by senses was a notation form adopted by a number of children and sometimes suggested by the teacher. It avoids "I hear" and "I see" but automatically forces out thought and feelings, unless, as one teacher told her pupils to do, they add a column for this. Pupils who use the column form once or twice should then try other forms. For one thing, it encourages the minimizing of linguistic structures, reducing them to nouns coupled with an adjective or a present participle. The more dispensable parts of speech such as articles and auxiliaries are virtually eliminated; adverbs, prepositions, and conjunctions are rare. Consequently, a lot of details and relationships are lost. As one should expect, the sound column consists of action, the smell column of things, and the sight column of both. Here is the revision (assignment 4):

> I can see the little bugs fly through the air and great big gray rocks sit in the same place all the time. I can hear a dog collor shake when he walks. Just smell the fresh air. The rich soil. Thoses birds tweeting and bees buzzing. The trees swaying and the bright green grass. The whole field with a yellow blanket covering it. The tree house way up high. I hear leaves rustling when the wind blows the wind knocks twigs off of trees and I hear the twigs fall to the ground faint noises from cars and a plane overhead.

It is worth noticing how phrases were joined and expanded into sentences, or expanded merely into longer fragments that do not quite become sentences because the obvious predicates were unnecessary and because there was too little action to warrant other predicates.

Now compare this revision with those by two other girls who were recording at the same time and same place as the first girl:

> The sound of little birds singing fills the clean fresh air. A field of green and yellow is at one of me. Silence fills the air exsept for the pretty birds singing and a few cars going on their way. There goes an airplane roering through the sky. It is quiet and peaceful now. The sun gleams as we write.

> We walk into the woods. The birds are chirping loudly. A car is going by very fast. Up above me is a tree house. The air smells fresh. Look at all those bright yellow dandelions. I wonder what Terry and Kathy are thinking. There goes a bird. Here comes two dogs. They must be repairing a road somewhere. There goes an airplane. It feels dark and creepy in here.

Only a few items were noted by all three children — the birds, the airplane, the fresh air, the car, and the yellow field. (Only one identified the yellow covering as dandelions.) Only two mentioned the tree house. Several things were mentioned by just one child — the bugs, the rich soil, the gray rocks, the sun, the bees, the twigs, the wind, the sound of road repairing. I do not think that sensory recording should become a contest to see who can cram in the most details, but, without *invidious* comparisons, children can see what items their companions caught that they missed or deliberately left out. Discussion may show that some of these discrepancies are due to differences in physical vantage points. Part of discussion can consist of inferring the time, locale, and weather as implied by the details (such implications are characteristics of haiku poetry). The mood established at the end of the second and third papers is very different — one of sunny peacefulness, the other "dark and creepy" (is one observer in the field, the other in the woods?).

All three versions above are essentially miscellaneous enumerations, the hardest kind of material to shape into a unity. Mood is perhaps the best possibility. Real moments of being are made of just such miscellanies, but one should not expect children to be able to compose more than a mood from such a scene. All three revisions are of the simplest sort. Little more than verbal expansion has taken place; tense and point of view remain in the present; selection and arrangement are slight, probably because the children could see nothing central to focus on, as they might have had there been more action or had they added more thoughts and feelings. These are notes in more presentable form, nice writing of a sort but probably not lively enough for most children.

From what looked like rather unpromising notes, a boy very consciously composed a mood piece:

ON OUR SUN PORCH

Hear: Birds singing
Airplane
Trees rustling
People talking
grinding of sand under peoples
    shoes
cars
doors slaming

looks like: everything looks
    gloomy
Houses
birds
people
cars
neighbor swings and play area
air plane
trees waving

I feel like I am lonley and cold
everything smells like pine sap

As the day wore on the clouds had grown dark and thicker. All the children were in their houses and the only person in sight was the mailman as he slowly walked his route.

The birds that had been singing earlier had stopped and all was quiet.

Now there same a rustle in the leaves. Slowly it grew louder and finally it fell into a steady rythm.

The twitering in the trees gradually ceased as the birds settled down in their nests from the night and the rain.

Besides shifting the tense and creating sentences, this boy deliberately omitted all details that did not suit his purpose.

Of course, there are always a few professionals, like the girl below, who can scent a good story a long way off and begin composing when they select the time and place. As her first sentence shows — these are the *notes* — she achieved her unity when she chose the occasion:

We're eating outside tonight. General bustling and "organized confusion" to bring all plates, food, etc., outside. Dad supervising and cooking steak over coals at same time. Mom making rest of food and telling people what goes where. Kids bringing food outside, running back and forth, bumping into each other. Occassional fights break out, e.g., who sets table, who sits where, whose napkin that is, why did you bring the tape in the house when I needed it, etc. etc., but good feeling prevails. Mom asks "Who's cutting up the pickles?" My sister gets them out. Mom yells, "Oh, the rice is boiling over! !" At the same time Dad yells, "Oh, the steak's burning!" and rushes to turn it over. Now the table and food's ready. Dad yells "Sue! We're eating!" Sue, who is doing homework, yells "Coming!" and thunders down the stairs. We sit down to eat. The steak smells good. So do pickles. Too bad no potatoes. We sit down to eat. Now I have to sit down too.

All this needs is paragraphing, indicated by the appropriate symbol, and occasional inserting of an auxiliary (*kids* [*are*] *bringing food*) unless the decision is made to shift all of the verbs into the past (a very dubious move here). If required to do another draft, it is quite likely that this superior student would cut out a lot of detail and ruin a lively sketch. That she was organizing *as* she recorded can be seen in the abstractive device of summarizing repeated or typical action in a series, especially in the sentence "Occassional fights break out, e.g. . . ."

Think of a title for the following piece, a revised recording by a girl:

Cars zooming down the highway looking like little toy cars going down a little toy road. Light taps of rain coming down on everyones windows. Splashes going up then down with children watching them gayly.
Once I heard one child say "What would it be like to be a rain drop?"
His brother Tom he asked "What would it be like to be one of those stiff people?" pointing to a tree.
Thoughts just filled my head with answers but they had gone away.

The first half establishes a setting with several images; the second half relates an incident that either happened in that setting or was recalled to the child by it. The piece seems split, but the halves are joined by raindrops. In proposing and discussing titles for it, other pupils would have to determine what kind of notion would contain it, how sharp or vague the title would have to be. I think also that they would ask the author if the second half were a memory or an observation, and he could clear up the ambiguity of "Once I heard one child say . . .", if indeed they think it should be cleared up (for the whole piece reads like an impressionistic reverie and reminds one a bit of some of Dylan Thomas' evocations of childhood). The author's own title was "The Highway," which might have been an unconscious metaphorising of the composition itself — the inner trip that begins in one place and ends somewhere very different — or may well have been simply a reference to an initial image from which he carelessly strayed later. But in discussing his title, his classmates are helping him know what he wrote and at the same time tackling the whole business of coherence.

Whatever one thinks of it, the composition shows how sensory data can become subjective by individual selection, personal reference, and thought association. It could have made a good poem, especially the second part and perhaps all of it. The last line has the climactic stuff of which a last line is made in a poem. And this possibility is one that I have not brought up before. We did not try it out in the experiment, but as I read the papers I wish we had. The teacher could project either a recording or a revision, say that he feels it would make a good poem, then suggest to them that they keep the possibility in their minds as they comment on each other's papers in small groups. Branching out into the poetic mode may prove to be at least as important as most of the possibilities I have discussed here.

One of the reasons that I have dwelled so long on sensory recording is that it can be the gateway to more kinds of writing than one would expect at first. It is best thought of not only as a thing in itself, for data gathering and personal reportage, but also as a springboard for invention. For imaginative writing it has two advantages: it makes stale imitation more difficult, and it makes getting an idea easier. The point of departure is a real and fresh one, and it is a definite one. The girl's composition below illustrates one direction a revision may take. Her invention here is not in fictionalizing but in typicalizing the specific events into a generality about herself:

"SATURDAY MORNING"

There's one thing I "hate" to do. That is to get up in the morning. One morning I just despised. That was June 4th, 1966. I think I'll tell you about it.

It all started the night of June 3rd. The whole week had been very hot and sticky. Like I always did, I pushed my blanket to the end of the bed, lied down, cuddled up, and fell asleep.

I slept like a dog, and probably wouldn't have woke up at 7:30, but would have slept to 9:00 or 10:00, if . . . someone hadn't got married, and drove down our street, with, or about ten to fifteen cars honking after them. But someone did get married, and they did drive down our street, about 7:30 and I woke up. I was cold and pulled my blanket over me.

Just as I settled back down, taking a good breath of fresh air, the milkman came. The bottles were clinking and making too much noise. The man pulled open the door, and shut it again making a louder racket then before.

Finally, when I was half asleep again, and everything was quiet my father got up and started to shave. In a few minutes I got used to the soft buzzing sound, and almost fell asleep again, when . . . my grandmother, decided she had to go to the bathroom. She went stamping through the hall, and woke me up again. The toilet flushed. Then my shade went up. I had to get out of bed to pull it down again.

When I finally got settled, a crow went by, and started to caw. He probably was screaming, for he sure was cawing loudly. By this time I was thoroughly distressed.

When my mother started the vacuum cleaner and the crow came by again I pushed down my blankets, gave a loud scream, and got up. (that's a good way to get me up. Just go through all the things I mentioned again. Otherwise you'll never get me up.)

This personal essay issued from these notes:

> tweet, chirp
> Honk, Honk
> trees, grass
> I see a window, a table
> I smell fresh air.
> clink, clink, bottles clinking
> quiet. . . . . .
> . . .clap, puff, footsteps, rattle
> rattle, clink. everything is
> getting up. A misty morning
> coldness
> swish, swish, peep, peep
> caw, caw
> lightness
> a vacuum cleaner
> Honk _____
> Honk _____
> Honk _____
> screech — eeeeeeeeeeeeee
> cold, you, who — whisler
> slam, bang, of car door
> tweet caw.

As a point of departure, this recording is much superior to an abstract topic given by the teacher such as "Getting Up in the Morning," which would probably not have stimulated this girl to write so fully and richly or with so much real interest. This way, the details crystallize into a topic and the child creates his own category of experience — Saturday Morning or whatever — instead of trying to fill in a prefabricated category by "racking his brains" and coming up with stereotypes of school compositions.

Some children, like this boy, invented a fiction based on their notes.

1. I can hear my friend slurping on a watermelon.
2. I can smell the freshly cut grass.
3. I can see and hear my nextdoor neighbor squirting his hose on his new grass.
4. I can see and hear my friend laughing.
5. I can hear in the distance, cars going along rt. 2.
6. I can hear the wind blow against the trees.
7. I can hear one of our neighbors hammering away at his house.
8. I can hear my friends yelling down the road.

OLD FARMER BROWN

Once upon a time, there was a farmer, his name was Old Farmer Brown. One sunny day he planted a seed. He did not know what kind of a seed it was. Farmer Brown had other jobs to do besides planting seeds. He had to cut and water the lawn, and he had to fix the steps that broke in half the year before. After a few months, he went back to see how his mysterious seed was growing. All of a sudden he started laughing. He found that his seed had turned into a plant that looked like a green football. He decided to see what it tasted like. It was watery and tasted somewhat like a melon. "I know what I'll call it!," exclaimed Farmer Brown, "I'll call it a WATER-MELON!" After that, Farmer Brown went running down the road telling everyone about his discovery.

Apparently this boy amalgamated his slurping friend and his busy neighbors into the single figure of Farmer Brown. Besides taking for his central object the watermelon that opened his recording, he employed also the cutting and watering of grass and the seasonal setting. Although he probably borrowed from other stories the name of Farmer Brown and the theme, he has created a fresh story of his own.

The next boy capitalized less well on his notes, I would say. I think he could have benefited from more commentary than his one partner could give him. Here is the story:

Billy was trapped inside an old building. He saw nothing but darkness! Bill screamed for help but no one heard him. Suddenly he heard foot steps comming closer, closer, closer then faded away. Bill screamed and yelled again untill he couldn't scream any more. Then there was scilence. Bill listened to the "shh" sound of the water pipes. Then he heard the loud "clip-clop" noise of the policemen as they came to the rescue.

And here are the notes that preceded it:

(I am in the Celler)

I hear foot steps, coming closer and closer the stoping and walking ferther away.

I hear the heater   The heater sound like water going thrue a drain that is partly cloged.

I hear the fawsett. It sounds like someone saying "shh".

I hear a high srill sound   I don't know what it is a "super radar ray" on T.V.

I smell paint It smells like turpintine.

I see darkness.

I hear a noise like an airplane out of gas.

I hear foot steps coming towards me.

I hear water going into the drain as a jar cover falls to the floor.

I hear the refrigerator door open. I feel coldness when the refrigerator door opens.

The dog comes in for breakfast and smells like damp grass.

I see the kichtion

These details are rich and he might have used more of them, spaced throughout the story, to emphasize the suspense of Billy's waiting. But he did insert the footsteps and the "shh" of the water pipes for this purpose, and no doubt his experience recording in the cellar put him in the right state of mind for this story and enabled him to give the situation reality.

To help this boy's spelling, the teacher could diagnose for him the kinds of errors he makes. *Ferther, fawsett,* and *turpintine* are all logical errors based in fact on his understanding of sound-letter correspondences. For example, *er* and *ur* are both possible spellings for the sound; to be wrong with *ferther* and right with *turpintine* is a matter simply of memorizing the troublesome parts of the words, for nothing else can tell him which alternate spelling to use when the sound is in that position. The same is true regarding the *aw* and the *s* in *fawsett,* which are alternates in English for *au* and *c,* given the position. Unstressed *in* and *en* (*turpintine*) are also logical alternates. But doubling the consonant after a short vowel and before the verb ending is a regularity of spelling (*stoping* and *cloged*), and mentioning that regularity would help the boy. *Srill* and *kichtion* belong to a third category of error, I would guess (not knowing the child): they probably stem from faulty pronunciation, since he seems to write pretty phonetically. The teacher would ask him to pronounce the words, in order to check this hunch; then he would pronounce the words in the standard dialect, by which they are spelled. The point is to classify for the pupil his various errors so that he can go on to recognize them himself and thus to attack each kind in the special way it requires.

The girl's story below was also done in the class where the teacher suggested a very free-wheeling way of rewriting the notes. The effect of this suggestion can be seen on both the author and her partner. The notes read:

1. I see a kitchen full of cooking things.
2. Water driping, it is like rain.
3. refregerato sounds like a humming bird with a cold.
4. I smell ham
5. hammering, it sounds like the wolf trying to get into the pigs house.
6. birds singing like they are lost and scared.
7. I smell some coffee
8. I see a pitch black cat out of the window that looks like a spooky house
9. door shakes, like on a old spooky house.
10. a loud drill sounds like a bearser.
11. trees moving in the wind look like the green giant sneezed.

12. I see cupcakes that look very good
13. clothes on the table
14. I see some different kinds of plants in the windows that make me think of a jungle.

The partner's comments read:

14, 2, 5, 9, 11, 10, 6, 8, 3, 12, 13, 4, 1. You could have notes in this order. I think this starts high up then comes to the Kitchen. You will have to add some things inbetween. It has good possibilities because you compared it to something else or what you thought it was like.

The suggestion is to reorder these sensations completely and to place last the general statement that opens the notes. Partly, she is proposing an inductive description that would start with particulars and let the reader identify the setting for himself. Actually, the author declined the suggestion in favor of making up a story, which may have been another pupil's idea.

A Hide And Go Seek Game

"It's your turn to count while we hide."
"All right. One two three four five." ect.
"Where will we hide?"
"I'll hide in the kitchen behind the door. (he is behind the door).
It sure is dark in here. Look at all of those pots and pans.
The water dripping gives me the chills.
And the refridgerator sounds like a sick humming bird.
I wonder if Tom is going to invite me to lunch? Because I smell ham.
Here comes Tom. He's looking for me. *WOW!* he just passed me. I see Tom, he is looking for Wendy now. Tom's father must be hammering. He is making a lot of noise.
That window has a lot of plants in it. It looks like a jungle.
Tom must be thinking about inviting me to lunch. Because there is some good looking cupcakes over there.
I guess Tom found Jane. I can here her laughing.
That coffee smells real good.
I think it is going to rain. The wind is blowing so hard that trees are almost falling over, the door is shaking too.
I think Tom found everone but me. They are all looking for me. Here they come. *WOW!* The just passed me again. oh! the door squeeked, now Im sure they'll find me. They're back again. They're looking around.
"THEY FOUND ME!"

This draft benefited from the following corrections made by her partner. Quotation marks were put into the opening exchange of dialogue with a remark explaining the need to differentiate speakers. "It sure is dark in here and look at all of the pots and pans" was broken into two sentences by cutting *and,* placing a period after *here* and capitalizing *look.* I *here Tome* was changed to I *see Tom,* correcting both a spelling and an author's lapse of attention. An inadvertent omission was supplied — I [*can*] *hear* — and *pased* was corrected to *passed.*

Let's look now at a rather complicated bit of collaboration:

In my playroom 4:20 PM May 17, 1966
Gong! ! ! Gong! ! ! like a herd of elephants crossing the boarder
Crying, like a Baby girrafe
Laughing, like a laughing hiena
Water falling sounds like a SWISHING waterfall.
A gold glass ball that tingles and looks like the reflection of a mirror.
A sweat peppery smell of "Mothers Best soup"
The end of my mothers apron string that looks like the tail of a BLUE
    donkey

One commentator wrote, "It could be rewritten as a funny story. The spelling needs help!" Another wrote, "It could be rewritten about a main character 'Mother' — about a mother and 8 confusing children, all sizes!" The last added, "Rewrite it as a story, take turns, writing chapters." He meant for the author and the second commentator each to write a chapter of the story that the second commentator had suggested. So the author rewrote:

MOTHER AND HER PROBLEM, "8 CHILDREN!"

Chapter I

Gong! ! Gong! ! Goes my sister Jana, playing with the door-bell. Boy. It sounds like a herd of elephants crossing the boarder! I heard Jeanie crying like a baby giraffe, because she didn't have her two-oclock feeding yet. Next I saw mother walk into the kitchen. She opened the cabinet, and saw little Robie playing with his tool kit, on the water pipe. I *never,* in my life, heard her scream so loud! ! I just heard my big sister Vicky telling a joke, and brother Stevy laughing like a laughing hiena! Well you can guess what happens next, just turn the page over to the next chapter and see! ! !

A colleague changed the placement of the title and the chapter in order to space and to center them (as here), told her to indent the first sentence and to start new paragraphs with I *heard Jeanie* and *Next I saw Mother,* and deleted the comma in *playing with his tool kit, on the water pipe.* The next chapter, written by the other pupil, was:

Chapter II

CRASH! I knew it would happen some time. All day Billy just sits with a glass ball on his finger. While twirling the ball on his finger, he tries to look in to see his reflection. He had to drop it sometime.

I wonder what that smell is? As I walked into the kitchen the smell got stronger. "Oh NO!" Jeanie had spilt the soup that takes Mother a whole day to make. It was all over the floor! ! When mother saw it she suddenly had a headace that lasted a week!

Tammy, the baby of the family, was tugging at my mothers apron string. She is all right. She does't do anything bad. Well Ive told you about my family, good luck to yours.

I end anti-climatically with a modest story by a much less sophisticated boy:

PLAYROOM

1. The vacum cleaner sounds like a eleghant.
2. The rug looks like a green on a golf course
3. The T.V. looks like a martians head and the antena for his built in walkie-talkie (in his head).

John and Paul were playing outside. Then Paul said, "Let's go to my house and play in the playroom."

John and Paul started to play. John said, "Let's pretend we are martians and the T.V. is the chief martian. They played that for a while.

Then Paul said, "Lets pretend we are golfers and golf on the rug. They golfed for a while. Then John's mother called and he had to go home.

(Judiciously, a partner deleted *They golfed for a while.*) He is trying a bit too hard to get in those similes, and yet the third one provides him with the fantasy part of his story: comparing the TV set to a Martian's head is a piece of imagining that resembles closely the pretenses of children's games. His achievement, like that of other children who write briefly and perhaps not very maturely, may not be so impressive or so much fun to show other teachers, but at the level of the boy's own development it may represent just as much learning as pieces that adults would value more. Sensory writing allows a child to work and learn in the way that is right for him at the time. He cannot fail to do the assignment right, because any pupil can observe and put down something of what he sees. He cannot fail to make some changes during rewriting and to produce some kind of composition. The task is quite definite and yet accommodates itself to all capacities.

Advantages for the Slower Pupil

The experiment indicated other advantages of sensory writing and of phased writing in general. The relaxed nature of note taking helps many less able children simply to put down words. They are relieved of the technical and formal aspects of writing that seem so formidable to unsure pupils who are accustomed to having trouble spelling and formulating sentences and shaping a presentation. They do not go blank trying to get ideas for what to say. The phasing and the collaboration allow them to work up a composition gradually and with help. The whole process is less threatening and opens up some otherwise very inhibited children. It feels reassuringly structured to the child and yet is in fact quite open, since neither a subject nor a certain kind of final product is stipulated. It is the sort of thing a child will make whatever he can out of.

These assets are especially important if one teaches disadvantaged children. My experiments were done in a suburban school serving middle-class children of educated parents. (There are many reasons I will not go into here why it is difficult to get such experimentation going in inner cities.) The participating teachers felt, like all teachers, that they had plenty of verbally backward pupils who did not write well in any sense, and they reported that the informal writing helps these youngsters to get going. It has always been my intention to devise assignments that automatically adjust to the capacity of the pupils. I believe disadvantaged children can do any of the assignments in this program and learn as much from them as more verbally developed children. But timing and other aspects of sensory writing may need adapting. Most of all, what any pupil can do at this age will depend enormously on what he has or has not done before. Disadvantaged pupils who have been following this program up to here will probably be able to do many of the things with sensory writing that the children quoted here have done.

Recapitulating Pantomimes and Improvisations

Recapitulating is not, strictly speaking, recording, since the pupils write down *afterwards* what they saw happen before them. A small group does a pantomime or an improvisation before some classmates, who write an account of the skit as soon as it is over.

When we first tried sensory recording of dramas in Lexington, we found that watching and writing at the same time was too much for the children. We then settled for recapitulation, which in fact is an interesting kind of writing. By the time the story is over, one knows considerably more and interprets differently than he does in the middle of registering the events. A recapitulation reads much more like a summarized, connected narration. The important things are sifted out of less significant details, the behavior of the actors is understood in terms of the outcome, premature inferences are corrected, and the series of events is economically coded as a totality. Learning about such abstractive differences is one purpose of the assignment. But the main point is writing narrative.

PANTOMIMES

The greater ambiguity of pantomimes makes them better for comparing differences in inference and interpretation. The accounts may vary as regards not only the action but also the motives of the characters and the circumstances one should assume as background for the action.

In small groups the pupils read aloud and discuss their versions. What are the differences? Which account do they agree on most? The accounts should be entitled so that overall interpretation can be focused on. The acting also may come under scrutiny. Which particular gestures and movements led to very different inferences by spectators? Since the narratives are sure to vary in length and therefore in the ratio of detail to summary, some of the discussion could be about such variations. Then the actors are asked to remark on the discussion points.

Some pantomimes, of course, will not be ambiguous, and certainly the players should not try to confuse the audience. Their intention is to communicate. But some stories will inevitably lend themselves to double or multiple interpretation, and acting without dialogue means renouncing the explicitness of language. Players can thus learn how much language can prevent ambiguity and in what ways body English must compensate for the loss of words. (It goes without saying that these pantomimes dispense with introduction and narration.)

Writing recapitulations in small groups is a particularly intimate and intensive way of sharing and reacting (using an audience of three pupils). The pantomimists get a full and explicit response to their efforts, and a written story is the product of the activity. The writers know that the same will be done for them. Ensuing discussion can, in addition to clarifying the exact effects on the audience, help the writers revise their papers for further use. That is, if the pantomime communicated well, as shown by a high consensus of the spectators, then the group collaborates in putting together a publishable version that draws on all of the papers. If the versions are very different, then each spectator's story could be separately revised and distributed, the writers even being encouraged to carry the story further from its source by inventing along the lines of their original divergence. In this case, recapitulating a pantomime becomes one more point of departure for original story making.

IMPROVISATIONS

Improvisations are less ambiguous than pantomimes and need a different emphasis. Two actual accounts will demonstrate the tacks that may be taken.

One night as the Jone's family was about to watch T.V. there was an argument about what to watch. It all started like this.

"Whats on T.V. tonight children?" asked Mr. Jones.

"Lost in Space!" the children shouted all together.

"No I don't think that program is good for children". answered Mrs. Jone's

"Ohhh but we want Lost in Space its such a good program"... And it was just at the good part please"

"I'll see what on" said Mr. Jone's "Let me see here's a good program" (Mr. Jone's had been turning to different chanels as he had told the children not to do) "Lawence Welk its very educational"

"Ohhh we hate Lawence Welk ick!". said the children

"Children eather you watch Lawence Welk or go to bed." said Mr. Jone's "OK". answerd the children and that's how the Jone's family settled their problem.

This girl ably reproduced a lot of the dialogue. Except for the opening and closing generalizations, this came close to being a play script. The laconic summary below should be compared both with this and with a detailed account of the same improvisation on page 172.

Report Card Night

The Smith family is sitting at the table with their report cards. The parents said what did you get? and they all got bad marks. The father gave them all some chores to do.

For some purposes this account would be better; it is succinct and just.

The emphasis, then, in recapitulating improvisations would be on reporting differently for different purposes — on the varying degrees of narrative summary or dramatic elaboration. After one round in which the chips fall where they may, and after which the teacher projects samples such as those I have reproduced here, each pupil could next be told to write his account for a specific purpose. Groups are formed so that besides the actors each group has three spectators who do not know what the actors will do. One will write a very short synopsis, like the last example, to serve as a minimal situation for another group to improvise from; the second will write a longer narrative account, merely sampling the dialogue, to go into a class newspaper as a news item; the third will write a version that would as nearly as possible enable another group to use it as a script in putting on the skit for themselves.

Eventually all pupils would do all three kinds of recapitulation as well as be the actors. All these pieces of writing would have a function that would actually be carried out. In the groups, the pupils would read and suggest changes to the authors before the papers are handed over for improvising, printing, and acting out. These changes could include the adding of more detail and verbatim dialogue to the version that is to be used as the script. In effect, what pupils do is write narratives and plays, but without inventing the story, which is settled on by the actors. At the same time, the whole cycle of acting, writing, and talking is turned over in another way.

Chapter 14

Memory Writing

I would like to introduce now a kind of writing that will be new to pupils following this program. The composing process, however, is in many ways similar to that of sensory writing, and much of what was said about the latter will apply here. Student response to this assignment has been very good at whatever age I have tried it. Writing memories, I am convinced, should be a continuous activity throughout school. The main thing for the pupil to learn now is how to tap memories, as he did sensations, for their fresh material, and how to select and shape this material into compositions.

Memory writing was tried out by the same group of Lexington teachers (the Omega team) and with the same fourth- and fifth-grade pupils who were involved in sensory writing experiments. Generally, the teachers reported that the children liked writing memories very much and that getting them to stop was often difficult. The appeal, as with imaginative writing, lies in the highly personal content, to which significant feelings are attached. Memories tie into these feelings. But whereas the actualities of his past refer rather explicitly to experience the child is willing to acknowledge, his far-fetched stories allow him to refer obliquely and symbolically to feelings he cannot acknowledge. Both kinds of writing are important.

From reading a lot of children's memories, I would say that pre-adolescent children have natural defenses to suppress material that would be embarrassing if seen by others. Thus exchanging spontaneous memories is no exposure now but will be in later years. This makes it important to teach the process now before privacy becomes an obstacle.

Account of Trials

Again as a basis for commentary and recommendations, I reproduce here the directions given in the experiment. The remarks to the teacher are enclosed between parenthesis.

Directions

Spontaneous flow
of memories.

1. Look around the room at different things until something you see reminds you of something from your past — a place, person or event. Write that down. Now what other memory does that person, place, or event remind you of? Once you get started, keep writing down your memories. Don't worry about their being jumbled or jumping from one time to another. Write the memories in whatever way captures them quickly; these are notes for yourself. Don't worry about spelling or correct sentences; just record as many memories as you have time for. You will have about fifteen minutes. These notes will not be marked, but you will need them for a later assignment. For right now, it is better to get a lot of memories than to go into detail about one of them.

(1. The main purpose of this three-assignment series is to work with the *process* of composition. Starting with apparently random material—in this case, scattered recollections of different times and places connected only by private associations — the pupil shapes the material by stages of *selection* and *focus* into a finished narrative that allows for an outside audience.

Assignment 1 should produce a lot of material; at least that is the point of it — to get a jumble of fragments from which the pupil may select. In Assignment 2 he should narrow down — sacrifice coverage for elaborated detail. The recollection should begin to take on point or purpose: whatever determines the pupil's choice of *this* recollection rather than another carries with it some unity, some central feeling or idea. I assume that we remember things for certain reasons — they were a trial or a pleasure, a jolt or a relief — but that the pupil may very well not know consciously what kind of importance or value makes him prefer that recollection. Discussion and collaboration should help this *core experience emerge* so that he can organize around it. This core experience or dominant feeling is what will interest the reader. Assignment 3 should accommodate an audience by providing necessary information, making references public, perhaps explaining background, stripping away irrelevant and therefore misleading details, and making the vocabulary and sentences conform to universal understanding and expectations.

To launch Assignment 1, before handing out the assignment slips, demonstrate the association process yourself out loud to them. Look around the room, settle on an object, tell them something it reminds you of that happened once, then say what other memory that brings to mind, and so forth. If more illustration seems needed, ask a pupil to volunteer to do what you just did.

For discussion later, continue the procedure, used before in the sensory writing, of selecting a couple of papers and placing them before the class, dittoed or projected.

Discuss the different ways used by pupils to note down memories, using the sample papers and also asking the rest of the class to look at their papers and say how they went about it. Again, the relative advantages of list, telegraphic, and full styles might be discussed, including the issue of coverage vs. detail, but the assignment calls for coverage, and also, since they are registering their own memories, they can control the speed of the material better than when recording external events.

Focusing first on the sample papers and then on their own, get them to discuss the *sequences* of recollections: why memory A led to memory B? What are the connections? What feeling, idea, or mood seems to go with certain of the memories? The class can speculate about the sample papers, then ask the authors for corroboration of what they have said.)

Expanded single memory.

2. Look over your Assignment 1 paper and pick out a memory of some incident that interests you and that you would like to do more with. An "incident" would be something that happened on a particular day, unless you feel that what happened on two or three different occasions goes together as one memory. Now think about that memory and write down, as notes for yourself still, all the details you can recall that are connected with it. In other words, for about fifteen minutes, write down everything you can remember about your incident and about your thoughts and feelings at the time.

These notes will not be graded but will be used in a following assignment.

(2. Discussion of these papers should center on:

1. The narrowing-down process, the focusing. This is critical for helping the author to get the point of his selected recollection to emerge, and each pupil can look at his own paper and apply the discussion to it. Sample papers should be dittoed or projected with Assignment 1 so that comparisons can be made between Assignment 1 and Assignment 2. Ask what things the pupil selected *out* in doing Assignment 2. Then ask what new material he added. Once the selection of memory and its expansion in detail have been clearly established, ask the class why they think he chose that memory over the others. Then ask the author.

Now ask what more he might do to it for an audience. Does he still need more detail about some aspect of it? Does some of the detail seem unnecessary? Unnecessary for *what*? What seems to be the main point or feeling?

At this point break the class into small groups for collaboration. Have them continue the issues raised in discussion by reading and writing comments on each other's papers (see assignment sheet 3.) They should have both Assignments 1 and 2 with them. They will need a good half hour for this collaboration. The final writing, or Assignment 3, can be done in or out of school. Make sure they hand in Assignments 1 and 2 along with Assignment 3.)

Composed memory.

3. Go to your group with your Assignment 1 and 2 papers. Exchange these papers with another student. After you have read his, write comments on his Assignment 2 that will help him to rewrite it as a finished composition. You will all rewrite your Assignment 2's for the whole class to read. Your comments can be about any of the things just discussed with the sample papers. Do you think he chose the best memory? What things about the memory do you think he should bring out most when he rewrites? What would you like to hear more about? What things do you think he should cut out? How about his choice of words and the kinds of sentences he uses? The amount of personal thought and feeling?

Then exchange with other students until you have been all around the group. Afterwards, you may talk with them about their comments on your Assignment 2.

Finally, rewrite your Assignment 2. Follow the suggestions the other students made, when you agree with them. Make all the big and small changes it takes to make your memory clear and interesting for the class.

Hand in this last paper along with Assignments 1 and 2.

(3. Ditto or project all three papers of a couple of students, so that the class can survey the entire process by which those students got from first to last stage. Discuss the decisions and changes they made between Assignments 1 and 2, and between Assignments 2 and 3. In one case, you might show Assignment 3 first, then 2, then 1 — work backwards from the finished product. When moving the other way — from 1 to 2 and 3 — ask the class to guess what choices the student is going to make between one stage and the next; then show the next paper. Get them to relate the writer's progressive decisions to their own judgment about the final version.

It would be good to have a number of the Assignment 3's read aloud to give the class an idea of some of the different results of memory writing — different points and moods — and also to carry through the idea that the whole class was their audience.)

Here are three final compositions (Assignment 3) that are good but not among the best, chosen rather for their representative subjects and treatment. The first is by a girl, the other two by boys.

First day of School

I had to take a test to get registered. As soon as I was registered, I started to get ready even though it was weeks before. I was supposed to be waiting for the bus at 8:30 am but I was ready at 8:00 am. I ran out to wait for the bus thinking that I would be able to read as soon as I got home. It was half days for the first week. When I got home I started crying because I couldn't read. And that is all I remember.

A long time ago I got a "Revell" weather forcasting kit. Since I was wearing my Sunday suit, I quickly changed into jeans and and old shirt just to find that there was no more glue.

After a five day wait, I rushehed upstairs to my room, got the "duco cement" the new glue and got to work on the oarnge, white, and clear, plastic pieces. I did all the easy parts first then came the hard part, the annemometer. But finally after about 2 weeks it was all finished. I was all through Boy was I glad.

My First Turtle.

I remember the day that I caught my first turtle. It had been a fairly warm day and my sisters and Peter Flynn had decided to go to the swamp. We though we might catch a snake or some other animal. This time would be different.

I was wearing a black coat with some tall green boots. I can't recall what anyone else was wearing. It was a warm day, with a clear blue sky.

As we were walking by a murkey pond, I saw something that looked interesting. I was following my sister, and she steped over something that looked like a unripe pumpkin with yellow spots on it. I picked it up and all of a sudden feet and a head came out of it. Startled at this, I dropped it. But when I saw it was a turtle, I picked it up again. I told everyone else and they conguralated me on my good luck, and we continued our journey.

Results and Problems

Making the assignment clear. The teachers found that demonstrating Assignment 1 orally before the class themselves was not hard and helped the children to grasp the process. Starting a chain of memories presents no difficulties to the children, whatever their ability or intelligence. They seem to fall into Proustian procedure with ease. Two possible confusions can arise with some children, however, as experience has shown. One is to mistake mere thought associations for memory links, so that *flag* might lead to *patriotism* and to *soldiers,* etc. The other mistake is to restrict oneself to memories associated with items in the room and thus to keep returning to the present setting in an alternation of sensations and memories. It is true that the assignment begins, as sensory recording does, by looking at one's surroundings, but the teacher can make clear that present sensation is only a springboard and that once in the past one stays there unless the chain breaks, at which time he returns to the surroundings for a new point of departure. Especially if forewarned, as we were not of course, the teacher can easily ward off these misunderstandings by clearly demonstrating a memory chain of his own, perhaps noting a few memories on the board, and by getting a volunteer to do the same. After a good demonstration, no pupil is likely to misunderstand the assignment.

Timing and grouping. For the whole series, several other practical matters came up. First of all, several teachers pointed out that if the chain of memories (Assignment 1) and the expanded memory (Assignment 2) occurred too far apart in time, the children lost interest in following through. This is only natural, is likely to be true of all phased writing, and can be easily remedied by giving Assignment 2 as homework that night or as in-class work the following day. Organizing a folder in advance, with directions and blank pages stapled in, might help more careless children to keep the papers intact and in meaningful order. So be it, so long as the folder does not acquire the mechanical aura of a workbook.

A number of teachers felt that pairs were much better collaborating units for revising Assignment 2 into 3 than groups of three or four. About this I remain somewhat skeptical, since their finding may merely reflect the children's lack of experience in commenting on each other's papers in small groups. The reading and discussing together of three or four papers gets more thoroughly at the issues in the assignment and reduces any possible misleading of one pupil by another. So I suggest that other teachers try out both pairs and larger groups.

Phasing the writing process. The most problematical matters concerned whether three stages are necessary. My original idea was that, if suddenly asked to write a memory in one stroke, the child might either draw a blank (which Assignment 1 is designed to prevent) or tell the gist of the memory so quickly that it would be lifeless (to be headed off by Assignment 2). Conventional assignments try to solve the problem of getting an idea by specifying topics such as "My Most Thrilling (Frightening, Surprising, etc.) Moment," or "The First Time I Learned a Sport." The problem of giving body and detail to an incident is, like most writing problems in a one-stroke assignment, not handled until the teacher's postmortem commentary comes along, when the pupil is confronted with the should-haves and made to feel in the wrong. And I think blanket topics make for canned themes. Not only do they work poorly as a stimulant but, in categorizing pupils' experience for them in advance, they by-pass the most worthwhile compositional issues that pupils should engage with. They always stipulate the abstract classification of events and usually also the feeling or mood that is to provide coherence. All the child does is fill in the blanks with an event — which reduces writing issues to a rather low level. And here begins the long years of nagging about detail. Elaborating and giving particulars appears as an obsession of teachers rather than as an organic development.

The original purpose of spontaneous memory writing, then, was to let the child do his own abstracting and decision making, to keep composition on a deeper, cognitive basis, since at heart it is the classifying and ordering of experience — information processing, if you like. By spreading the composing over three stages, I hoped to lay bare for examination and influence the internal processes of writing that in conventional assignments remain more hidden and less tractable, if they are put into play at all. Selecting one incident would come as a meaningful narrowing down of the first, miscellaneous array. Expanding into detail would follow, before the final draft, as a filling in of what one had staked out, like pointing to a city on a map and then looking at the inserted plan of that city. Stage three would again be a bit of selective abstracting, this time around a "core experience" that discussion with partners would have helped to emerge. Thus the pupil would be plucking from riches rather than fleshing abstractions.

The point of any assignment is not to avoid problems; it is to engage with the right problems in the right way. Memory writing does this well, and is an activity I can recommend with great confidence, but the experiment seems to show that the three-stage procedure goes a step too far for this age. In most cases two stages were enough, and a third resulted mainly in copying. That is, most pupils either wrote so fully on a few memories in Assignment 1 that only one other effort was needed to select and shape; or else, if Assignment 1 consisted of many short fragments, their expansion of the single memory in Assignment 2 was itself so close to a final composition that further revision did not warrant another copy. When we tried two stages only, the results were as good. This was so for a good reason, I think.

Most of these children naturally composed the memory at the same time that they expanded it, so that separating these processes into two additional stages merely made Assignment 3 into a brushup job of Assignment 2. I suspect a developmental factor here, however. Adolescents with whom I have also tried three-stage memory writing were more willing to elaborate first for the sake of garnering more material and less inclined toward an early closure. Whereas Assignment 2 seems like a natural end to elementary children, it can be viewed by older students still as preliminary note taking. I attribute this difference to the younger children's general tendency to elaborate little and revise little. Pushing downward into detail is as hard for them as pushing upward into generalities. They will expand some and shape some but only enough to justify one occasion for both. The chief result of Assignment 3, then, was the incorporating of sentence revisions made by other pupils, which means that by the time an author began writing out his Assignment 3, with these minor changes, the learning was all over and only copying was left. As with unwarranted last drafts of sensories, many pupils deleted good things to spare themselves labor.

IMPROVEMENTS TO BE MADE OVER THE TRIALS

Several differences in our experiment might have changed the results a fair amount.

Creating books of memories. The compositions were not destined for any particular use later. The printing of a class memory book, besides serving as a final copy of the slightly revised Assignment 2's, would have stimulated more cross-commentary and revision and led to a meaningful and motivated Assignment 3, as perhaps would also a much longer prior experience with small-group exchanging of papers.

Fuller use of workshop. The full benefit of group process in writing — class projections followed up by smaller discussions of each member's paper — is still unknown. My teachers had far too little time to work with this and often skipped or made short shrift of these sessions. And of course the cumulative effect of such experience over several years could affect considerably what sort of activities expanding and rewriting turn out to be. Despite some very good comments at times, our children, like most, were still strangers to collaborative responding. The high quality of what they can say about each other's writing even without much background is very persuasive evidence that they can learn to comment very well indeed, but, like the other verbal arts we try to help them learn, this one grows slowly with practice over a long span. Whereas our children's enthusiasm, very high for Assignment 1, declined with each additional step, more interactive stimulation among them, set off by teacher-led demonstrations and sustained by a goal, would probably have made Assignments 2 and 3 appear as equally exciting forays.

Freer rewriting. It is the amount of purposeful change proposed by other pupils that keeps the writing alive for them. In this respect, my experiment was badly lacking, for we did not raise the possibilities for free rewriting that in fact could be raised by the teacher and carried into the groups, such as converting the selected incident into a poem or fictionalized story. Or pupils could return to Assignment 1, pluck out another incident, and expand it also; if they *began* with a kernel memory from the old Assignment 1, then the fullness so often found in Assignment 1 might pour forth instead in an expansion of this kernel. In that case, an Assignment 3 might become well warranted and motivated. Or Assignment 3 might become a possibility rather than a requirement, a valuable option for pupils to consider and discuss with each paper. The option would be a means of thinking about how much change a given paper needs, even if Assignment 3 is not ultimately recommended.

Finally, we did not relate memory writing to drama. Acting out a detailed memory as a pantomime or with dialogue would add a lot of interest to the writing of it, if this possibility were announced in advance. In fact, the obvious need for detail in that case might motivate expansion (Assignment 2) considerably. Very succinct memories could be used as "minimal situations" for improvisation, which would in turn elaborate the memories and thus point the way to written expansion. Relating drama and memories will supplement publication with another writing purpose, and will provide excellent material for drama. Some revisions might even be in script form, another option the teacher should feed into the groups.

These are reservations about our trials, not attempts to salvage the three-stage procedure, which, so far as one can tell now, should be reduced to two steps until further experimentation with the factors above indicates otherwise. At any rate, when introduced abruptly, the assignment will probably go better in two stages. The following samples may help other teachers to judge somewhat for themselves.

Samples

Influenced by discussion, a number of pupils elected the pyramidal form of note taking (below) because it obviates writing "I remember" and "That reminds me of. . . ." One girl's memory chain began with spotting a flutaphone in the classroom:

<pre>
                        Flutaphone
        boring music   practicing at home
   Miss Brown   practicing   having to take
                           piano   time for it
           chorus   piano lessons   recitals
   performances   getting up early   riding lessons
                     for practices
</pre>

Actually, these capsule memories are noted in a dryly abstract way, none of them being an incident, and yet from these she reconstructs a very specific underlying incident:

Piano lessons remind me of a recital I had this year.
The room was full of chairs, each occupied by either someone's mother or a student. I was to play fourth.
"Merry is now going to play an english folk song," my teacher announced. I stood up and walked up to the piano. I could hear and feel my heart pumping and wondered if the audience could. When I was done I heard a lot of applause.
"Now Merry is going to play a composed song, she composed it." My piano teacher announced, "The name is 'memories.' "
I played my short minor song and turned around to get up.
"Please play it again, its so short and I think the audience will enjoy it more."
So I did, got applause and left the piano seat happily.

Preadolescents are not inclined to state feelings as explicitly as this girl does; they either assume that such things are self-evident or are not introspective enough to identify and name them. A composed memory that others feel is pointless and uninteresting almost always fails to make clear the core experience that made the memory stand out in the first place. Discussion can be helpful in indicating that more explicitness, or perhaps just a more emphatic handling of facts, is needed. The core experience here is obviously pleasure, the flush of success and attention. It is rather hard to find a meaningless memory, and the meaning engenders the coherence. This children intuitively understand, but an egocentric failure to allow for the reader, among other things, can obscure the coherence. I do not include here the above writer's Assignment 3, because it reads exactly like Assignment 2 except for the deletion of the last three paragraphs, more of a loss than a gain, though conceivably she felt that the announcement of the song title was the high point and the rest anticlimatic.

At the other extreme of note taking, many of the spontaneous streams of memory are more copious and colorful than the compositions derived from them. Such rich notes give one pause: How much should teaching push for the standard coherence that defines a composition? At this age do the losses sometimes outweigh the gains? When the notes are mere lists of words and phrases, these questions do not arise, but when I read the easily flowing memories and sentences of a paper like this girl's, I wonder if we shouldn't just let be, regardless of our preconceptions of the assignment, or else make the assignment more flexible:

> As I look on top of a radiator I see a gallon jar with dirt on the bottom of it and with dirty water. That reminds me, once I was swimming in salt water and I was laying down but then I got up.
> Suddenly I found me walking in freezing water. Suddenly I fell into a drop by the wind. Which reminds me of a green type of fly that stays near water, and when you are on sand It comes along and stings.
> Once I was playing in some sand near water and one came along and landed on my arm.
> I was so excited that I ran and jumped into the water and that scared him away.
> That reminds me, once I was one a raft (floating) in the salt water and I was drifting into a drop with one of my friends, she pushed me off. Some one had to come and get me out.

Though scattered in time, her memories connect easily, forming a natural psychological continuity, and yet are kept distinct by the paragraphing. It is this spontaneous flow that the children like so much. For her Assignment 2 she took the last memory:

> Once I was on a plastic floatable raft. I was on the raft with my friend in the salt water. We were going with the curent going into a drop and there was no possible way to stop. My friend got excited and by mistake she pushed me off and the curent was to strong and my friend's parant had to get in their boat and come get me out.

The gains of expanding were: more detail about the raft (*plastic, float-able*), more explanation of the situation (there was no way to stop drifting, and her friend pushed her off *by mistake*), and more specification of who rescued her and how (*friend's parant, in their boat*). These are all good changes and additions, fulfilling the purpose of Assignment 2 and showing the ability to "fill in" for the reader's benefit. But the sentences are hardly improved, the first one being choppy and overlapping as though she had suddenly become overformal. In doing the last version (Assignment 3), interestingly enough, she tightened up the sentences by herself; a partner broke the last run-on sentence into two. Though it is only stylistically different, I reproduce here this last version and suggest that the reader compare Assignments 2 and 3 to see how important sentence development can occur without teacher intervention. The direction of these revisions that she did on her own is toward a mature economy of construction.

> Once I was on a plastic floatable raft with my friend in the salt water. We were going with the curent, into a drop and there was no possible way to stop. My friend got excited and by mistake she pushed me off and the curent was to strong. My friend's parent had to get in their boat, and get me out.

These are typical of the gains and losses that the teacher needs to be alert to and to weigh when working with serial assignments. Compare the notes and composition below, done as a two-stage assignment by a boy:

> I saw McGath a then I thought of my brother when it was his first birthday when he stuck his hand in the cake and took a big gob of cake out and ate it then it was SyClops the one eyed, 25 foot man then it was Voyage to the bottom of the Sea when down went inside the inside the whales tummy, the spider too, a snout comming out of a nose, JoHanna Katy disecting a frog disecting a crayfish, throw up (sick), spit, an old lady some messy (soming that comes out of your fannie.

If I am not mistaken, this is what critics mean by "visceral writing." Among the good qualities required of language arts teachers a strong stomach is perhaps too seldom listed. This is a child writing in freedom and with relish. There is naturalistic realism and literary allusion side by side, strung together by private associations but in an obvious continuity. What the piece lacks is grammatical coherence and a more definite focus, both of which he achieves in the composition:

> When it was my brothers first birthday he stuck his hand in the cake and pulled out a big gob of cake and shouved it in his mouth. He had a mouth covered with chocolate cake.

The sentences are good, he "sticks to the subject," and he has even expanded slightly. (He replaced *ate* by *shouved in his mouth*, and added the whole last sentence, which makes the point of the anecdote — his baby brother's comic appearance at the moment — a core experience that hardly needs belaboring.) As a succinct summary of a single incident, this is admirable. But what have we traded for it?

Actually the question is a bit false. It is possible to have our cake and the spiders and frogs too: instead of thinking of serial writing as stages toward "the real thing," called a composition, both teacher and pupils should probably conceive the related pieces as things in themselves, all equal in worth but for different reasons. The fact that one is base for another should not debase it. In fact, to distinguish, and to value accordingly, the variousness of writing is an important goal of the language arts. While discriminating between writing for himself and writing for others, between notes and a public composition, the child can also appreciate each for its own sake. This means that speaking of a staged assignment is using a misnomer, and that the teacher would do better to consider each piece of writing as an end in itself and not merely as a means; what we really mean by staging or phasing writing is that one piece is used as stimulus for another, in the manner of chain reaction.

The following memory chain shows, I think, how pell-mell writing encourages children to spin out the longer, more complex sentence constructions that they will try out freely when talking but will not often risk in writing. I have italicized two especially exemplary passages:

I see a top of a house and it is white. It reminds me of going up to maine at My grandparents cottage. That reminds me of the time Gail, Robin and I and Nancy were in maine and hid in someones pyle of hay when they came bye. The White on the house also reminds me of the ski slopes when I first when on them. That reminds me of up in maine when we went to bonds. *We called to 17 year old tommy manahan who lives two houses away in maine a boy scout as he went bye. That reminds me of when My Family and I went to the end of the lake and saw the lake and the ocean be divided by a huge metal that was aquad shape and sliding down the slide that lead to the ocean.* That reminds me of when I first learned to water ski I fell and fell and then I Finally got up and made it First time around. That reminds me of when I caught my First Fish. It turned out to be a gold Fish. The remind me of when we went to canipe lake Park and I went on the biggest Rollar coaster in New England. I also went on the house of seven gables and you see statues and *I saw a statue of a man having his head sawe in half* and going throw the huge barrels. That remind me of when I was four and went to boston with my mother. The reminds me of when I First learned to dive at Hayden day camp. That reminds me off the time Gail, Robin, and me went up the dirt road in maine and picked Blueberrys and rasberrys. That reminds me of the time I almost Drownded watersking. That reminds me of the time gail and nancy and I went in Mrs. Pratts canal

The first italicized sentence contains three modifying phrases (*17 year old, in maine,* and *a boy scout,* the last being an appositive), a relative clause (*who lives two houses away*), and a temporal clause (*as he went bye*). This represents the embedding of five potentially independent kernel sentences into the main kernel sentence, *We called to tommy manahan.* Of course the sentence is badly ordered and is overloaded with information, but the girl has usefully exercised her developing sentence-building ability. In the next sentence she tries out a construction involving a verbal complement of the predicate — *saw the lake and the ocean be divided by a huge metal. . .* An adult's first impulse might be to use a participle here (*I saw the ocean being divided*) but the girl is intuitively following a grammatical regularity, since she would say, using the active, *I saw something divide the ocean.* In not using a participle, she has merely analogized from the active complement and thus written the passage *be divided.* In the other italicized passage — *I saw a statue of a man having his head sawe in half* — she does use a participle in what is a subtly different grammatical situation, the case of a verbal form modifying a preceding noun rather than complementing a preceding predicate.

Such an accurate intuitive discrimination between constructions that one would expect a child to confuse makes me marvel at the powerful cognitive operations at work in language acquisition. Rarely if ever do teachers of any grade attempt to explain grammatical distinctions as fine as this. Such linguistic feats, which greatly surpass the expectations of any grammar teaching I have heard of, are persuasive evidence that the child's perceptions about what he hears and reads are the real teachers of grammar. But my point here is that he needs a lot of free writing practice in which to rehearse and recombine these constructions on paper without fear of correction.

The girl's expansion and composition, assigned as only one additional piece of writing, went like this:

The Boyscout

One time a year ago in the summer. My Family went to maine. We go to maine every year. We live in our grandparents cottage. In Front of the cottage is a lake. We Have a motor boat, sailboat, rowboat and water skis. We go to bonds a store usally by boat but this time we went by car. My sisters Ellen and nancy went with me. Tommy manahan a 17 years old boy past and we said "Hey boyscout are you going to help a lady cross the street. When my mother came to the car she said that he told her what we said and we all started to laugh.

Again, I suspect that the choppy, overlapping "baby sentences" of the first half stem from an over-concern about writing correct sentences, which may very well have caused her to open with a sentence fragment. The backfiring strategy in that case was to parcel out speech in short and therefore "safe" units. The result is less mature writing. The sentence in Assignment 1 about the boy scout, which becomes expanded and framed here as an anecdote, has undergone an interesting transformation. No doubt realizing that her former construction was overloaded and unreadable, she took out the dependent clauses, simply dropped some information, shifted *17 year old* from the adjectival to the appositive position, and converted what had been the appositive before — *a boyscout* — into a quoted direct address. Certainly children should get a chance to flex their intelligence and ingenuity in linguistic ways by reworking their own sentence structures, but if fear of error plays a part, they will regress instead. This paper shows both aspects.

A few miscellaneous points on these two papers. First, another pupil gave considerable and helpful attention to this girl's problem with capitalization. Second, the original title of the piece was "The Hey," apt but neutral; either the girl herself or another pupil — I don't know which — changed the title to "The Boyscout," which has the same playful irony that inspired the incident itself. I can only urge, again, the strong emphasis on titling and revising titles as a way of helping the children both to make explicit their core experience and to compose a coherence around it. The girl here has more information than she needs to tell in her anecdote, but, given her starting point, she has already focused considerably, and she will have plenty of other occasions to practice further.

Finally, examining papers from such assignments, as I have examined these two, can give teachers many useful insights about how their children's minds work and how they come to do the types of things with language that they do. In this way teachers can conduct their own research — not essentially different from that of some linguists and psycholinguists — that can help them think about what they are doing and ought to be doing.

It is for a child like the next girl that the second stage of expansion seems right:

My Memries

The ratiator reminded me where my brother was fooling with the iron and he burnt himself.

The tres remind me of camp when I was going into second grade.

The spots on the celling remind me when the water from are tub leaked though are celling and made a mess down stairs.

She chose to expand the last memory, which a classmate thought was most promising:

A couple of years ago my brother was taking a bath. While he was waiting in the living room the water was getting higher in the tub when the water was just about at the top he ran in and shut it off. Then he took a bath. As soon as he was in the water started to overflow in the bathrub but it went so slowly you couldn't notice it. About 15 minutes and there was a big puddle on the floor. When are housekeeper went down stairs and saw it she told my brother to stop taking a bath then she took a bucket, and put it there in a few minites it stoped and dryed up the next day

In this case, writing a second piece based on a first had only positive results. She seems to be writing zestfully, and with high motivation and an anticipation of audience appreciation. Sentences are mature, and the incident is sharply focused. All she needs is transcriptive practice for punctuating sentence stops.

The final samples indicate a possibility of memory writing that, while allowed for by the experiments, was not really explored. If a pupil puts together in one composition two or three incidents that happened at different times but are related by an idea or category of which the incidents are instances, then the unity of the piece becomes automatically something general. A critical first step is made toward essay and away from pure narrative. That is, when instead of telling an anecdote one juxtaposes several shorter anecdotes, the question is: What heading do all of these incidents go under? What logic is replacing pure chronology as the linking and organizing factor? Below are two pieces demonstrating this transition; unfortunately I do not know at which of the three stages they were done. The first contains two incidents, the second, three. In both, the connection among incidents is obvious but unstated, and the heading or category of experience is still at a low level of generality:

> The grahm crackers remind me of one day when my grandmother was visiting us. She made me graham crackers for breakfast. And one day she gave me a plate of six whole graham crackers she went in the other room for napkin. When she came back in the room I had finished. The amazing thing was that I ate them in around six seconds. Another time I had a breast of turkey and 5 scoops of potatoe and good helping of peas and finished before everyone else. And waited outside while I was waiting I went out to the tree hut. I got up on weak side fell down broke thumb and sprained my rist didn't have to write in school.

> One day I brought my snake to school. After art I came in and he was gone. I thought someone had taken him I looked around and Russel found him in the shelf.
> One day I went to a place called Turtle Pond. On the bank I saw a thing that looked like a turtle, It was a turtle. I went a picked it up and it was asleep. All of a sudden he stuck his head out. And tried to swim away from me.
> One day we went to Watham Pond. And we found fresh water invertebrates. In about ten minutes my freind fell in and five minutes later my other freind fell in and fifteen minutes later I fell in. The water was cold.

It would be interesting to have other children propose titles for these. For such a kind of essay a title normally names or suggests the generality that the instances exemplify; in these two cases, something about speed-eating and hunting animal specimens would come to mind. Titles might in turn suggest a more explicit frame for the incidents — phrases or sentences that say something about the unifying connection.

This movement toward essay can be prepared for by discussing the association between one memory and another in Assignment 1, before any further writing is done. Clearly the two boys here arrived at their unity just by exploiting the category responsible in the first place for the thought association. Quite likely, they had originally included other memories which they subsequently deleted as irrelevant to the category. At any rate, such would be the selection process for further writing beyond Assignment 1. The teacher would project an Assignment 1 and ask: How did this writer get from one memory to the next? Can you follow the jumps? Where does a new train of thought begin? Which memories here would you clump together as being about the same thing? Is there another clump about something different?

If, in answering these questions, some pupils classify the same memory differently, the discrepancy could make good discussion, involving finally the author. "Which would you rather see this writer do — tell more about one of these incidents or tell about several of them together? In each case what might a working title be?" In other words, pupils carry into the small groups another possible option to consider in making suggestions to each other. The possibility gives rise in a most natural way to writing of a more abstract sort. These two boys, and a few other children, inadvertently anticipated an assignment that I had already been trying out in secondary school (Chapter 29 in the K–13 edition). It explicitly asks students to do just what these boys did but without prior memory notes. Ringing this variation on memory writing would set up the later assignment very well. What will vary with growth is the abstraction level of the "theme" or category. (The concrete themes of these two papers may seem trivial to adults.) In this respect, again, by stipulating process, not content, the assignment adjusts to individual capacity.

We did not have time to try out the writing of poems and fictions based on memories. This is an extremely rich possibility, as with sensations, which the teacher should raise periodically in leading discussions of projected samples. Not only, I think, would memories solve the problem of getting an idea for imaginative writing but they would exert an influence away from imitation toward more originality.

Summary

I have presented the experiment in its original rigidity to demonstrate the wisdom of flexibility and the possibility of variations. The neat unit, the definitive syllabus, would violate what has been learned. Even the original formalism was based more on the needs of experiment than on principle. But it is possible to conclude with some definite suggestions for staged writing that might apply reliably to the composing of other material than memories.

1. As regards individuals, let the decision about pursuing a subject into another stage depend on teacher-influenced group consultation.

2. As regards collective growth, add stages as children mature.

3. Treat any piece of writing both as an end in itself and as a possible stimulus for another piece (notes may turn out as compositions, and compositions as notes).

If one thinks about how much of traditional theme writing in the later years, and of adult writing, draws on memory for its material (including, later, the memory of what one reads), and if one acknowledges the universality of the compositional issues entailed in memory writing, then perhaps the space devoted to it here will seem well warranted. Together, sensations and memories are the individual's storehouse, from which — however bizarrely imaginative or abstractly formulated — all his writing must necessarily proceed. Not all of our recordings and reportings get written, but they occur inside anyway, and we further abstract these into the generalities according to which we see the world and according to which we take action.

When these processes are themselves the basis of assignments, then writing becomes an external and explicit replica of what ordinarily happens inwardly and hiddenly. A pupil can thus gradually become aware of how he knows what he knows, and of how his experience shapes his thought. As for his fancies and fictions, they are merely a less direct mode of recombining and synthesizing these same raw materials. Asking a child to write down sensations and memories not only shows him that the real stuff of speaking and writing lies all around him and within him at any moment, but it validates this stuff; it says plainly that his individual experience is of great worth, something to turn to, not away from. At the same time, the group process lets him air this experience and his expression of it before other people of his own development but of different experience. This gives him the perspective of public reality.

Chapter 15

Writing Fictions

All good writing, of course, is imaginative, even when the point of departure is as factual as sensations and memories. What is meant here by "fictions" is simply a greater degree of invention. And, invention *is* a matter of degree. As I have indicated, sensory and memory writing may take an inventive turn into fiction. "Pure imagination," on the other hand, does not exist; inventions are some more or less indirect recombining of experiences, either from real life or from books, television, and so on. For the kind of writing dealt with here, children set out to invent fictions, regardless of how real or fantastic the results.

Ideally, a teacher would simply say, "Write a story about anything you like," but teachers of even very able pupils say that such an open assignment is very hard to respond to. Writing fictions seems to require a context, a stimulating situation of one sort or another — involved discussion, reading around a subject, dramatic activity, a concentration on literary form. Some of the stimulants suggested in Chapter 7 for the lower grades — caption development, cartoons, song writing — might, in the teacher's discretion, still serve well for inexperienced or verbally undeveloped children of this age. Certainly, writing lyrics for songs and filling in various metrical forms with one's own ideas is not limited to the lower grades.

Here I would like to make further suggestions with the understanding that if assignments to "make up a story" or "write a poem" work well for some children, then they may as well be given just that simply. The goal is self-initiated writing, but some of the stimulants used to reach this goal also have value in themselves, such as learning what forms are available and how different subjects may be treated.

Fictional writing, too, is read, discussed, and revised in small groups, then printed up into booklets for exchange. Revision would not be required but would, rather, be proposed by workshop colleagues and motivated by the writer's desire to prepare the best possible copy for printing. To ensure that the cross-commentary is perceptive and useful, lead model class discussions

231

on papers selected for a variety of reasons — for range of expression and invention and for compositional issues they raise. These discussions are for appreciation and exhibition as much as for critical commentary. Ask for the natural responses of the class to a paper, then play from these responses by a few impromptu questions and observations of your own, until the pupils relate their responses to specific features of the paper that elicited them.

Writing About Pictures

A picture stimulus is still appropriate but can be developed. One fourth-grade teacher asked his pupils to make up a story by placing themselves in a scene, depicted in a magazine advertisement, of a camel standing in a New York City street:

> But this we were just driving along when suddenly we stopped. I was in the back and didn't know what was going on. When I looked out I saw a camal right in the middle of the road. We waited about an hour until the camal moved. The plain we were supposed to catch had lefted. Mom and Dad were fighting over why didn't Dad get out and move the camal. And Dad said why didn't you?! Then Mom started crying and telling us about the dum camal. I bet she was so mad she made Dad cry. I said I didn't want to go home cause Susy was going to beat me up. After that I said I'd walk a mile for a camal! Mom was still crying when we got home and Dad was still yellen at us and the dog was howing and barking. And I told all the kids at school about the camal and how we missed our plain. I took the camal with me.[1]

Other developments of the picture stimulus are accomplished by specializing the type of picture used, so that the following questions can be asked: What are these people saying to each other? What is this person doing — or thinking? What might happen in this place? Or children can simply bring in their favorite pictures from magazines, exchange them, and choose one to write from. In one sixth-grade class using a variety of self-chosen pictures, I once saw, accidentally arranged side by side on a bulletin board, three picture stories told in the three different persons — *I, you,* and *he.* The assignment had, curiously enough, stimulated a variety of story-telling techniques, probably because pictures may be associated more flexibly than most fictional material with any one of the three pronouns.

Writing Memories of Literature[2]

This assignment is not purely inventive but will prime invention. The children recreate in their own words an especially memorable scene or mo-

---

[1] My thanks to John Talbot, Cochituate Elementary School, Wayland, Massachusetts, for this paper and for his experimentation with other assignments in this program.

[2] For this assignment I am indebted to Frank Lyman and Kayda Cushman, of the Estabrook Elementary School in Lexington, Massachusetts. They devised it and provided the samples printed in this section.

ment from a book, play, or movie without looking back at the original text. Emphasis is on choosing a scene that stands out later because of the strong feeling it aroused in the child when he read it or saw it. The key is vivid involvement, and the source may be any that the child knows, regardless of whether it relates to schoolwork or not. He is directed to write the scene by putting himself back into it, becoming part of it, perhaps taking the role of a character in it, making it happen again.

The purpose, of course, is not to recapitulate accurately the original; in fact, the teachers who developed and tried out the assignments were casting about for a stimulus for imaginative writing because they found that their children could not easily make up a story from scratch. These fifth- and sixth-grade pupils liked the assignment very much and wrote better stories than they had in other attempts. Besides endorsing the assignment for its own obvious value, I see helpful connections between it and other activities in this program.

Some of the samples reproduced below bear a subtitle that names the main feeling of the recreated scene. In some cases, the teachers who were trying this assignment had the class designate a theme in advance — some emotion or quality that might give the pupils more to go on when selecting their scenes. In other cases, the pupils chose a theme for their scenes *after* they had written them. I am inclined to think that such focusing of the assignment is unnecessary and, when the theme is pre-selected, possibly obstructive. But other teachers might do well to run the same sort of mixed trials and judge for themselves.

This is by a low-grouped, underachieving fifth-grade boy:

SINK IT RUSTY
SADNESS

Rusty blew the whistle and said "foul on Perry." he struck Joby's wrist when he stold the ball from him. THen Rusty came over, took the ball from Perry and handed it to Joby. Then Rusty said "two shots." Just then Alec Paws came over and everybody stoped playing. Alec was much older than the other boys. Rusty had never seen him before and he kept staring at the black glove on his left hand. THen all tha boys said hi to him. they where glad to see him. Rusty could see the boys didn't want him to play so Rusty said "Here Alec you take the ball." the boys said "come on Alec" so Alec took the ball and the whistle and Rusty walked off sadly. The End.

A fifth-grade girl of superior ability recreated this moment from the well known film:

SOUND OF MUSIC
FRIENDSHIP

Maria sits quietly and thoughtfully on a bench near a glassed-in room. Crunching through the leaves, Captain Von Trapp sits beside Maria. "I want to congratulate you and the Baronese," Maria said standing up.

"Can you marry someone when you like somebody else more?" questioned the Captain who was growing used to Maria.

"No, I guess not." replied Maria softly.

It is clear that each of these two children has chosen a personally meaningful bit of action involving someone they could identify with.

Not all of the stories were done in third person. The teachers' emphasis on the possibilities of taking a character point of view was undoubtedly what influenced some children either to use the first person or to go into a character's mind in third person. These two girls wrote interior monologues — a case again of pupils' involuntarily anticipating a much later assignment (Chapter 20 in the K–13 edition). The first, by a sixth-grade girl of superior ability, contains one unsignalled line of dialogue:

Lucy

That no good brother of my he will never learn. There he is lying out there freezing to death. . . , I have to get him. Get in bed stupid. His shoes are hard to get off because they're ice! Stay there now. I don't know why he does it. If he does it next year I will kill him!

The second is by a fifth-grade girl considered to be of average cognitive skills:

I better not let that Cinderella try on that slipper, it just might fit her. My daughters have to fit the slipper, they just have to! If they don't my life will be just ruined, just ruined. (Knock-knock) Oh I better let him in. It will be sure to fit me or one of my daughters. Darn it didn't fit one of my daughters. Oh No! he wants Cinderella to try it on' It FIT! Oh No! I'm ruined, Oh dear! I'm simply ruined! The End

The dramatic possibilities of all of these are splendid. The last two could be acted out as soliloquies, the silent roles being done in pantomime. The scenes from "Sink It, Rusty" and "The Sound of Music" read almost like play scripts; they contain only movement and dialogue — no author commentary or character thoughts. The playability of these papers is a happy effect of the emphasis the teachers placed on recreating a *small span of action*. As I have suggested before, one of the chief difficulties with children's written stories is that, because they cannot write at great length, if they encompass the whole of even a moderately long action they are forced to oversummarize it in a dull way. By stressing a scene or moment, and by directing the children to put themselves in that scene, the teachers effectively steered them away from synopsis toward detail.

In discussing their papers together in preparation for acting them out, the children will discover, however, that some stories are not readily dramatizable, even though they cover a short duration. For example, this story by a sixth-grade girl of high ability:

WITCH OF BLACKBIRD POND
"COMFORT"

She ran without reason or decorum, past the houses of her pupils, past the townhall, past the loiterers at the town pump. Without having chosen a destination in her mind, her feet had. They lead her beyond the outskirts of the town, into a Great Meadow. She took a path that led off into the meadow and flung herself down on the long, earth-smelling grass. Slowly, the meadow with its vastness began to fulfill its promise.

This girl does not employ the wholly external viewpoint of a movie, nor the wholly internal viewpoint of an interior monologue; using a common novelistic technique, she tells the story in the third person but from the viewpoint of a single character. Thus the load is on narration, description of scenery, and accounts of feeling in the author's words but as perceived by the character. This is hard to dramatize and therefore presents a special opportunity for learning. In sifting stories for those that can be fairly readily acted out, pupils will learn about various fictional techniques in a very pragmatic, intuitive way. If a story does not lend itself to acting out, they have to think about why this is so. Too much description? Too indirect a relaying of the character's inner life? Too much commentary by the author? Does such a story have to be read and only read? Could it be *adapted* in some way for dramatizing or for filming? An advantage here of reading a lot of each other's papers is that children will borrow various first- and third-person techniques from each other. As a secondary effect of doing the assignment, such exploration of technique can be expert and concrete; to push the study of fictional methods for its own sake, however, would be too academic. Reading and writing stories done in various techniques, and, especially, trying to determine their relation to drama, would teach quite enough for this age. Technique is better done than talked about, except when the talking is of a problem-solving sort.

Generally, I see this assignment as an extension of memory writing into the realm of reading and fictive creation. The extension allows for second-hand experience and for imaginative rather than factual material. It is a repeatable assignment because the content is always different. It engages pupils because this content is essentially personal feeling conveniently projected into a scene which the child makes his own. It is the only kind of literary appreciation that makes sense to me for this age. To ask a pupil to write, in a book report, what he liked about a book will not get anything like the same quality of response, for all a child can do in a book report is summarize the plot and make a couple of shallow generalities.

Points of Departure for Inventing

Either content or form may launch an invention. Observations in nature study, discussion of social studies material, reading of nonfiction, and many other subjects dealt with in class could inspire stories or poems. Playing by ear, the teacher seizes a moment of high enthusiasm for some content, takes the spin-off from that activity, and turns it toward writing: "Write a story about such an animal (somebody in such a situation, something taking place in such a region)." By "story" children understand virtually any kind of writing they are capable of doing that has characters, setting, and action. The possibilities of different forms — poem, ballad, playlet — are mentioned.

Though involvement in subject matter is a good and natural stimulus for writing, it seems to me that trading on children's excitement about certain holidays has been very much overdone. One sometimes has the impression that the elementary curriculum is founded on Halloween, Thanksgiving, Christmas, Valentine's Day, George Washington's Birthday, and Easter, and that if these occasions were to cease being celebrated, elementary education in this country would collapse into a rubble of paper ghosts and hearts. To guard against repeals by future presidents, it might be sound to tap other sources of children's enthusiasm. Such typical assignments as "Do a Thanksgiving poem" fill the bulletin boards with papers that gobble terribly like those one read last year on another bulletin board in some other school. Even "Write a poem about autumn" becomes no more than an annual invitation to turn over the leaves of old clichés. We can be sure that children will celebrate at the slightest excuse anyway, without the sponsorship of schools. For writing, more spontaneous and less stereotyped subjects would be better.

An Unfinished Sentence

A provocative, unfinished sentence has been used very successfully by some teachers. In England, Sybil Marshall gives this starter: "Nobody knew where it came from, but there it was, a big red _____." A low-ability class of mixed fifth- and sixth-graders began their stories with this unfinished sentence but added a sentence of their own that all stories were to include somewhere. With capitals and punctuation adjusted, this is one boy's response:

> All of a sudden there it was, a big red sign that said Ghost Realty. Just then a man walked in. He said that he was looking for a haunted house. The man in the chair said that there was one house on a iland about a half mile from Long Iland. The owner died about a week a go and the man (buyer) said, "I will take it." "*Wait.* In order that you may buy the house you will have to spend the night in the house." "Ok, I will spend the night in the house." "Ok, than it is settled." "Fine, then you will take me out in a rowboat tonight." "Good."
>
> Out in a rowboat that night he rowed him up to the iland and when the man let him of he rowed back as fast as he could. He looked back and then went up the stairs and went in side. He looked all around then he saw a

stair case. He went up it then he herd a voice. It said, "If the log rolls over we will all be dround," and then he ran in a room as fast as he could and there siting in a washbowl sat three ants on a mach stick saying, "If the log rolls over we will all be drowned."[3]

The children themselves can propose such starters.

LOADED WORDS

One fifth-grade teacher asked her pupils to think up several interesting words, then to choose one to write a poem, story, or script about. One word was "mysterious":

MYSTERIOUS

There's a mysterious house on our street
It's where Oak and Flag Street meet.
People say they hear noises when it's dark.
And the creaking of gates, when chirps the lark.

It's very old you know.
It's where all the weeds on Oak St. grow,
I went there once to see what it's like.
And I almost fell off of my bike.

For, there from the back window,
There came a giant frog.
He didn't look like any I'd seen in the bog.
He was really quite frightening.
He held a sword, and threw it like lightning.

Well that sword just missed me,
And I ran home fast.
And my bad dreams stopped only
The night before last.

My advice to anyone
Whom it may concern
Is stay away from there
For if you don't, say a prayer.

Another word was "fish":

THE FISH STORY

The ocean was a silver cup
With a deep scalloped rim;

[3] My thanks to Rose Arnone, Cochituate Elementary School, Wayland, Massachusetts.

And all the fish I took up
Were big enough to swim;
And had speckled tails.
There were not any in between
The rest, I guess, were whales.[4]

Song and Verse Forms

Inspired by the East coast blackout of 1965, and fitted to the tune and meter of "Sweet Betsy from Pike," this ballad shows the stimulus of both a subject and a form (done by a group of Omega children in the Franklin Elementary School in Lexington, Massachusetts).

Ballad of the Blackout

At half past five Tuesday, November the ninth,
The lights went out and it gave me a fright.
We lit all our candles.
'Twas a spoo-ooky sight,
When the lights went out o-on that Tuesday night!

(*Chorus*)
The people were all right when candles were light.
But electricity is a much better light.

"What happened?" said Sally.
I said, "I don't know."
"What happened?" said Willy
While tying a bow.
They pushed the wrong button and turned to reverse.
The main truck line shorted with one great big burst.

(*Chorus*)

The li-ights went ou-out.
The hou-ouse got dark.
The moo-oon came ou-out.
The do-ogs did bark.
The babies cri-ied,
The pe-eople sighed.
And tha-at's what happened on Tu-uesday night.

(*Chorus*)

---

[4] My thanks to Rose Merzon of the Happy Hollow Elementary School, Wayland, Massachusetts, for these poems and for her extensive trials of other assignments in this program.

I was i-in the bathtub when it happened to me.
The water went o-off and I was freezing.
Yes that was what happened
And now you will see
The rest of the thin-ings that happened to me.

(*Chorus*)

I was washing my hai-ar when out went the lights.
I cried to my mother, "what a terrible fright!"
"Now what will I do? There's shampoo in my eyes.
And the lather is growin-ing double its size.

(*Chorus*)

I was doing my homework that Tu-uesday night.
When all of a sudden I looked at my light.
It flickered and flickered. Oh what a sight!
Oh what a terrible Tu-esday night.

(*Chorus*)

We were out at our friends' house when the li-ights went poof!
The TV went blurry and we were so shook.
We sat and we sat there a-waiting for help.
And then we found out that it was a black-out.

(*Chorus*)

So when the lights went out
It all was quite black.
I thought I heard Martians
So I hit the sack.
And then I heard scre-eams
Upstairs in the hall,
And found that my brother had started to bawl.

(*Chorus*)

Oh whe-e-en the li-ights went out,
Fly-i-ing saucers came dow-own with doubt.
They crashed and they banged and they clattered and called.
They landed right i-in Nia-a-gra Falls.

(*Chorus*)

The Mars-men were coming
And coming they were.

They turned off our lights
With their ray gun rayer.

And away they all went and away they all flew.
They left us with nothing but fuses that blew.

(*Chorus*)

After concentrating on a form through considerable reading of instances of it, the pupils try their hand at this form, the subject matter being stimulated by such structural features as metrical and stanzaic patterns of rhyme, rhythm, and repetition. Thus limericks, ballads, short lyrics, and longer narrative poems should all be read in large quantities, taking one type at a time, initially at least, until the form is fixed in their minds. The teacher does not need to explain the form or point out the technical characteristics of it; that is the point of reading many instances together. The best way to know literature is to practice it.

FABLES

One form in particular that I would recommend is fable. Of course, fables might be written as either prose or poetry, but in either mode they represent a differentiated form of narrative — the story that illustrates an explicit general point. Besides being popular with children and available to them through a rich literature stemming from Aesop and LaFontaine, the fable has by definition a particularly strong learning asset that should be taken advantage of.

Whereas few children of this age are capable of, or even interested in, writing general truths in the sense of sustaining generalizations throughout a whole discourse, they are quite able and motivated to make single generalities and to insert these into their stories and descriptions. In two ways, fables act as a natural bridge between narrative statement and idea statement: (1) the whole story must be "pointed" toward the concluding moral, and (2) the moral itself must be an explicit assertion, in the present tense of generalization, of an idea that the narrative merely embodies. Thus fable acts as a hinge between two kinds of idea presentation — examples and generalities. While not asking the child to abandon his characteristic mode of narrative for abstract essay, it leads him toward a transitional kind of narrative that prepares for generalization writing. Later assignments in secondary school will more fully develop this crucial intellectual transformation of *what happened* into *what happens,* or *when* into *whenever.* What differentiates fable from other narrative is just this cognitive shift from pure story (once-upon-a-time) toward the illustrative story (typical of many times).

In "Teaching the 'Unteachable,' "[5] Herbert Kohl has given a very vivid and valuable account of the ways in which he tried to help Harlem children to start writing. Reading and making fables was one of the successful ways. Here is what one eleven-year-old Negro girl wrote for him:

> Once upon a time there was a pig and a cat. The cat kept saying old dirty pig who want to eat you. And the pig replied when I die I'll be made use of, but when you die you'll just rot. The cat always thought he was better than the pig. When the pig died he was used as food for the people to eat. When the cat died he was bured in old dirt.
>
> Moral: Live dirty die clean.

Both the tale and the moral show real native wit. *Live dirty die clean* shows how moral writing can help children practice the rhetorical devices and pithiness of epigrammatic statement. An eleven-year-old Negro boy wrote this one:

> Once a boy was standing on a huge metal flattening machine. The flattener was coming down slowly. Now this boy was a boy who love insects and bugs. The boy could have stopped the machine from coming down but there were two ladie bugs on the button and in order to push the button he would kill the two ladie bugs. The flattener was about a half inch over his head now he made a decision he would have to kill the ladie bugs he quickly pressed the button. The machine stoped he was saved and the ladie bugs were dead.
>
> Moral: smash or be smashed

The allegorical aspect of fable allows the boy to express impersonally the painful conflict, probably only too familiar to him, of having to hurt another to save yourself. In short, fable is an excellent form to put experience into and for making statements about that experience.

Parables can be read and written along with fables, as a similarly pointed story but without a *stated* moral. By treating both as specialized kinds of stories, the teacher can make clear that not *all* stories are to be read for their moral, an incorrect idea that many children now have. One reads different kinds of tales differently, according as they invite one to savor events for their

[5] Printed by *The New York Review of Books,* 1967. The following two pupil papers and one in Chapter 16 are reprinted from this booklet with the permission of Herbert Kohl. The Teachers' and Writers' Collaborative, of which Mr. Kohl is director, is putting together a complete curriculum unit on the fable. The unit will include a discussion of the fable form; a compilation of fables from various countries and cultures; a selection of children's fables; reports by teachers on the use of the fable in the classroom. Preliminary material can be obtained by writing to Teachers and Writers Collaborative, 249 Macy Annex, Teacher's College, Columbia University, New York, N.Y.

own sake or to distill conclusions from them. Fables and parables encourage readers to infer a generality — either a truth or an imperative — and to interpret symbolically, but this way of reading comes as an appropriate response to the purpose of the writing — often signalled by its form — not as an indiscriminate reaction to all stories.

General Ways of Stimulating Creativity

The secret of stimulating children to write inventions lies not in any one or two sorts of stimulants (many kinds will work well) but in the teacher's ability to capitalize on provocative forms and passing subjects, and to point out to children the writing possibilities in their improvisations and in their previous writings. This takes flexibility and alertness. It means that the kernels of story ideas are lying about everywhere and that once children are licensed to convert a sensory description to a short story by imagining an action in that setting, or to start making up something from the random meanings of rhyme words, or to transpose a "minimal situation" into a narrative, they will solve for themselves the problem of getting an idea. The teacher should be a storehouse of ideas — for transforming one piece of writing into another, for transposing an action, for converting body English to written English — that can pass into small groups and become part of the individual's thinking.

The only essential requirement is that the children be involved in the writing; otherwise all snappy ideas will fail. The children have the feelings; all they need are materials and forms, some stuff they can shape and project their feeling into, and some structures of language and literature that fix feelings "out there," impersonally before them. The teacher does not have to give these things to the class; it is enough to point them out, for materials and forms exist independently of schools and teachers. But the children have to be awash in good literature, imaginative writing that has art and wit and bite. They have to hear it, see it, read it, take off from it. A true commitment to letting children write will solve more problems than volumes of advice.

This is perhaps the place to plead for "creative writing" as a staple of learning, not as Friday afternoon fun or the luxury of lucky "advantaged" children who are mastering the "basics" on schedule. The testimony is ample from many hard-working teachers in urban ghettos that deprived children can learn "basics" only *after* they have become persuaded that the world of letters has something in it for them.[6] As *Programs for the Disadvantaged*[7]

---

[6] A lot of such testimony was given at the Huntting Conference of Writers and Teachers, June, 1966 (from Sonny Jameson, Elaine Avidon, Florence Howe, Ira Landess, and many others working in Manhattan "600" schools and other schools with seriously deprived or disturbed populations).

[7] Edited by Richard Corbin and Muriel Crosby (Champaign, Ill.: National Council of Teachers of English, 1965).

pointed out, the greatest formalization of instruction and the least self-expression occur in the urban schools, where children can learn the least from formalization and most need self-expression. *The "basics" for children are feelings and motives.* The more deprived he is, the more a child must deal with feelings *first* and objective, technical matters afterwards. A ghetto child needs more so-called "creative" writing, not less of it, because so little opportunity exists in his environment for learning how language can help him handle his feelings and manage his life. Once persuaded of its personal value for him, he will attack its technical aspects.

Chapter 16

Idea Writing

The emphasis of this section is on what is generally called essay and exposition. It includes practical writing and direct statement of ideas. But no effort is made to draw a sharp line between narrative and non-narrative, or utilitarian and imaginative. Of the four points of departure treated here, it is clear that at least two would sometimes lead students into imagined material and chronological writing.

Verbal Stimulus

The best stimulus is probably the spin-off from discussion and reading. The results are all sorts of explicit assertion of opinions, attitudes, wishes, and ideas that are neither fictional nor factual. Whether cast in prose or in poetry, they constitute what is really personal essay, though the appellation seems stuffy and certainly need not be used in class. When group concentration on a subject reaches a peak of intensity, and everyone has more to say, the teacher sends them to paper, where in a sense they continue the discussion in written monologue.

In Herbert Kohl's sixth-grade Harlem class, feelings were running high in discussion of their squalid neighborhood. He asked them to write about what they would do to change things. An eleven-year-old girl wrote:

If I could change my block I would stand on Madison Ave and throw nothing but Teargas in it. I would have all the people I liked to get out of the block and then I would become very tall and have big hands and with my big hands I would take all of the narcartic people and pick them up with my hand and throw them in the nearest river and oceans. I would go to some of those old smart alic cops and throw them in the Ocians and Rivers too. I would let the people I like move into the projects so they could tell their friends that they live in a decent block. If I could do this you would never see 117th st again.

245

Sometimes a well chosen abstract word will evoke thought and feeling. Borrowing again from Sybil Marshall, one teacher gave her fifth-graders "wishing":

MY WISH

I wish that I could ride around the world
On a big fat tiny fish.
He'd swish his tail and we would have to bail out all the hail.
The hail was heavy and not so light.
As a matter of fact it was a might bit light for the two of us.
We huffed and we puffed as we stuffed it off board.

We are in China now.
Look, look there are some indians having a pow wow.
Wow they must be cow corn pipes.

We are in India now.
I see a cow.
Bow wow brown cow.
Up in the air jumped my big fat tiny fish.
No come back wish fish come back.
It was only a dream —
Now isn't that mean?

WISHING

One doll, one book
That is wishing
A fire truck with a ladder & hook
That is wishing too.

Make a wish on a star
Way up afar
Don't feel blue
Make a wish too![1]

If the teacher makes up a topic, it should be open like this one, which gives the illusion of specifying but in fact leaves content to the child, or else one like Kohl's which merely gives a loose frame for a topic that has already in fact been shaped by class activity.

A strong possibility for involved idea writing is to take to paper a spirited but unresolved small-group discussion. The topic is whatever the unresolved issue is about and would hardly even need to be framed by the teacher. Such writing gives everyone a chance to rebut or get the last word. The main things to avoid are the "old chestnut" topic that invites cliché, and the loaded or narrow topic that dictates content or position. Ideally, the writing of

[1] Happy Hollow Elementary School, Wayland, Massachusetts.

opinions and personal views arises from the classroom drama of ideas and comes at moments of light and heat. Papers can be fed back into discussion by projecting and distributing them. Rather than thinking of a topic in advance and prescheduling it, teachers would do better to seize the moment when a topic does not have to be thought of: it is staring you in the face. This may happen on an individual basis as well, not always with a group. If a child has just lost a pet, let him write an epitaph for it (another idea from Sybil Marshall).

Diaries and Letters

The children are issued softcover notebooks and given five or ten minutes nearly every day to make entries in them. They write the date and anything else they want to put down — reminders, past events, thoughts, or ideas for stories. Such a diary is also a kind of writer's notebook, not a strict record of events. Emphasize personal freedom. The child does not even have to write anything at all on some days. He does not have to show his notebook to anyone.

A diary is a superficial structure into which a miscellany of things can be comfortably written. It is a daily habit, a period of meditation and self-collection. It is also a time to rehearse one's writing alone, just as small children learning to talk rehearse speech alone in their crib before falling off to sleep. It is relaxed practice. The pupils can make of it what they want — and what they make of it may continually change. But because they will write under the influence of present circumstances and in a particular state of mind, the entries will inevitably become in some sense a record. All the teacher does is open all the possibilities: "Put down things in the past or the future that you want to remember, ideas you don't want to slip away, feelings you want to express, whatever is on your mind or comes to mind that you want to put into words. Maybe you'll think of a good idea for a story, song, poem, or improvisation that you can use soon."

To whom is a diary written, and for what purpose? Many people who keep diaries on their own are writing to their future selves, or to an image of some ideal reader, or unconsciously to a real and meaningful figure in their life. The purpose may be practical but it is often just self-expression and fantasy communication for its own sake. It may often happen that a child will want someone else to see what he has written — to call the teacher over or show his notebook to another child. This should be permitted so long as he does not disturb the others. But especially, the option of writing a letter instead of an entry should be kept before the class. A child who feels on some day that he would rather write what he has to say to a friend or relative understands that he may do so. A stationery pad and envelopes might be kept in a "mail corner" along with a poster model of the heading, closing, and addressing of a letter, and perhaps even a mailbox and stamps to buy. The teacher is on call to help with mechanics if the pupil asks for help, but does not otherwise intervene or "check out" the letter.

Of course, for pupils who have done calendar keeping and letter writing before (Chapter 8), none of this will seem strange. They will be used to associating the two and to looking over their diaries and seeing how pieces of them might be summarized for someone in particular. Both kinds of writing — for oneself and for another individual — are personal and will be best fostered by setting aside time in an atmosphere of personal freedom. Assigning impersonal courtesy letters, stressing proper form and etiquette, makes of letter writing just the sort of onerous duty that makes so many adults say, "Oh, I just hate to write letters." If letter writing is kept a matter of self-expression, more children, I'm sure, will write them. Since the diary contains plans and practical reminders, it may often suggest to children the need to write a "business" letter to order something, ask about something, and so on. Instead of always beating the children to the jump, and teaching a unit on business letters, it would be much better to have them ask the teacher for advice as a real need for help arises. And who knows? Some may even *want* to thank the firemen for the nice visit.

Writing up Show-and-Tell

As I suggested in Chapter 4, show-and-tell can take several directions — toward narration, information, explanation, or personal essay. It should continue indefinitely. There is nothing inherently childish about it; the pupil before his group is doing essentially the same thing an appliance salesman or science demonstrator does. But teachers would do well to give it a new name when referring to it in grades four to six.

Emphasis should be on showing objects to which long histories, deep personal involvement, or complicated explanations are attached. Since the period of ages nine to eleven is when crafts, hobbies, collections, and sports get under way, these should be capitalized on as much as possible for explanations of construction, operation, and procedure. The object itself becomes merely a prop, a conversation piece, a pump-primer, as children become capable of ranging far beyond it. The reason for continuing to hold these sessions in small groups is to enable more pupils to hold forth in a given amount of time and also to stimulate more questions and interaction than is likely to occur when one person speaks before an entire class. The size of groups might be enlarged, however, to nine or ten, clustered in three parts of the room, to provide a larger audience. The teacher moves from group to group. It may be necessary to separate boys and girls sometimes if an object is of no interest to one sex. Actually, since the practice in explaining something to an outgroup is very valuable, non-segregation is preferable, if it works.

After sessions in which all members of the small groups have spoken about and answered questions on the items they brought in, allow them time to write up what they said as influenced by feedback. This need not occur every time, but perhaps only when the session is specialized in the direction of, say, explanation — "Bring in something of which the purpose, use, care, or operation can be explained" — since the memory assignments allow for writing reminiscence. Having rehearsed while talking, and having received from their audience an idea of how to explain some things better and what emphasis might be most interesting, pupils should be ready to write. The personal choice of the item should ensure motivation. Announcing the intention of printing the papers would add interest. These booklets might be specialized according to how the show-and-tell assignment was stated ("How to Operate . . ." or "How to Play . . .").

Writing Directions

Giving directions is an excellent way to engage with some of the general problems of verbal communication. The natural egocentricity that causes us to assume information and viewpoints that our listener does not have is revealed to us when directions misfire. And because directions are translatable into action, there is little chance of miscommunication remaining unnoticed as it so often does in other kinds of speaking and writing, where sender and receiver may think they understand the words in the same way when in fact they do not. Far more than is commonly recognized, egocentricity is a central source of writing problems — from punctuation and phrasing to paragraphing and overall organization. Just as we know how our written sentences should be spoken, we know in what sense they are to be taken, forgetting that the reader does not. Developmentally, egocentricity decreases with age, but it is clear that the problem is lifelong. The solution is more awareness, and awareness can come only through feedback from other people. (Looking over one's own writing after a lapse of time, much like an outsider, one often catches his own egocentricities.) So while gaining experience in a practical kind of discourse, pupils writing directions can begin to de-center (allow for the receiver) in ways that will help them in all of their communication.

ORAL DIRECTIONS WITH PUZZLES

To reap the most benefits from the assignment, the children need to know what happens when others attempt to follow their directions. Furthermore, translating words into action will make the assignment more fun. As a game, the directions can at first be oral. The class breaks into groups of six to eight, who cluster around two children seated back to back, one of whom is sender and one of whom is receiver. The sender has before him a few pieces of a very simple puzzle that when assembled forms a familiar shape. His pieces are in fact assembled already, and his job is to talk his partner through an assembly of an identical puzzle, the pieces of which are scattered before the receiver on his desk. The point of not letting the two see each other is to enforce a total reliance on words. In such situations children will still try to express directions egocentrically, by gesturing, even though they should know that their receiver cannot see their signals.

For the first time or two, the communication is restricted to one-way talk, in a pretense, for example, that one is a boss giving a worker directions over a one-way intercom; then the "worker" is finally allowed to ask questions. Withholding two-way conversation for a while demonstrates its great advantage, which is the receiver's feedback in the form of questions of clarification and requests for omitted information. The onlookers of the group are told that kibbitzing spoils the game and that they should watch silently so that they can observe the causes of miscommunication and try to avoid these mistakes when their turns come to give directions. Depending on the difficulty of the puzzle, a number of children may have to act as sender before the receiver can assemble it successfully. Sets of puzzles are exchanged and children rotate roles.

The puzzles will probably have to be made in school in order to have simple shapes of few pieces in identical sets. Cutting the figures into common geometrical shapes is a variation that enables children to put into play the vocabulary of geometry. Odd shapes, on the other hand, stretch the imagination for ways of describing. When I tried out this game once in a fifth-grade class, I used the "Fractured T,"[2] a large block-letter T cut into five irregular pieces, and found that it was a bit more difficult for beginners than is desirable. Although the game can be set up so that each sender expects to be replaced in mid-game by another, still there should be progress across different senders and not too much frustration.

A graded difficulty in puzzles can be achieved by gradually increasing the number of pieces (starting with three) and by making the component shapes harder to describe and to position. The point of having the completed puzzle form a familiar figure is that, if he thinks of doing so, the sender may state at the outset: "We're going to put the pieces together so that they look like a house." Omission of this general framework can create the same communication problems here that it can in a piece of written exposition, since in either case the receiver lacks context for relating particulars to each other.

ORAL DIRECTIONS WITH OTHER MATERIALS

After children have become aware of at least some of the factors that make for success and failure in the game, variations are introduced. The goal is still to match senders' and receivers' materials by means of verbal directions, but, to vary and generalize the communication issues, puzzles are replaced by other things. One child who has learned how to do some Origami crea-

[2] Obtainable from Advanced Seminars, 1725 Beverly Boulevard, Los Angeles, California.

tions (paper-folding) talks another child, or perhaps his group, through the procedure. They can compare the success the sender has with his directions when he is speaking from memory with his success when he is folding as he speaks (sender and receiver are still back to back). Or: the sender looks at an abstract picture composed especially for this purpose and tells his receiver how to draw it. The children themselves might bring or suggest other materials to use. A variation in the game situation is to let one child give directions to the whole class. But all pupils should have plenty of opportunity to watch the process also, for onlookers get good insights from observing, simultaneously, what the sender intended and how the receiver took the message.

WRITING DIRECTIONS FOR HOW TO MAKE AND DO THINGS

Some direction-giving once a month for these three years should lead to marked improvement in thinking and communicating, but at some point directions are shifted from speech to paper. Each child thinks of something he knows how to make from common materials, writes the directions as clearly as he can, and exchanges with another pupil. They all follow out the directions as homework, and bring to school what they have made. Any problems or uncertainties about the directions are noted down on the paper, which is returned to the author. This assignment could include cooking recipes, an issue in that case being whether to list ingredients separately or just to mention each as it comes up. Quantities and measurements will of course enter into many manufacturing directions.

A secondary general benefit is that children learn from each other how to make things. Revised after feedback, these papers could be printed together in a classbook called, "How to Make . . ." Or children can take turns inventing a board or a card game for their group to play, and then observe them playing it. They would make the materials and write the goal, procedure, and rules. An interesting feature of this assignment is the unforeseen situations for which the directions do not allow. Revised, these directions could be affixed to the game, and the games exchanged and taken home. Generally, it is important that a direction writer either get back written comments or have a chance to talk with whoever excuted the directions; sometimes both would be in order.

WRITING TRAVELING DIRECTIONS

Traveling directions constitute one of the best assignments but are difficult in practice to carry out because children would have to go after school to unfamiliar places. The assignment is simply to write directions for getting from the school to one's own house, or from one part of town to another. Maps are not allowed in this case, because, we'll pretend, the directions are coming over telegraph or will be read over the phone. In small towns, perhaps, where distances are small and buses not used, children might exchange directions and go to each other's houses. Directions for getting around the school plant would be the next best possibility.

Some directions should be projected and discussed. I sat in once on a fifth-grade discussion of home directions that was very lively and interesting. In every paper there were some directions the class felt sure it could not follow. For example, "then turn up Linden Street" indicated only a turn, not the direction of the turn, since *up* expressed nothing but the writer's subjective mental picture of aiming himself where he wanted to go (this kind of egocentricity is equivalent to the puzzle-director's saying, "Now pick up the next piece," or "Put the funny-looking piece against it." Since the children frequently did not know the names of streets, locations were often identified by ambiguous descriptions that more accurate word choice or better vocabulary would have cleared up. "Store," for example, could have been one of several retail places, but there was only one supermarket on the street. Since improving directions often requires replacing some words by others, this is another important place to work on vocabulary. Then, later in the discussion, a paper referred to the Western Building, at which point it occurred to some of the children that only someone familiar with the town would know that landmark. Who were these directions written for anyway? Suppose a stranger had to follow them. So they themselves brought up the issue of adapting directions to different receivers.

At this point the teacher should ask them to look at their papers, check for directions that a stranger would not understand, and change them so that he would. For another occasion a story situation based on the problem could be imagined: an out-of-town visitor is staying over night at such and such hotel, and the next day he is coming out to the school to show a film. What directions should the principal give him when he telephones him that evening? Will he be walking or driving? These directions are read and discussed in small groups.

A final suggestion is that pupils write directions for getting from one place on a map to another, revealing the starting point but not the destination. The object is to see if classmates wind up at the place the writer had in mind by tracing a route on the map according to his directions.

Unrecommended Writing

This is the place to indicate exclusions. One cannot take a stand on curriculum without negative as well as positive recommendations. Besides doing damage, some kinds of assignments simply take up time that would be much better spent doing other things. In judging whether a writing assignment is worthy, I ask these questions. (The sense of "writing" here is "composition," of course, not "transcription.")

CRITERIA FOR JUDGING A WRITING ASSIGNMENT

1. Is it given for punitive reasons? (There are teachers today who still make children "write an essay on _____" as punishment for inattention, failure to follow directions, etc.) If we wish to kill writing, setting up such negative associations is a splendid way to do it.

2. Is it given essentially as a check to prove that something was read? I have in mind here such tasks as reporting on a book or paraphrasing reference books.

3. Is motivation intrinsic to the kind of writing assigned?

4. Does it have, at least potentially, an authentic audience besides the teacher?

5. Does it require cognitive abilities too advanced for the age?

6. Is it given mainly as a vehicle for teaching something extraneous to itself?

It takes honesty to answer these questions, especially since tradition has heavily rationalized some deeply entrenched assignments. Applying the criteria above to certain conventional assignments, I can only recommend that they be dropped.

BOOK REPORTS

Perhaps the most common kind of writing done in most elementary schools today — and the most time-consuming — is reporting on books one has read. This takes two forms, the "book report" on individually read works and the social studies, geography, or science paper comprised of information pieced together from reference books. I realize that some teachers have tried to make both assignments more meaningful by asking the children to put more of themselves into them. But if the children's interpretations or views are wanted, then papers of thought and reactions should be assigned, and the copying aspect eliminated. Both assignments are severely faulted by the criteria.

It seems clear that the book report is designed as a check on what children have read. It is a nervous by-product of individual reading programs. Jacket blurbs, plot summary, and bland endorsement of the book are about all I have ever seen in these reports. The exceptions, the occasional sentences of personal response or assessment, did not make the whole assignment worthwhile and in any case are, when written, unnecessary and unmotivated. Sharing and discussing responses to books in small groups would serve the purpose much better. Children do not like book reports (except as a way of getting good marks), and indeed what motive or audience could there be for them at this age? I interpret book reports as partly a false effort to give children some writing practice and partly as one of many artificial tasks that are generated out of school routine, for the teacher's benefit, having virtually nothing to do with learning.

REFERENCE PAPERS

In some ways, reference papers are even worse. Although book reports encourage some copying and paraphrasing, the task of collating information from encyclopedias, newspapers, magazines, and other sources openly invites plagiarism. Quoting and citing references looks scholarly, but most children just hastily paraphrase, and in any case they are hardly writing in any real sense. We all know that the point of the assignments is to get children to read about a certain subject. It is just this abuse of writing that I deplore. If this is the only way that children will read about science, people, current events, and foreign lands, then something is seriously wrong with the whole approach to these subjects, and no deforming of the writing process will solve the problem.

Children should not be allowed to think that such inauthentic discourse is writing. At the very best, they are lightly summarizing and editing other writers' passages, a subsidiary researcher's skill that does not belong in elementary school. The assignment, furthermore, has no purpose to the child and no audience but the teacher. Since there is practically no composing involved, and since the content is information straight from the horse's mouth, all a teacher can do with such a paper is close in on the mechanics and presentation. It does not teach, it tests, and I do not think that writing should be used to test. Because the assignment is boring and meaningless, many children resent both the reading and the writing. There are better ways to stimulate children to read, and to let them use what they have read. Informational reading should not deadend in a chore for the teacher; it should feed into small groups where it can be exchanged, recalled, thought about, and extrapolated. Writing comes out of these discussions, as interpretive issues arise from the facts. When children demand evidence from each other, books are referred to and further consulted.

LITERARY ANALYSIS

There are other kinds of writing about reading that also break good teaching principles. These fall under the heading of literary analysis or criticism. A sample assignment I have seen given will illustrate.

Some fifth-grade children were asked to compare, in a single paragraph, a poem and a short story that handled the same theme in somewhat different ways. To the teacher this probably seemed like a sophisticated assignment that would prepare for many similar assignments to come in later years. But sensing, correctly, that the task would be cognitively difficult and would require guidance, she directed them to cover, in this one paragraph, eight points of comparison. This in effect furnished the organization and dictated what virtually every sentence should be about.

First of all, the over-structuring was a give-away that the assignment was too advanced. If children have to have that much guidance they should not be asked to do such a thing. Second, since she had previously emphasized that a paragraph was about one thing, she confused the children by asking them to put eight things in one paragraph, the problem here being both in the original attempt to define a paragraph, like a sentence, as "one idea," and in the unnecessary injunction to make one paragraph contain all they had to say. Third, for children such an assignment has no point or purpose. They have already appreciated and responded to the poem and story. However the teacher may conceive the task, the children can only see the paper as a kind of test. Far from increasing appreciation, such unpleasant after-chores drive children away from literature. Fourth, it is not the mission of schools to teach for its own sake literacy criticism and analysis, which is a college specialty. No evidence supports the strong current belief that direct and explicit critical analysis aids comprehension and appreciation. Much more likely is that it interferes with response, which is the main goal of schools. Response can be deepened and sharpened by small-group discussion based on native reactions and touching on literary technique as it becomes a natural issue (and it will, because content is partly a factor of form). What schools should do is develop intuitions, through authentic writing and through discussion, so that children do not *need* vivisections and postmortems in order to understand and respond to literature.

Chapter 17

Playing Games of Language and Logic

For some children of this age certain word and sentence games described in Chapter 10 will still be appropriate. The sentence-building game especially, on p. 155, would remain very valuable for grades 4–6 and is strongly recommended.

Chess

Chess is the appropriate game to follow up the playing of checkers suggested in Chapter 10. The purposes are the same as stated there.

Card Games

The following recommendations take off directly from the earlier discussion of card games in Chapter 10. One direction of further development mentioned there still applies at this age and would apply indefinitely. This is that decks can be made to match maturation by increasing the abstractness of concepts, the unfamiliarity of class designations, and the fineness of subclasses. The taxonomy of biology will provide an example of this development as well as a fitting content for decks at this age.

EXAMPLE OF CLASSIFICATION CARD GAMES

What can be taught of biology through print — that does not require laboratory work and observation — is essentially its system of classification, which reaches upwards into such abstract things as classes of vertebrates and downwards into discriminations among species of canines. It also introduces new designations, such as *arachnids* and *crustaceans,* that subsume the familiar spiders and lobsters according to scientific criterial attributes that are not always obvious. Part of the learning problem is to conceive spiders and lobsters as similar enough to be lumped together as arthropods and as different enough to part company into arachnids and crustaceans. The other part of the problem is not conceptual, but informative: before you can place a spider in the class of arachnids you have to know whether he has the four sets of jointed legs, the sac or breathing tube, and the segmented exoskeleton that qualify him for membership. Of course, students can memorize the fact that spiders, scorpions, and mites are all arachnids, but the true test of having learned a class concept is to be able to identify new instances of it.

Given these two basic problems, and keeping in mind that these problems apply to any concept learning, not just to biology, let us look at how special card games might help children develop their abstractive powers and learn a new content at the same time. The general strategy is to work a limited range of the biological scale at a time, moving gradually upward and downward from a familiar zone somewhere in the middle and gradually integrating these ranges into a full knowledge structure, depending on how much of the ground it seems wise to try to cover. At any rate, a number of decks would be introduced over several years. Individual children could progress at their own rates by staying with one deck as long as they needed to before moving to another. The teacher would pair or group children according to this need. The decks do not now exist, of course, but would be produced by educational publishers if teachers asked for them. Since a lot of the information needed for classifying plants and animals would be contained in the pictures on the cards, the illustrations would have to be of the highest accuracy and quality.

Form of the first decks. The simplest game would, as in grades K–3, consist of making "books" of members of a category. But the category might be at any level — class, order, family, genus, or species. For example, one deck could comprise the phylum *arthropods* and be called the arthropod deck. The cards would picture members of the crustacean, arachnid, insect, and myriapod classes but would not name the class to which each creature belonged, because pupils would then rely on memory rather than deduction. Instead, above the picture would appear *spider* or *centipede* and below it would appear a brief notation of the one or two criterial attributes that might not be visible in the illustration of the creature in its natural habitat, as, for example, certain behaviors or internal structures. Accompanying the deck would be a small placard bearing four columns — the name of each family and a short list of its criterial attributes without examples. The name and attributes establish the class concepts against which players match individual cards in their minds. The placard is presented and explained along with directions for the game and may be referred to during the game.

How to play with the first decks. Thus, playing is a matter of identifying instances (cards) of the four classes by recognizing such distinguishing criterial attributes as number of legs and presence of sacs or gills, and of grouping cards to form books. The main effect is to substitute biological classes for the conventional card suits. Whereas clubs, hearts, diamonds, and spades are arbitrary and have identical instances (the same symbol on all cards of one suit), crustaceans, arachnids, insects, and myriapods are actual substantive categories containing not identical but merely similar instances. The difference is that players have to *recognize* suits before they can play them. Of course, after playing with the arthropod deck once or twice, the children will have learned the "suits" and can play the game as ordinarily, without recognition being a problem.

Sometime after this point — and pacing is both an individual and an experimental matter — those players could start a new deck on arthropods, played exactly the same way but with all fresh instances of the four families. They do not have to learn new class concepts and attributes but would merely be identifying further instances. Since the number of exemplary creatures will be small for some classifications and very large for others, the deck could reflect this disproportion by containing more cards for some classifications than for others. Scoring could allow for this by crediting more points to the books for the scarcer classification, thus introducing some option in game strategy. And not all subdivisions of a category need to be included merely for the sake of systematic thoroughness, since many of the less familiar ones are definable in very technical ways.

Later decks. The next deck could go up or down, that is, could treat arthropods itself as one phylum among several others or treat the various orders of insects as a further subdivision of arthropods. Which vertical way to move is not something I want to predict without experimentation. It may well be that direction makes no difference in the eventual integration of a hierarchy. At any rate, if the next deck is based on a group of phyla, arthropods will be defined on the placard by their explicit criterial attributes, which will replace the implicit attributes pupils inferred for them in the arthropod deck. Also, since the instances of arthropods in this deck will range indiscriminately over all four of its classes, the pupils are focused on the similarities rather than on the differences among them, and can learn how a member of a given class is automatically a member of any superclass that includes the given class (an ant being not only an insect but also an arthropod).

If the next decks, on the other hand, treat the subdivisions among arachnids, crustaceans, myriapods, and insects, then the differences among arthropods are brought out while focusing on the similarities within each of the four classes, and an ant is seen not only as a member of arthropods and insects but also of the order *hymenoptera* as well. This logical principle of multiple membership in successively included classes is difficult for children to grasp because of its relativity: whether one calls the ant an arthropod, insect, or hymenopteran depends on the level of abstraction at which one is making distinctions.

GAMES THAT COMBINE CLASSIFICATION WITH SERIAL ORDERING

Somewhere during these years, the classifying aspect of card games should be combined with the aspect of serial ordering. That is, just as conventional decks have numbers as well as suits, special school decks could have, to push further the suggestion on page 158, both categorical and serial elements. In poker, for example, players have the option of trying for a straight — four, five, six, seven, eight — or for a flush — all clubs, all diamonds, etc. A more difficult possibility is a straight flush — four, five, six, seven, eight of one suit. Because it entails thinking along two dimensions at once, and estimating one's chances each way, playing poker itself would be a good exercise of mental powers. Some experience with it would also prepare for more meaningful games based on its principles. (I can see the newspaper leads now — Fifth-Graders Playing Poker in School. The moral concern of parents could be allayed, however, by explaining that poker playing will prepare their children for college. Failing this, change the name of the game.)

What might these more meaningful games, based on poker, be like? To answer this, let me say that there is a special and very valuable way to construe the notion of "more than" or "higher than" that underlies serial ordering. This is the idea of class inclusion itself. Thus successively broader classes, whose members logically include the members of subclasses, constitute a serial order to replace mere numerical succession. In this way, the categorical and serial dimensions of card playing, which are arbitrary in conventional games, would become organically related under the logic of classes and class relations.

To use the taxonomy of biology again as an illustration, the cards in the school decks might each contain a labeled picture of an animal and a smaller insert in one corner with the name of a phylum, class, order, family, genus, or species. The animals would be chosen from all levels of, say, the vertebrate scale. Dealt a hand of five cards, a player may either try for a straight, by lining up insert names so as to get a succession, or try for a flush by assembling five animals of one kind. But since "kinds" could themselves be of any level of classification — five mammals or five canines — the scoring would have to credit more points to flushes of the lower levels (canines), for which there would be fewer instances, than to those of higher levels (mammals), for which there are increasingly more instances the higher the level of classification.

This further option about which level of classification to try for would reinforce the principle of all logical hierarchies — that larger classes comprise the combined memberships of their subclasses. In deciding whether to play a wolf as a mammal or a canine, the pupil confronts the very issue mentioned above of classifying the same item variously according to the level at which the classifier wishes to make distinctions. This game presupposes, of course, that students have already learned the class concepts from playing with previous decks of the sort described before.

I am aware that designing such card games raises a host of technical problems — calculating game probabilities, selecting biologically sound material, and determining the order of difficulty befitting children's ability. The games would have to be developed by teams of mathematicians, teachers, and subject-matter specialists. I should emphasize that biology is only an example. All I wish to do here is suggest what I feel to be the enormous and untapped potentiality that card games based on the logic of classes have for developing abstractive ability, deepening concepts, and enlarging vocabulary. The subject matter is secondary, but such games offer an unusual opportunity both to present a particular content and to foster a general cognitive capacity that is critical for the language arts. Actually, something like the hierarchy of class inclusions would be better taught as a thought process if the content changed, so that it was embodied one time in the evolutionary scale and another time in something else.

GAMES FOSTERING ORIGINAL CONCEPT FORMATION

Some card games, however, should invite free and original categorizing. The games above would help a student *attain* concepts established by convention. But the taxonomy of biology has changed considerably over the years, and the classifications of some plants and animals is still very controversial. The issue, there and elsewhere, concerns which of the many attributes of a thing shall be deemed criterial for the classification. Color, shape, structure, function, behavior, are only a few possible kinds of criteria. The increasing ability to categorize an item in different ways, to create fresh categories, and to make explicit one's hidden categories is a major dimension of mental and verbal growth.

Though limited of course to pictorial things, a deck of very mixed and unlabeled pictures has one advantage that characterizes all card games — a random hand. (Such a deck can be made from cutouts by the pupils.) Let us say that four children are dealt a meaningless mixture of three cards each. The rules say to think of some way in which the three items pictured are all alike — any way at all. Some categories might in fact have to be "mineral" or "man-made" or "can't be seen through" or "has moving parts." But the object of the game is to tailor the category as specifically to the three items as possible. This is done, first, by allowing eight or ten rounds of drawing and discarding during which the players attempt to narrow down their hand so that others would have the most difficulty playing on it. Each time they draw, they try to replace one of their three previous cards by one that will permit a more specific category. After the eight or ten rounds, they place their hands down and declare their category. The rest of the game, in effect, is spent determining who has the narrowest or most specific category by drawing from the rest of the deck and trying to add cards to the others' hands according to the categories they declared. (Cards they cannot place are simply laid aside.) When the deck is used up, the player whose tabled hand is smallest — whose category is most specific — wins. The idea is that the rules should cause pupils to create original categories and to classify the same items in different ways.

GAMES FOR DEDUCTIVE REASONING

Wiff 'n Proof. Especially developed for elementary children at a Yale project supported by Carnegie Corporation, *Wiff 'n Proof: The Game of Modern Logic* (Layman E. Allen, Box 71, New Haven, Conn.) is a kit of 21 graduated games intended to "encourage a favorable attitude towards symbol-manipulating activities in general, and, incidentally, to teach something about mathematical logic and provide practice in abstract thinking." Players learn how to "recognize 'well formulated formulas' (Wiff's) and how to construct proofs of theorems in propositional calculus."[1] Essentially, these games further the growth of logical analysis and deduction of the sort one needs in order to draw correct conclusions from complicated verbal problems. I strongly recommend trial of this kit because it provides the possibility of joining mathematics and English.

Guessing games with cards, similar to the experiments described in *A Study of Thinking,* could help teach thinking strategies involving the logic of combinatorial possibilities (the deductive process of elimination). Although psychologists seem to agree that this kind of logic comes into use among children only around the age of twelve, I include it in grades four to six, because that is where these games might begin. They might, of course, have to be deferred to junior high school.

If someone points to a pen and says, "That's an example of what I have in mind," we do not know whether he means writing instruments, metal objects, a shade of blue, careless mislaying of items, or any number of other things. If he continues to point out instances, or if we ask him whether various other objects are instances, we can gradually figure out the concept he has in mind. This kind of inferring goes on all the time as people learn individual and cultural concepts by isolating out those attributes of an object or a situation that are criterial for the concept. The strategies we use may be more or less systematic or random, cautious or hasty. The kind of games that could embody the deductive process and give play to its various strategies might go as follows.

[1] Introduction, pp. 1 and 5 respectively.

Conjunctive categories. One such game is based on what is called "conjunctive" categories, which are defined by the conjunction of two or more traits, as in the concept of "brave man" (both courageousness and maleness are required to fulfill the concept). Each card in the deck bears several attributes — color, shape, and figure — but all cards are different as to the combination of attributes. One player makes up a conjunctive category, which he does not reveal to the other, by combining two or three attributes — say the color blue and a circle. He places face up a card containing these attributes along with another. His partner holds the rest of the deck and chooses from it whichever card he thinks will yield the most information about the category when presented to the first player for him to identify as a positive or negative instance. The guesser may present cards containing the combination of symbols he thinks his partner has in mind, or try out blue in all combinations, circle in all combinations, and so on.

The game is a series of trials, and the object is to deduce the category in as few trials as possible. The number of trials can be reduced by noting what the initial card contained and what combinations are progressively eliminated. At the end, partners reverse roles. High-risk guesses may lead to quick victory, but if unsuccessful will take longer than a conservative, systematic varying of one attribute at a time, the latter being a logical procedure for checking out and keeping track of the various combinatorial possibilities.

Disjunctive categories. A similar game is based on disjunctive categories, which are defined by the presence of *either* one *or* another attribute. "Congressman" is a disjunctive category, since a member of Congress need only be either a senator or a representative, not both. The player is directed to make up such a category (*either* blue *or* circular) and to place down a positive instance of it. The partner proceeds as before, but the strategies are different now. Because of the strictness of conjunctive classes, negative instances generally yield more information than positive ones. For example, if blue appears in a card presented during a conjunctive game, and the maker of the category says it is not an instance, the guesser still does not know, from that instance alone, whether blue is a criterial attribute or not, for the card would be positive only if the other criterial attribute(s) also appeared on it. But if the categorizer says "no" to a card presented in a disjunctive game, all the attributes on that card are immediately ruled out, since by the definition of "disjunctive" the appearance of a single attribute is enough to make the card a positive instance.

I think it very likely that the learning of these strategies would proceed best if at some point the games were surrounded by small-group discussion. That is, each pair of players would have two or three observers who would join with them afterwards in discussing the strategy the guesser used and comparing it with alternatives.

Of course, most human categories are not nearly so clear-cut as those put together from colors and abstract shapes. Once pupils have practiced various strategies with such decks, however, they might transfer the strategies to decks with more human content. In any case, however fuzzy our everyday concepts, the logical processes by which we form and manipulate them are the same as those embodied in the games just described.

Chapter 18

_____

_____

_____

Review and Preview

What has been accomplished so far in this curriculum, and how will this work be followed out in later years?

Establishment of Learning Processes

Of most importance are the *ways* in which children have begun to learn how to produce and receive language. These ways are: dramatic play and interplay, small-group discussion, writing for real purposes and audiences, and actively responding to both books and the writing of other pupils. Underlying all of these has been group process — receiving and giving feedback, using language and finding out the results, responding to responses and thereby sharpening the responses. Learning through group process will not only continue into college — in the very ways established in elementary school — but will continue throughout the learners' lives, for it is the main means of "adult education." This process will have engaged the child with language by letting him learn about it through sociality. At the same time that the ultimately social origin and function of language has been stressed, an attitude of independence and initiative has been fostered, for children have taken over their own education and learned how to learn from each other.

The best way, perhaps, to look backward and forward a little more specifically is to take one at a time the main activities that are the goals of the curriculum.

Thinking

Being the most universal sort of learning, thinking has developed through all the activities.

Dramatic work and discussion have developed fluency of thought through the reciprocal prompting of one child by another. The mind was thus stimu-

265

lated, and pupils became accustomed to thinking on their feet without inner blockage; then they could think more fluently when alone. They attended to stimuli and produced ideas in response. The idea may have been embodied in a movement or in speech. In discussion, furthermore, each child has sharpened concepts and definitions, enlarged his store of points of view, developed and examined ideas, and participated in the particular cognitive act of summarizing. The key to thought development in oral speech was *expatiation,* collectively building ideas, and improvisation and discussion have given children this key.

The composition program has developed thought in two general ways. In the recognition that fantasying is thinking — and an especially important form of thinking for children — the program provided points of departure for inventive writing in which children could classify experience and syllogize about it through concrete figments. In poems and stories, children have symbolized implicitly those unthought thoughts that they are not ready to name and state explicitly. Also, in constructing their fictions, they have been recombining things in novel ways, which is the basis of thinking, whatever the things may be.

In fact, the view that composing is a conceptual act has been at the heart of the writing assignments. In recording and recalling on paper, the pupils have been merely externalizing natural inner processes that go on in them all the time. The selecting and summarizing of experience is fundamental to all abstracting, and determines the categories and generalizations the learner will create. Sensory and memory writing have provided the pupil a way to become aware of his own abstracting and a way to develop *choice* in how he will further abstract these lower abstractions. Feedback from peers, furthermore, allowed him to discover the egocentricity of his thinking, the hidden assumptions and points of view. One of the main contributions of cross-commentary in the writing workshop will have been the diminishing of egocentricity. In this respect particularly, the practice in giving directions has played a large role in the growth of thought.

Playing checkers, cards, and other games has nourished logic. The decisions necessary to play these come from figuring out possibilities, syllogizing, and predicting. Card games in particular have given practice in classifying and in concept formation. In objective and explicit fashion, the pupil has ranged concepts hierarchically and grasped class inclusion.

During the following years of schooling, the expatiation process will be further exploited for the growth of thought. Some dramatic improvisations will become topic-centered and veer toward discussion, which will evolve into improvised panels witnessed by a reacting audience. The dialectic element of dialogue will be more strongly emphasized. More of this dialogue will be continued on paper, some of it in the form of "socratic dialogue," some in the form of essay. The large experience with collective thinking will make possible both more fluent and more profound solo thinking.

Though the composition program will invite more explicit statement of ideas — the formulating of generalizations and finally of theories — it will continue to the end to allow substantial room for fictionalizing, so that concrete "story thinking" will continue to evolve alongside idea statement. The abstracting of raw experience is continued into higher-level kinds of writing, as described below, and remains the core of the composition program. In fact, one general sequence of assignments is based on the progressive abstracting of first-hand, then second-hand, material.

Card-playing continues into junior high school, but no new aspects of it are unfolded in this book because it is still too unexplored.

Throughout all the later years, discussion and composition converge directly on certain problems of thinking. One of these is the supporting of ideas with evidence of various sorts, factual and logical. A second is the qualification of ideas through the emendation of single statements. A third is the creation of syllogisms — combining given statements so as to derive new ones. These three conceptual matters become major issues in discussion and also come under special focus in certain writing assignments. Personal concepts and generalizations, private ways of classifying experience, are well scrutinized in other writing assignments for which they are the basis. Breaking through the limitations of egocentricity continues both in topic-centered discussion and in the cross-commentary on the writing, unchanged from elementary school except as the greater maturity of the students naturally raises the level of sophistication.

Speaking and Listening

The thrust of dramatic work and small-group discussion was toward effective interaction. Attending closely to the speech of others and responding relevantly to it were made basic to topic-centered talk and were naturally practiced in dramatic activities. The foundation for conversation was laid in early social play, where interacting began, and was built upon in dramatization and improvisation, where the action of one actor was cued by the action of another. Conversing and making up dialogue, *in small groups,* gave each child plenty of opportunity to produce speech, develop expressiveness, and benefit from specific reactions. Collaborating on projects, commenting on each other's writing, and monologuing for show-and-tell also provided constant oral practice.

The principle of learning to listen was that the listening should have a purpose and be acted upon by the listener. Thus scribes listened in order to take notes for later use. The literacy programs I have recommended had pupils speak, write, and build words with the sounds presented to them. Pupils took dictation from the teacher and from other children or recorded overheard conversations. The recording of non-human sounds helped train auditory attention and was also purposive. Listening, in short, was conceived not as a passive activity focused on in isolated exercises but as a preliminary to some action the learner was to take. It was thus interwoven with a variety of language activities.

For vocal expression, dramatic work was the main instrument of learning. For clarity and precision of speech, small-group discussion was the instrument. In dramatizing, role playing, and oral reading, the pupil adopted the language of others and thus enlarged his vocal repertory. Improvisation limbered his tongue and his native wit. He learned to say what he meant by trying to say it in discussion and in direction-giving, being misunderstood, and then restating his ideas under the influence of feedback. Show-and-tell monologuing allowed him to sustain speech, to begin to grapple with sequence and continuity, and to become aware of the needs of an audience.

In none of these activities was the child told how to speak, nor was he ever asked to deliver a prepared speech. Musicality, force, dynamics, volume, and even enunciation were considered factors of feeling and involvement that develop best in speaking situations that release feeling and tie into real motives. Thus dramatic work and spontaneous talk took the place of elocution lessons and declamation.

During junior high, two important shifts take place in dramatic work. The acting acquires an audience, first in a drama workshop, where small groups watch each other and give reactions, then in performance occasionally before students of other classes. In the workshop, spectators rotate with actors and feed back to each other as in the writing cross-commentary. Second, improvising is taken to paper. In fact, drama work becomes a critical means of introducing some of the new writing assignments. After improvising dialogues and external and internal monologues, students write the corresponding sorts of scripts — scenes, dramatic monologues, soliloquies, and short plays.

Enactment and improvisation continue throughout secondary school, providing the chief means of approaching dramatic literature of all types, not just plays but also many poems and short stories when they consist mostly of character voices. In senior high especially, a considerable number of poems are dramatized and performed, adding to students' spontaneous speech the enriched language of literature. Both professional and students' scripts are memorized and performed. Near the end of the program, a method called Chamber Theatre is introduced, whereby the narrator's role in fiction is acted and his relationship to his characters thus dramatized.

The "minimal situations" for improvising become more specialized so that emphasis can be deliberately placed on topical ideas, a borrowed situation, a situation in a literary work as yet unassigned, or original invention. Improvisation culminates in the freest, most "minimal" situation of all — an assignment to achieve a certain effect on a fellow actor when nothing else at all is specified. Far from being a terminal activity at the end of elementary school, dramatic work remains a major means of comprehending and appreciating, in addition to pursuing oral fluency and expression.

Small-group discussion, too, acquires an audience and hence a source of feedback from beyond the participants. While continuing to the end as staple activity in itself, it also evolves into panels. The panelists' talk is still unplanned, but the audience reaction adds to the activity the qualities of a workshop, wherein both the speakers' ideas and their interactions receive commentary. At the same time, in junior high, discussion and improvisation meet in the form of mock panels, for which students play roles — that is, pretend to be certain people or kinds of people engaged in turning over an issue.

As a process, small-group discussion changes little, or at any rate I have left these changes open for lack of knowledge. Increasingly, however, reading and writing provide subjects as students become able to pursue farther afield various points of content and technique drawn from these texts.

Constant practice and good interaction continue to be the best teachers of speaking and listening. Upper-level teachers will try to induce more awareness in their older students than was attempted before of the "group dynamics" factors operating to make and break communication. Whereas elementary pupils were not ready for much of this, the greater introspective tendency of adolescence affords a better occasion. But how much those teachers can help their charges to grow in speaking and listening depends tremendously on the experience built up through the elementary years.

Writing

Children wrote for each other and reacted to each other's papers in discussion and in marginal notations. This process of cross-commentary was called the writing workshop. Or they wrote in groups, composing together as a scribe wrote down the words. Either way, the teacher's role was to guide the process most effectively, not to read and mark papers. Writing was put to use — printed and distributed, dramatized, acted upon, or incorporated into follow-up writing. Literacy programs were recommended that would enable children to write very early by presenting to them directly at the outset the correspondences between English vocal sounds and their spellings. Punctuation was similarly presented as correspondences between features of intonation and written symbols. After the literacy program, spelling was learned essentially through writing practice, the use of a dictionary, and self-diagnosis set in motion by the teacher.

The writing assignments were authentic kinds of discourse, not school exercises. Sometimes these were notes for later writing — direct recording of sensations or of spontaneous memories. By a process of expanding or selecting, and of revising from feedback, this writing was composed in stages so that the composing acts could be externalized and made susceptible to learning influences. The more inventive writing of stories and poems, on the other hand, was usually done in one stroke, on a sudden inspiration, except perhaps for revisions suggested by other children. And some writing — journal entries and letters — was not seen by anyone else. Based on vocal directions, the writing of directions provided experience of a very important utilitarian sort. Inspired by discussion, the writing of opinions and idea statements was carried only to the length pupils spontaneously took it.

Comparable to the minimal situations of dramatic work, writing was triggered by various easy points of departure, or stimulants, such as ongoing sensations, or memories associated with them, the pupils' own pictures and pictures drawn from elsewhere, literary forms such as the fable or certain poetic patterns, melodies, provocatively unfinished sentences, discussion arguments, and story ideas from improvisations. In general, a richly stimulating atmosphere was created by permitting the release of feeling in dramatic activities and by steeping the children in felicitous literature to which they could respond enthusiastically and into which they could project feeling. These specific and general stimulants were preferred to topical assignments, which were considered inimical to the development of thought and expression. Essay writing was allowed to evolve from several of these points of departure in a self-directive manner.

A grasp of sentence structures and the ability to manipulate them was approached pragmatically rather than academically. Instead of learning grammatical classifications and analyzing given sentences, the children expanded, reduced, and otherwise altered their own sentences and those of other pupils. Knowing already how to put the parts of speech into proper syntactic relationships, the children explored the possibilities and limitations of the orally learned rules for making sentences. They expanded the kernel phrases of their notes into fuller sentences, wrote telegrams, expanded baby talk, played sentence-building games with word slips, and, if they followed the *Words in Color* literacy program, did similar sentence-building with word cards color-coded for parts of speech. But most of all, children have been rewriting their own sentences and those of classmates. The importance of this constant emending, a primary feature of the writing workshop, has been difficult to convey adequately in a book. But in a considerable amount of their composition, pupils have been joining and disjoining sentences, subordinating clauses, trying out variant constructions, rewording phrases, and generally exploring practical language alternatives. They did these things for those very practical reasons that have been thought to justify the teaching of grammar — to improve communication and expression. Feedback, reinforced by the writer's own proofreading and afterthoughts, has indicated the need for sentence changes and often specific alterations as well. Learning to master language consists, precisely, of changing one's sentences.

The *processes* by which writing is taught do not differ in the years to follow from what has just been summarized. Some big differences will be found in the assignments themselves, and yet these differences are but an unfolding of potentialities latent in the elementary assignments. During junior high school, when drama is taken to paper, there occurs a sequence of assignments in script writing that begins with two- and three-person dialogues and continues through dramatic monologue to soliloquy. Taking other tacks, that sequence leads also to whole plays and to "socratic" or idea dialogues. In other words, the basic small-dialogue situation used in improvisations undergoes shifts in emphasis that are stipulated in writing assignments so as to produce very different sorts of scripts, some of which emphasize feeling and human interplay, some of which feature the solo voice, and some of which deal with the dialectic of ideas. These scripts lead in turn to poems, stories, and essays.

A second sequence of assignments takes off from sensations and memories. The former become the foundation for eyewitness reporting, first-hand observations noted at a locale chosen in advance then written up later as a newspaper story. For this journalistic assignment the writing groups act both as city editors and as copy editors. Memory writing becomes differentiated into autobiography and memoir, to sharpen focus and point of view; then memoir subdivides into human and non-human subjects, to specialize focus even more. The time-space coverage of these narratives is limited to a single "incident."

Both the dramatic and narrative sequences lend themselves to poetry writing. In addition, concrete poetry of observation is specifically assigned, founded on the reading and writing of haiku poems. It proceeds to somewhat longer poetic renderings of direct observation and ties in with sensory notation.

A junior high journal-and-diary sequence picks up where this kind of writing left off in elementary school. The sequence begins with private, in-class diaries, followed by a couple of short, public journals to be summarized later, and climaxed by one long, miscellaneous journal that is also summarized afterwards. These assignments capture fresh material and at the same time pose good abstractive problems for the student.

The writing of fictions, in prose or poetry, can take any of the dramatic forms covered, model itself on the first-person assignments, or simply follow familiar third-person conventions. Idea writing can be either dialogical, as mentioned, or monological, the latter being stimulated usually by small-group discussion.

During grades ten to thirteen, autobiography and memoir culminate in longer writing assignments covering the time span of a "phase." Memoir focuses on the "third person singular" (biography) and then on the "third person plural" (chronicle). Reporting blends into research via this sequence: the write-up of an observational visit, as before; the write-up of a combined interview and visit; the write-up of a long interview-visit designed to give a substantial look at some enterprise ("reporter-at-large"); the pointed account of a series of visits and interviews recorded in a journal and later summarized (case); the distillation of information about some subject acquired from visits, interviews, and written sources, but told as what happens, not as what happened (profile); and finally, the distillation and interpretation of information from primary source documents similar to many that the student has himself been creating in his previous writing (book research).

Concurrent with these sequences run three other strands of writing. One is designed to tap spontaneous trains of reflections by asking the student to write down his actual interior monologues at certain locales and to compose these for an audience. For inventive writing, the repertory of fictional techniques is enlarged to the full by experience with Chamber Theatre and with a special sequence of fiction reading following the spectrum arrayed in *Points of View: An Anthology of Short Stories*[1] Free assignments to invent in any form are given.

The third strand concerns the forging of generalizations and theories and their development throughout an essay. Four repeatable assignments comprise a sequence that carries the student up the abstraction ladder. For the first he tells several pointed incidents, drawn from both real life and reading, that clearly illustrate the same thing or play on the same theme; some category or generalization underlies the paper. Then he writes, as independent compositions, a number of single-sentence generalizations such as maxims, epigrams, and aphorisms. The next assignment is to develop one such generalization through substatements and illustrations. After class work with syllogisms, the student writes a composition in which several generalizations are combined so as to produce new statements and to generate a theory.

Work with the sentence is pursued, at the concrete level, in the writing and revising of haiku and other single-sentence poems. At the abstract level, it is pursued in the writing and revising of epigrams and other one-sentence generalizations.

Since the writing assignments result in the same kinds of discourse that are produced outside of school, the outline just sketched represents a reading program also. Each kind of writing is accompanied by corresponding reading selections, created of course in the same way the students created their compositions. Thus the compositional issues of writing and the comprehension issues of reading are joined in each kind of discourse. In fact, though the reading selections are not at all held up as models or analyzed for the sake of rhetorical points to be applied to the writing, they strengthen tremendously the student's involvement with the forms in which he is writing and his understanding of how to master them. The teacher juxtaposes reading and writing but does not himself make connections.

---

[1] Edited by James Moffett and Kenneth McElheny (New York: New American Library, 1966).

Reading

The chief learning issue of beginning reading was considered to be the decoding of letters into familiar vocal sounds to which meanings were already attached. Accordingly, children following this curriculum have had an early, intensive course in sound-spelling correspondences. But phonics was complemented by whole-word and whole-sentence approaches, namely "language experience" and reading while listening. During the period of pre-reading and beginning reading, the teacher frequently read good poems and stories to the pupils. Except for some phonetically controlled texts introduced during the literacy program, the reading matter assigned to beginners was the highest caliber of folk and children's literature. The only readers selected for both younger and older children were anthologies containing such material.

No effort was made to structure a reading program around concepts of either form or content. A very large quantity of anthologies and single trade books were made available from which pupils could make selections for individual silent reading and for reading aloud to classmates in small groups. Reading in common was for the purpose either of discussion or of focusing on a literary form. Attention was drawn to such things as stanzaic form, incremental repetition, and story type simply by clustering a number of instances of each and then having pupils do similar writing. Literary terms and analysis were avoided, but many structural features of literature were brought out through expressive oral reading and through dramatization. The latter, in fact, was made an important instrument of interpretation and appreciation.

Comprehending reading texts was deemed a general conceptual matter that could be better learned in a variety of intellectual tasks than in courses of practice reading or skill building based on comprehension questions. Instead of answering the prepared questions of an adult, children asked their own questions. Further thinking about reading texts was inspired by enacting them, discussing them, or carrying out directions contained in them. Discussion in particular allowed children, collectively, to recall facts, make inferences, draw conclusions, and compare interpretations, so that each individual could improve his ability to do these things alone.

Oral reading was transferred from teacher to pupils, who read aloud in parts and chorally and also practiced expressive reading by taking turns reading to each other in small groups. The latter amounted to reading workshops, since variant readings could be compared and the content discussed in connection with the manner of reading it.

A considerable amount of the children's reading has been each other's compositions, which were naturally controlled for difficulty and interest by the fact of being peer-written. This kind of reading material allowed children to talk to the authors, to discriminate textual features by seeing the texts change, and thus to become aware of these features in a book. In other words, the locally written texts of classmates not only provided additional texts having a special social interest, but also brought reading down from the remote perfection of the printed page to the everyday realm.

As mentioned before, the reading program of the later years is more structured, but only in a general way. Following the principle that students write in the same forms they read, the recommendations for kinds of reading selections to be assigned are made under the same headings as the writing assignments. In surveying the writing program of grades seven to thirteen I have already outlined much of the reading. The "units" of the curriculum are kinds of discourse to be both read and written — dramatic and narrative discourse, which covers plays, poems, and fiction; reportage and research; autobiography, memoir and chronicle, which covers corresponding kinds of fiction and poetry; essays of generalization and theory; and essays of personal reflection. The various first- and third-person fictional techniques are arrayed in a reading sequence drawn form *Points of View,* and also dramatized in Chamber Theatre. Any performable literature is read silently in preparation for being rendered orally; sometimes it is memorized. Dramatic, narrative, observational, lyric, and philosophical poetry are all read in significant connection with corresponding kinds of composition. Reportage and research cover many important kinds of reading, such as eyewitness accounts, journals, and informative articles. Reading in the whole range of concrete and abstract essay is gradually accomplished through assignments made at appropriate junctures. Again, locating and sequencing particular titles was left to teachers to determine locally.

The matter of how students follow up a reading selection is solved in essentially the same way as in the elementary years: they do something with what they have got from the page; they improvise on, perform, discuss, or assimilate into their own writing (research) the texts they have read.

In sum, the rest of this curriculum attempts to acquaint students, as both readers and writers, with all the forms of written discourse, and continues to do so by extending oral discourse onto the page. It unfolds the whole spectrum of dialogue and monologue, literature and non-literature, invention and documentation, private utterance and impersonal formulation.